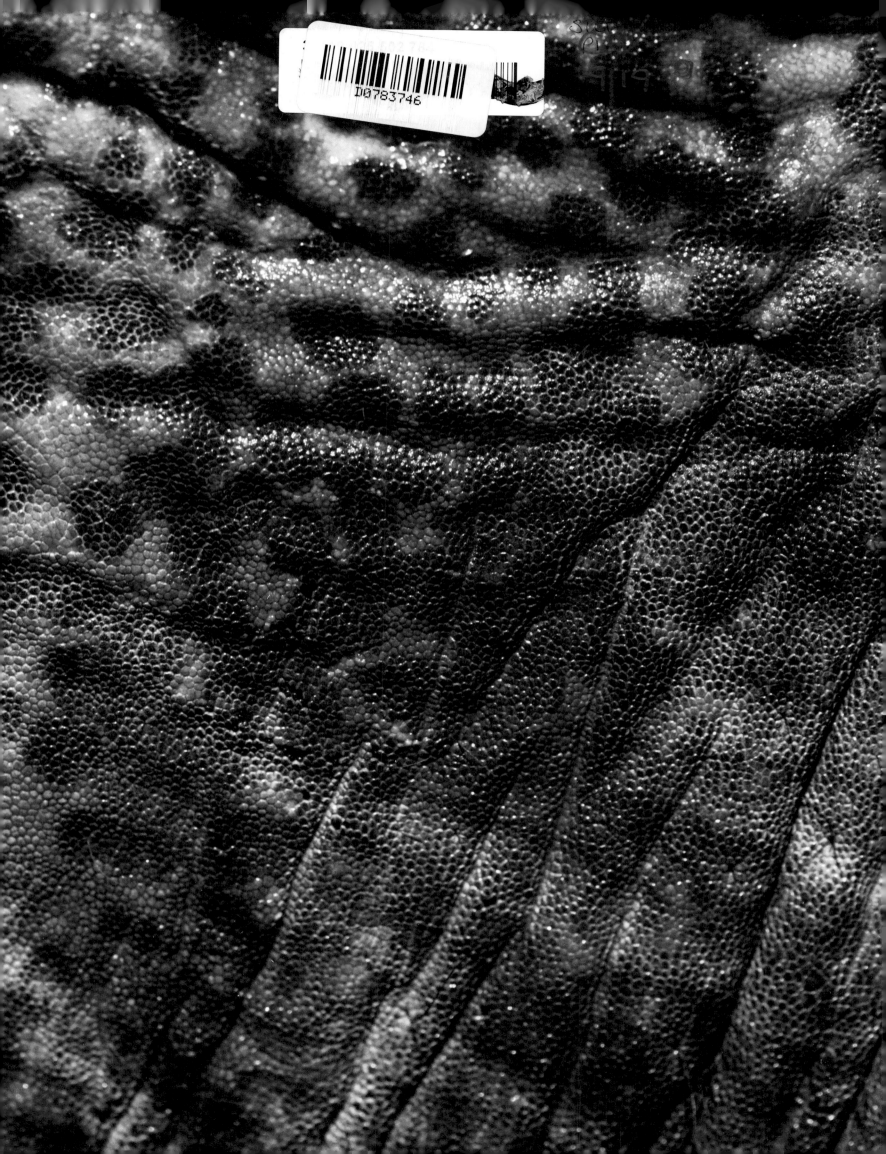

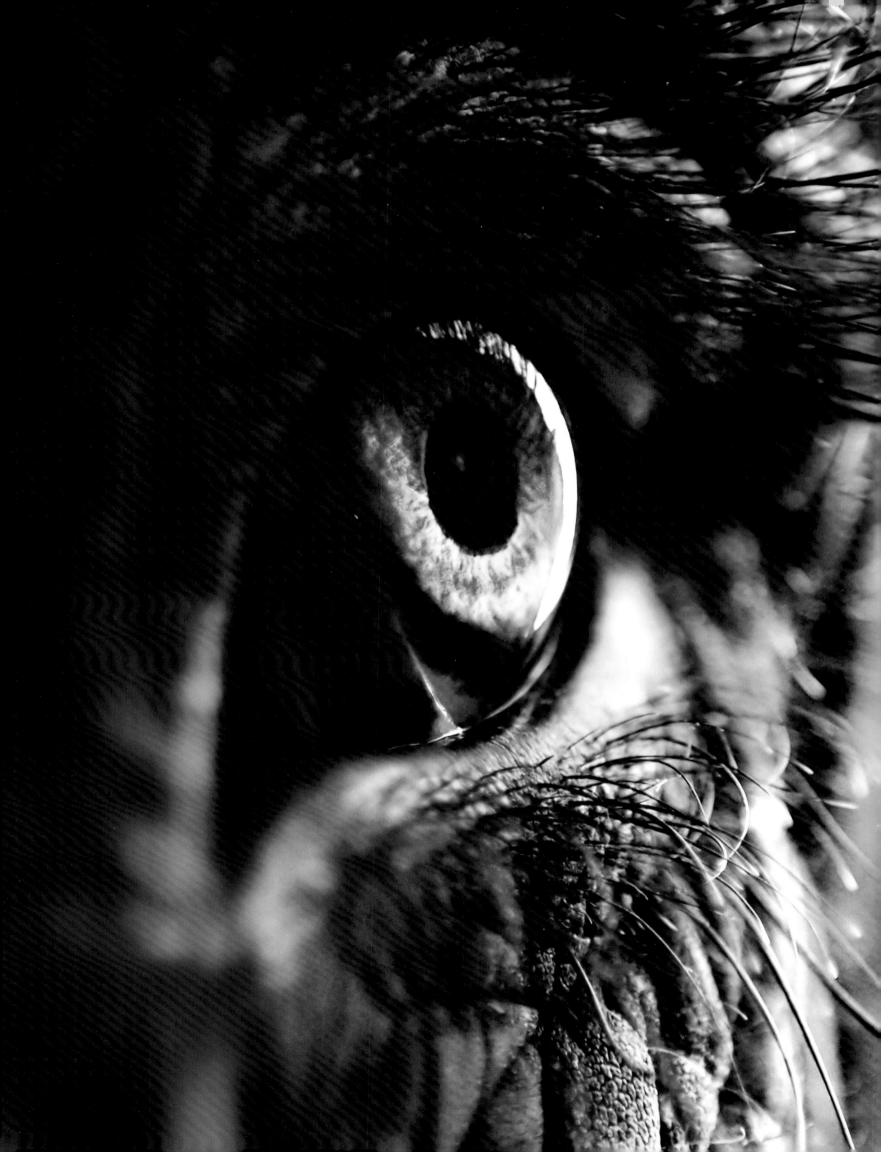

Thames & Hudson

ELEPHANT!

STEVE BLOOM

WITH 117 COLOUR PHOTOGRAPHS

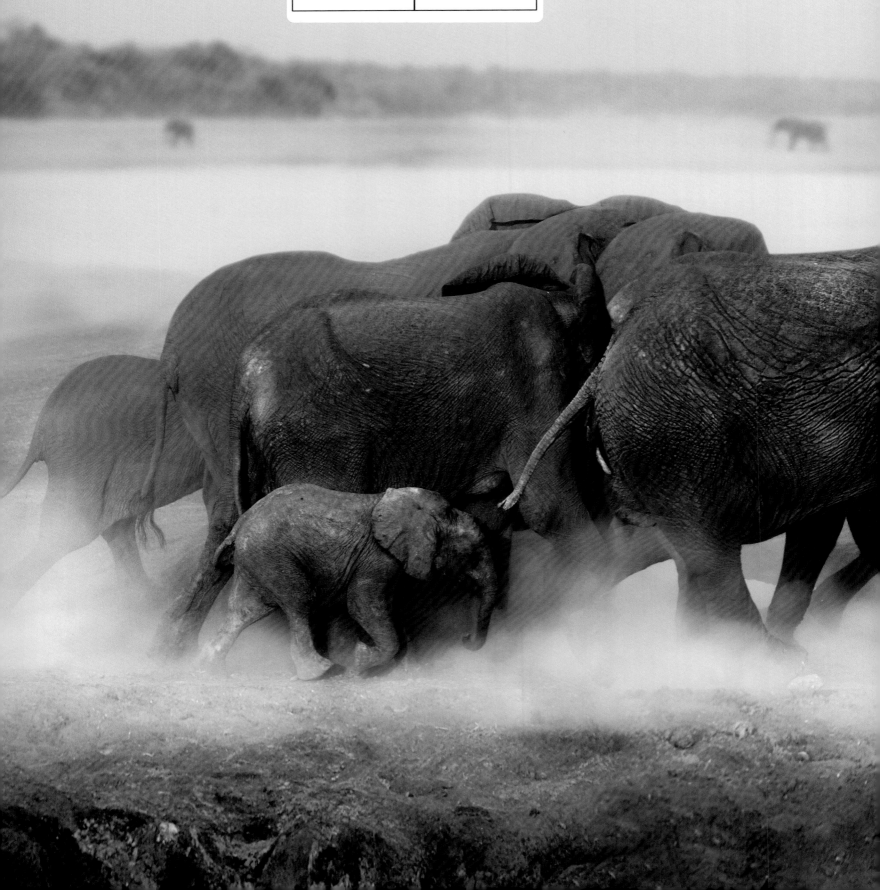

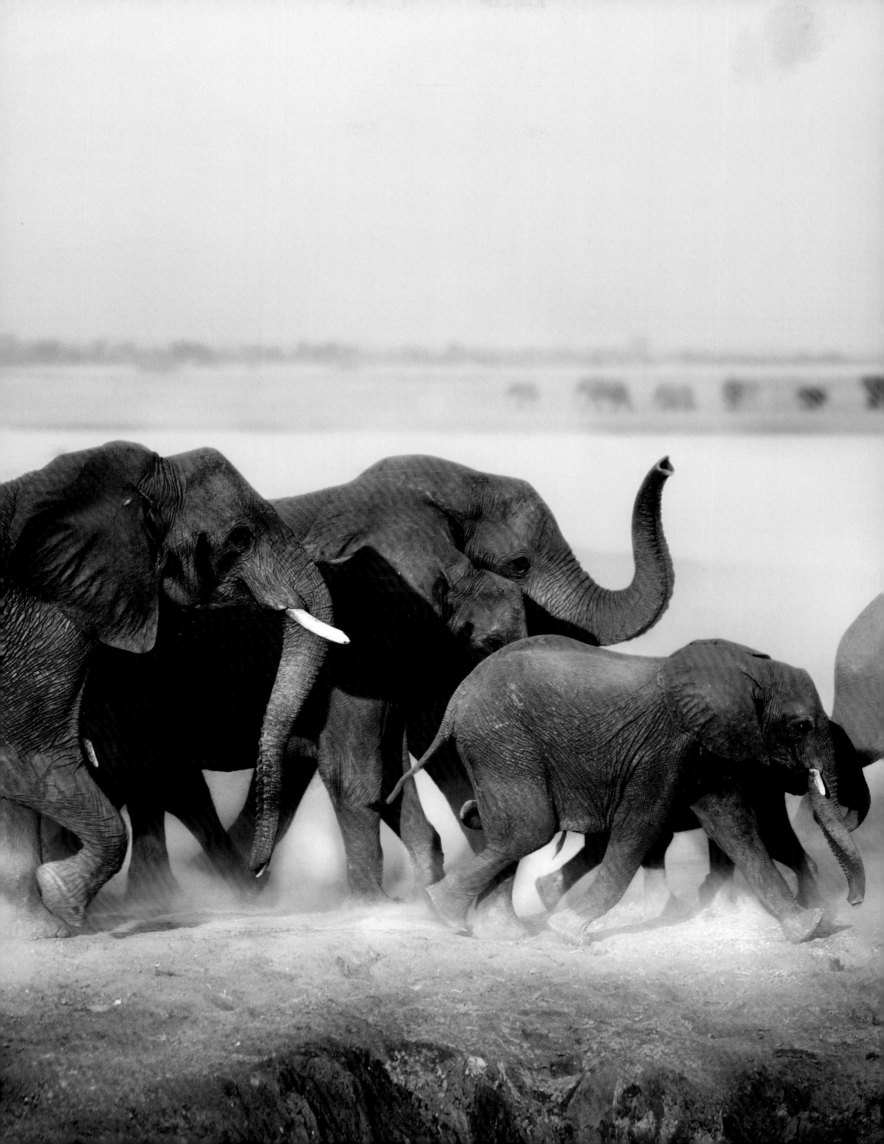

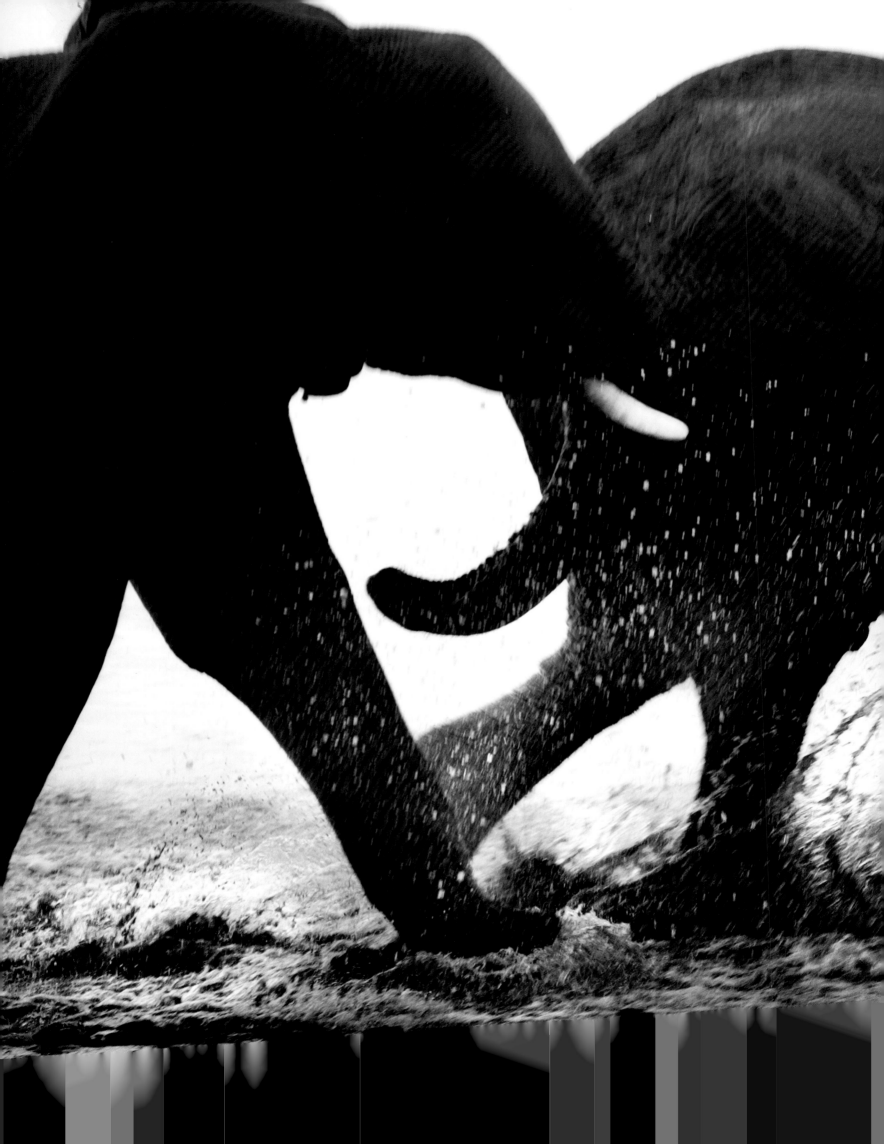

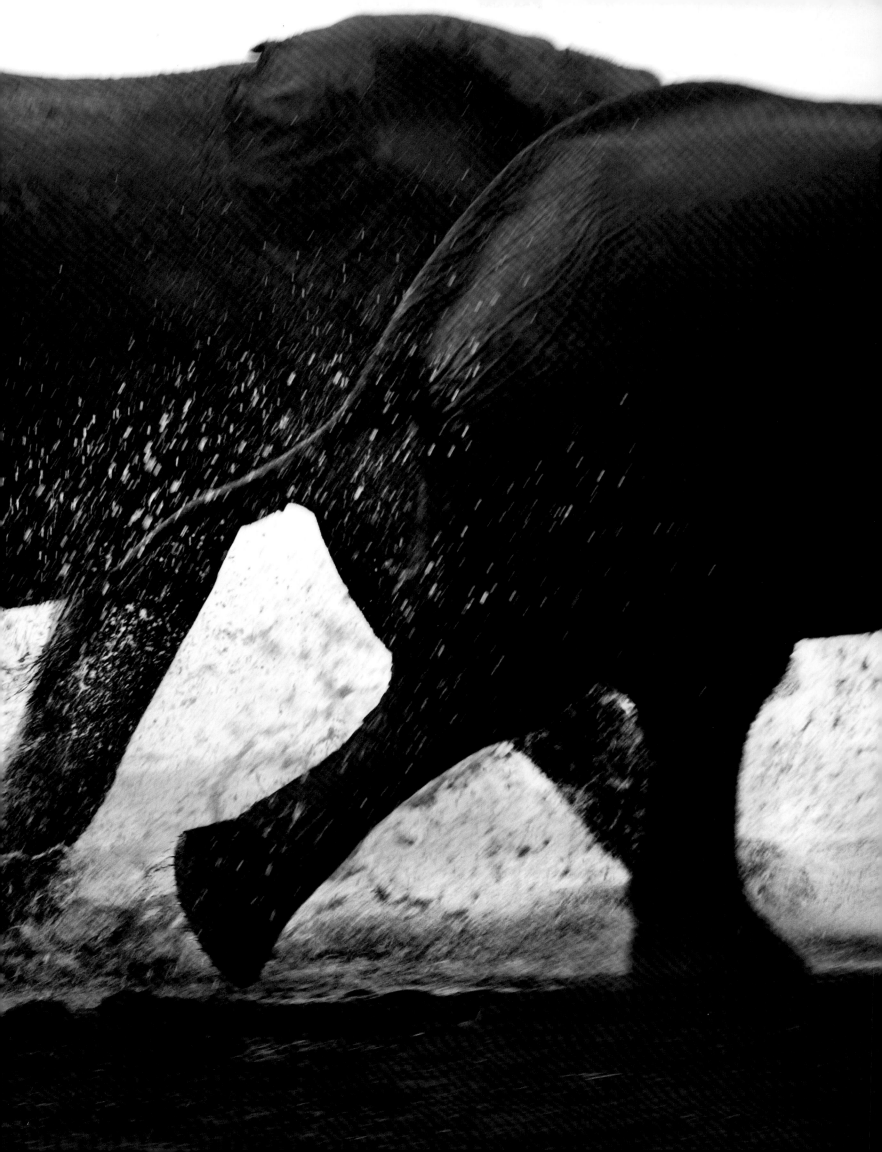

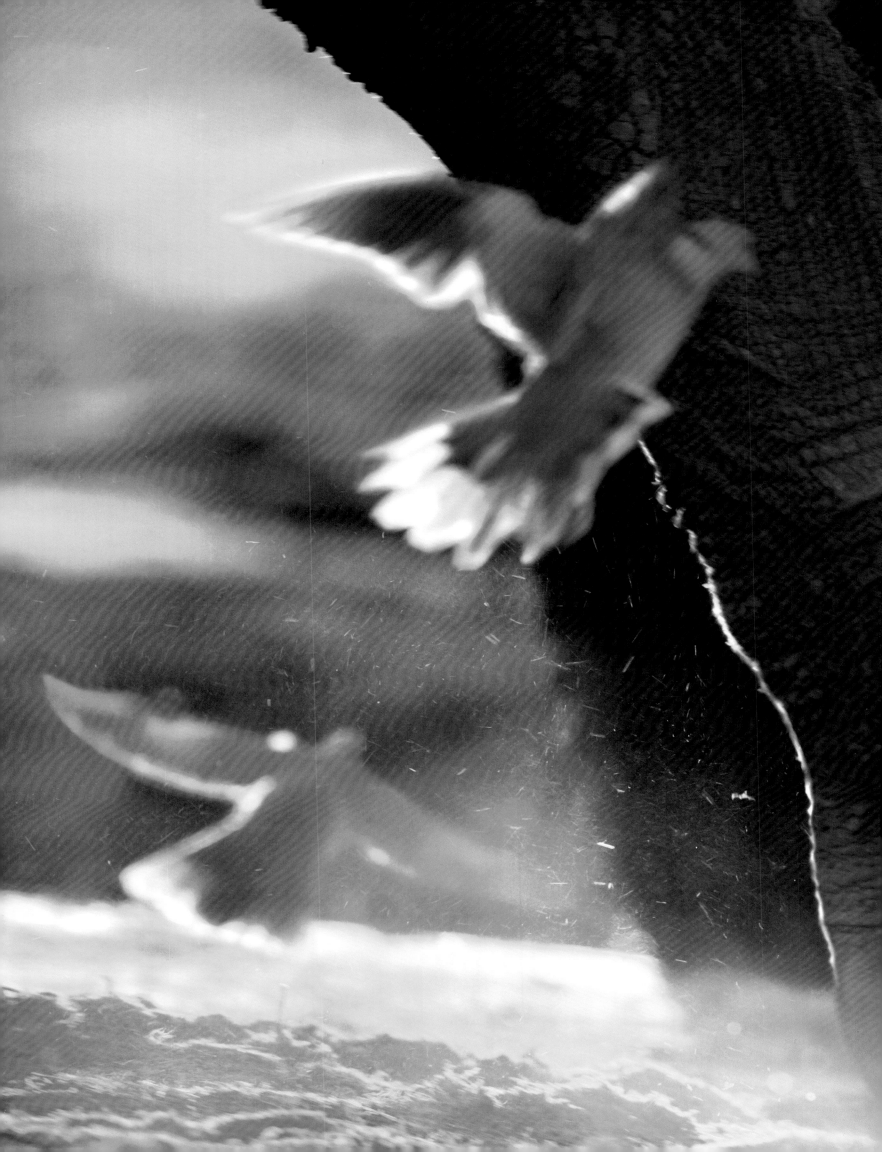

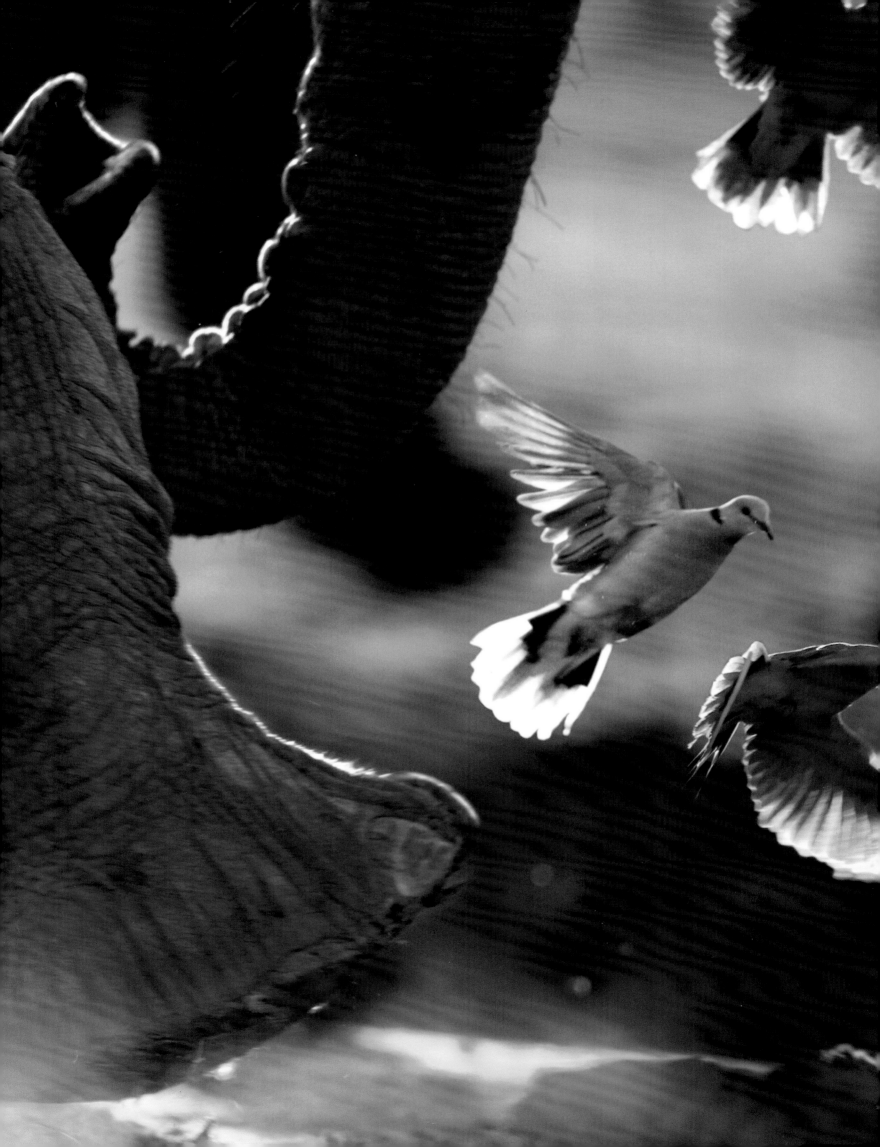

FOR KATHY

First published in the United Kingdom in 2006 by
Thames & Hudson Ltd, 181A High Holborn, London WC1V 7QX

www.thamesandhudson.com

© 2006 Steve Bloom
Author photo on jacket by Des Pretorius
Illustrations on pages 28, 31, 32 and 92 © 2006 Steve Bloom
Illustrations on page 188 are reproduced by kind permission of Mr Abdul Rasheed

www.stevebloom.com

British Library Cataloguing-in-Publication Data
A catalogue record for this book is available from the British Library

ISBN-13: 978-0-500-51321-7
ISBN-10: 0-500-51321-X

Printed and bound in Singapore by CS Graphics

CONTENTS

Elephants are silent.

They tread softly, like burglars in the night;

then they assail our nostrils with their earthy, musty odour.

Iron-willed and purposeful, elephants march

with the quietness and single-minded

determination of an army of ants.

They are true kings of the jungle.

STEVE BLOOM

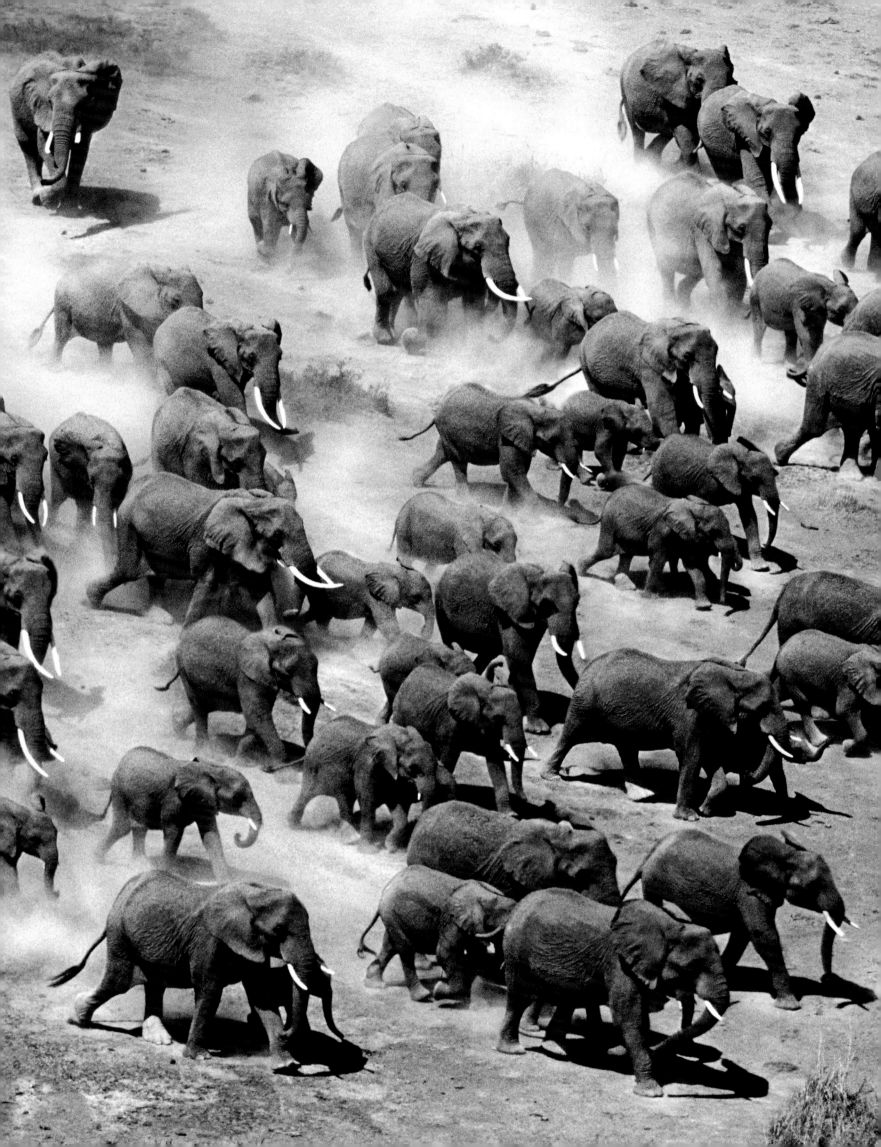

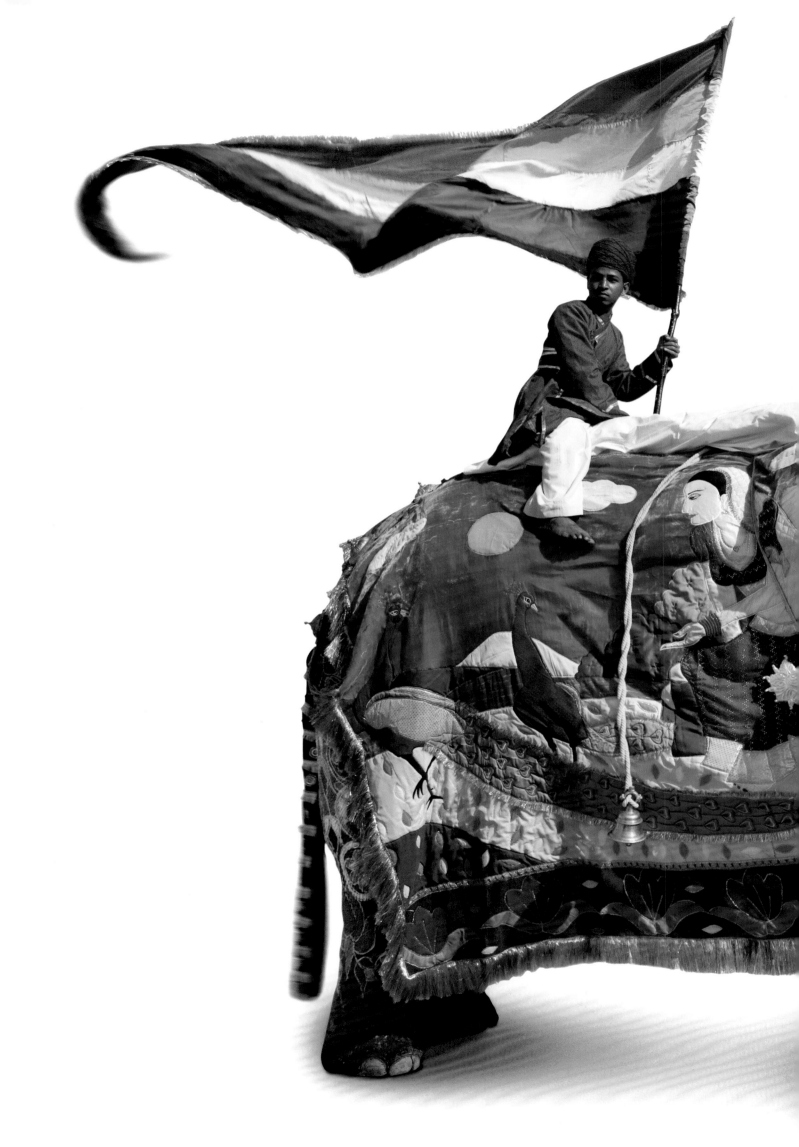

THE COLOUR OF ELEPHANTS

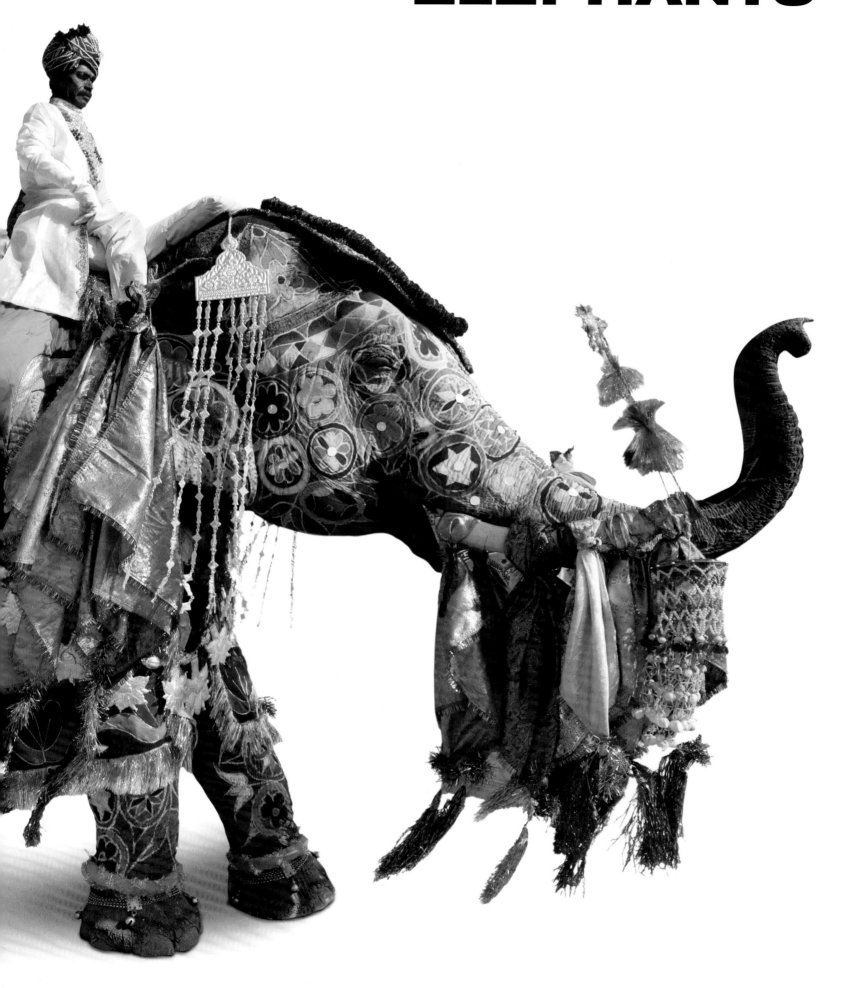

If you ask the average person to describe the colour of an elephant, you will most likely be told that elephants are grey. Certainly, on gloomy, overcast days, they can appear to be grey: but I have noticed many different colours emanate from elephants. As the light bounces off them, they seem pink at sunset, blue at night, orange in the morning and brown under a coating of dust. Photography reveals the emotional nature of subjects by exploiting the light that is reflected from them, thereby influencing our visual perception. Elephants are colourful subjects, and give off their own aura: an elephant splashing in the water in the morning, like a playful child, is a kaleidoscope of motion and colour.

If I search for a personal reason for creating this book about elephants, it is because, as a photographer, I am naturally drawn to subjects that appeal to me. I am decidedly attracted to elephants. At the age of six, I was given the exorbitant sum of five shillings to spend at a funfair and rather than go on rides, I spent the lot on a cuddly toy elephant. And so my fascination for these magnificent creatures was born, and the toy stayed with me until it disintegrated with age. Long ago I vowed that I would one day create a book about elephants, before I, too, disintegrate with age. And so this book is intended to be a joyous celebration of elephants, from the wildest outreaches of Botswana to the teeming cities of India. It is a reaction against all things grey, and an affirmation of the richness of colour and wide diversity that exists throughout the elephant world.

Elephants are similar to people in so many ways. They have family structures as we do. They show loyalty and allegiance, have individual personalities and even talk to each other with low rumbling sounds. The cry of a young elephant reminds me of a distressed child. When an elderly elephant stumbles and falls, and is helped to his feet by those around him, I realize that we are not so different from the animal world as we sometimes assume.

Elephants are awe-inspiring, and it is a great challenge to produce a book with images depicting their many facets. Over a period of twelve years, I have visited Africa and India, encountering countless different elephants with varying temperaments. I found them to be agitated in those areas where culling had taken place, and generally peaceful where humans posed little threat. It is the very recognition of their sentient nature that encourages us to become environmentalists and engenders a conviction that the only rightful place for ivory is on the face of an elephant.

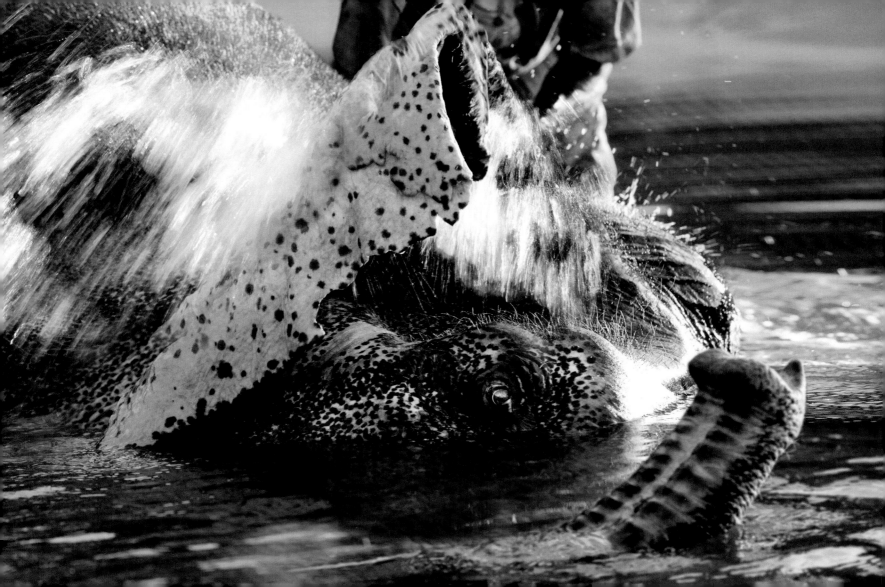

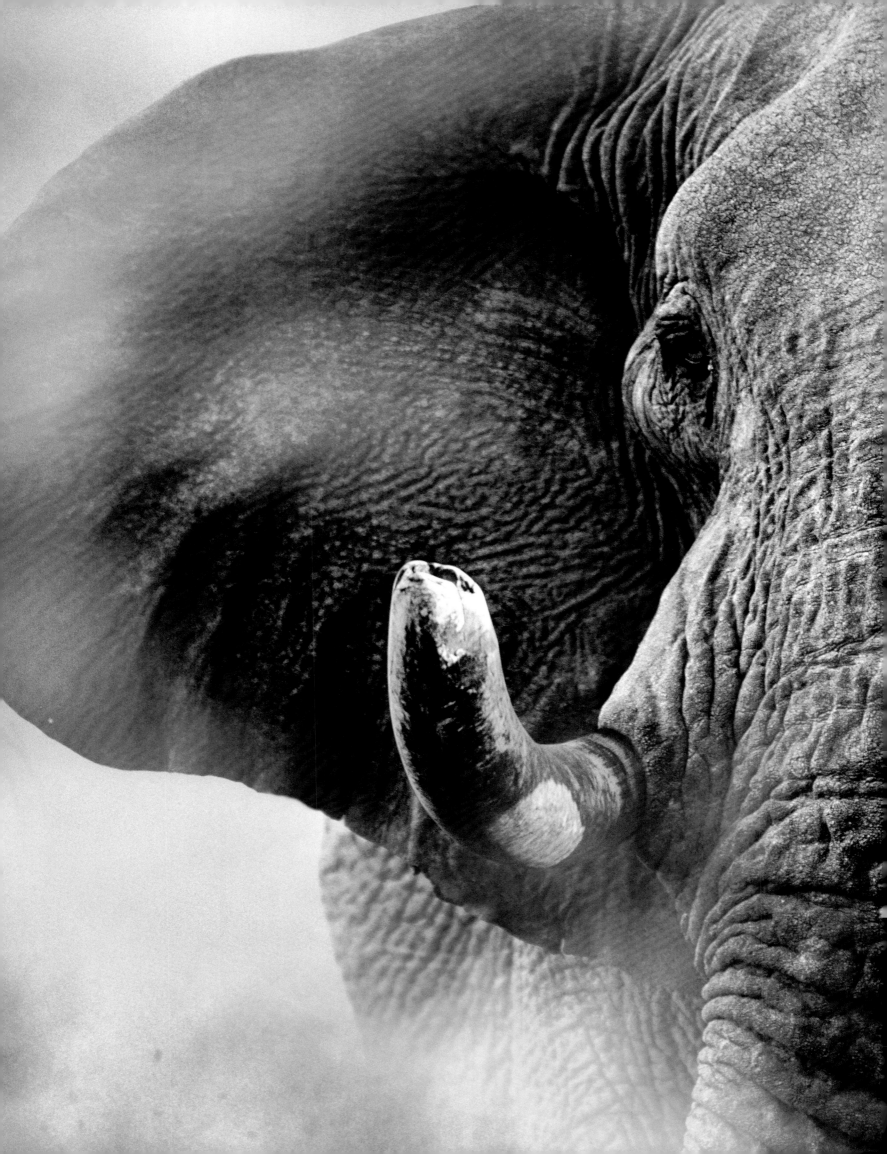

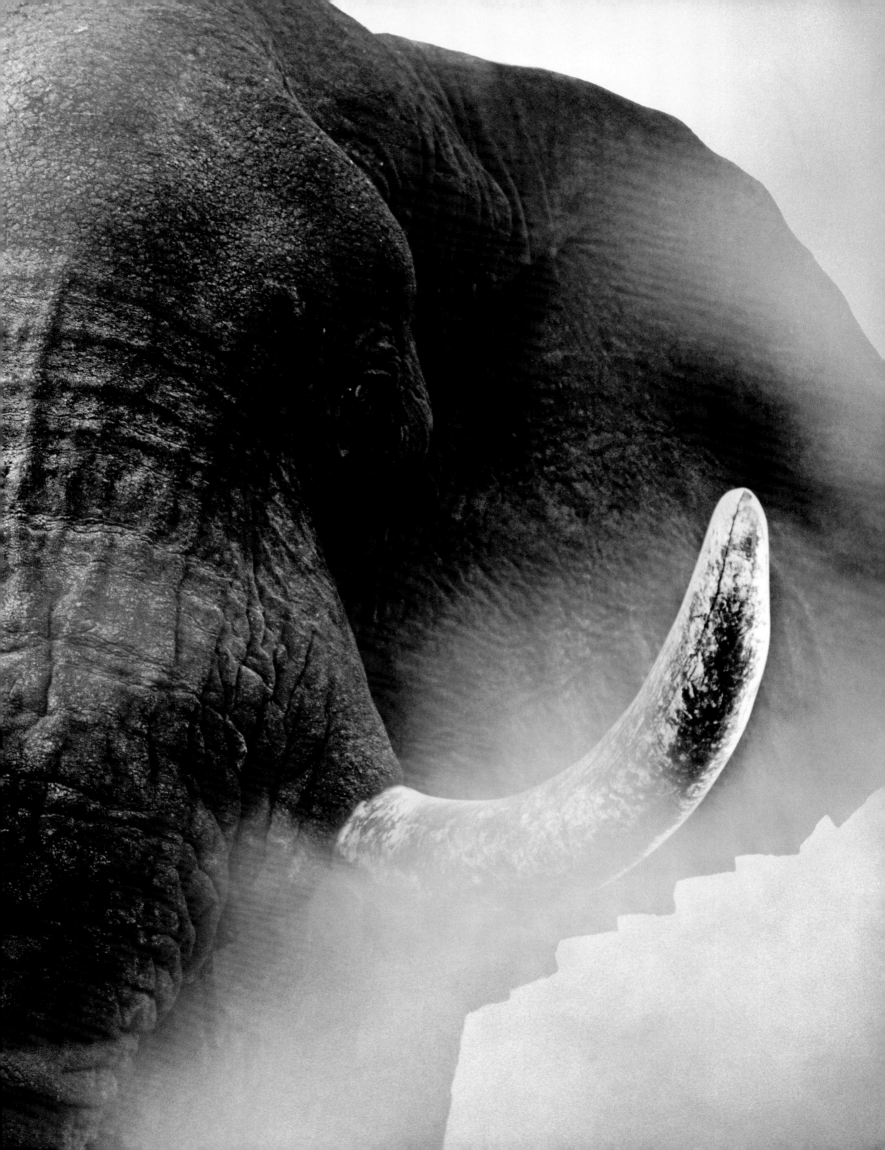

AFRICAN ELEPHANT

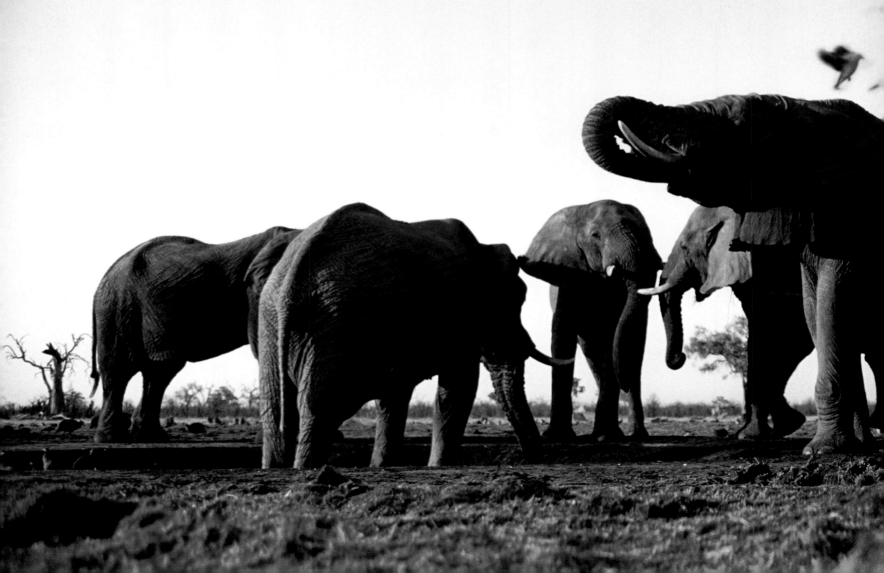

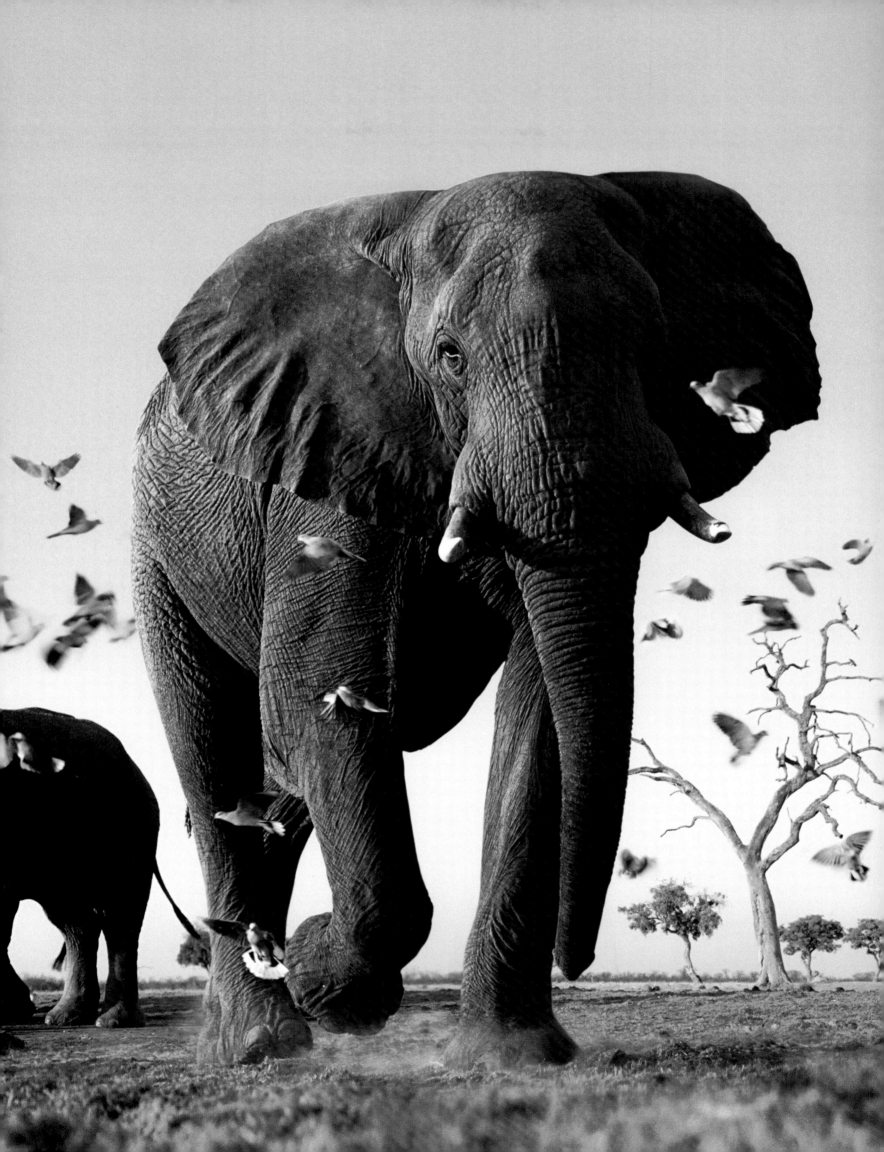

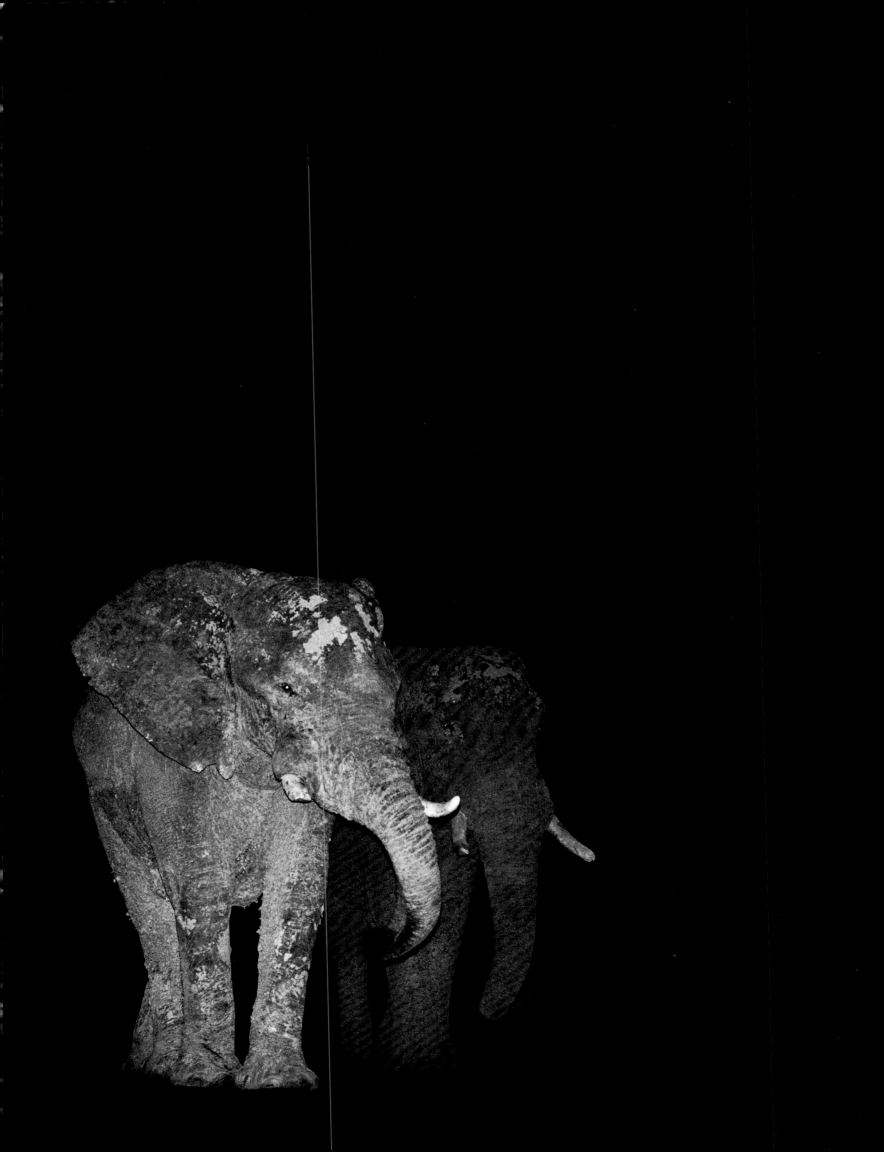

Water is scarce in Savute. Considerable time and energy is devoted to finding it in this remote part of Botswana where humans, in a display of compassion towards other species, lend a helping hand by sinking boreholes deep into the ground and pumping water to the surface. Such places are magnets for elephants, much to the annoyance of doves, jackals, lions, hyenas and many others who are equally thirsty, but not so massively imposing. Savute, I have decided, is a fine place to start my journey to search for something of the soul of the elephant.

I spent many nights watching elephants at a convenient waterhole. There was a constant bustle of activity as families came and went, each drinking as much as possible, always with a sense of great urgency before backing off to allow others to move in and take their turn. Generally the very young were allowed a free rein, though adolescents had to learn to be quite assertive if they, too, were to be given a chance to drink. One night I noticed an adult male on the periphery, nervously rocking back and forth while he waited for an opportunity to approach the water. In the moonlight, his huge size and enormous tusks made him appear physically intimidating and yet, whenever another elephant moved away from the water after drinking, he nervously took a few paces forwards, only to be edged out by others who rushed in ahead of him. Many of these elephants were comparatively small, but much more assertive. I watched him for many hours that evening, and by the time I went to bed, he had not yet been able to take the opportunity to drink. It was a hot night, and he must have been parched. Afterwards I sat in my tent, with a large bottle of water at my side, and thought about him. He looked strong, and all he had to do to get a drink was wave his trunk in the air and make a loud noise. Surely a path to the water would have opened up, had he displayed typical bullish behaviour?

Appearances can be deceptive, and elephants are deeply sensitive individuals. Though he was physically large, I sensed a damaged personality within. Inside the bulk of his fine strong body lay a frightened individual, someone easily intimidated, pushed to the sidelines of society. This particular elephant, a tormented soul, made me realize how, if we only look deeper, we can detect something of the inner psyche in other creatures. I wondered what it must be like to actually be him – to stand there, thirsty and tired, frightened of those smaller than himself; those who should by rights be his subordinates. What must it feel like to be an elephant with collapsed self-esteem?

I have photographed elephants in many places, and one thing that struck me about their behaviour in Savute was their general lack of hostility towards humans. Though families with young babies were nervous of me, and naturally dangerous to approach, large males in bachelor herds seemed quite relaxed in my presence. This was not surprising, as local people had built boreholes to help the elephants gain access to water. However, in places where culling had occurred, even years later, I felt far more threatened and the elephants were particularly sensitive in the presence of humans. In South Africa, I simply parked my car at the side of the road one day when a large bull came crashing angrily at me through the bushes, chasing me away. Like us, elephants never forget bad experiences. They vary in personality and temperament much as we do, and may be vengeful and harbour grudges, or be placid by nature. Their individual make-up – that mysterious combination of personality traits made from a fusion of genes and experiences – pours scorn on all the arguments about animals being unfeeling, devoid of self-awareness.

Our relationship with elephants stretches back thousands of years. They are the largest of the land mammals, and once roamed the world. Our fascination for them has consequently influenced our mythology and cultures. Worshipped as gods, regarded as bizarre curiosities, symbols of status and wealth, and used in warfare by historical figures such as Hannibal and Alexander the Great, elephants have been exploited throughout history. The Romans used them in gladiatorial competitions, and they have been pitted against each other for mankind's entertainment, with bouts staged right up until the early twentieth century. In Asia, thousands of elephants have been forced to work, hauling timber in logging camps, ploughing fields and turning forests into farmland, so destroying their own habitat for the benefit of people. Our reverence for elephants is perhaps eclipsed by our abuse of them.

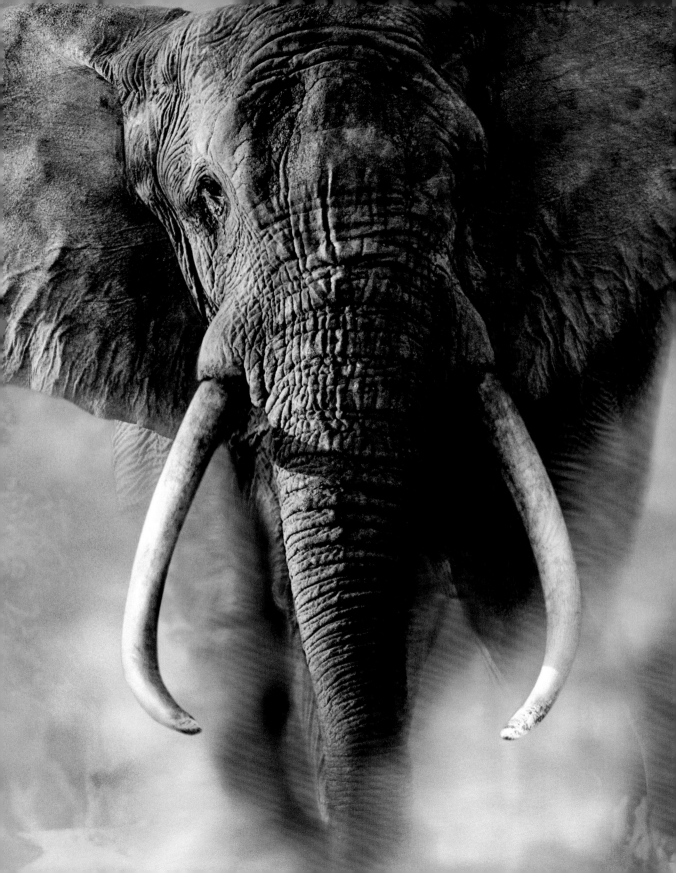

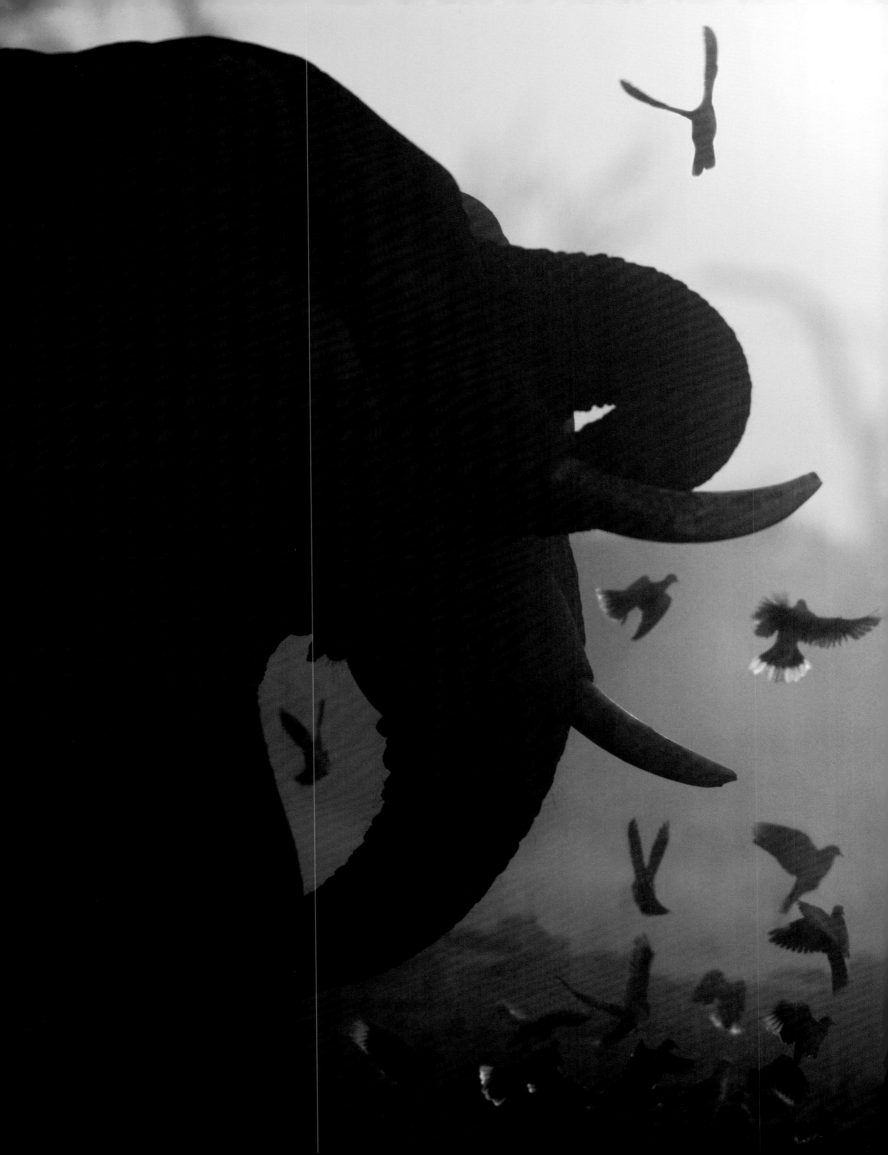

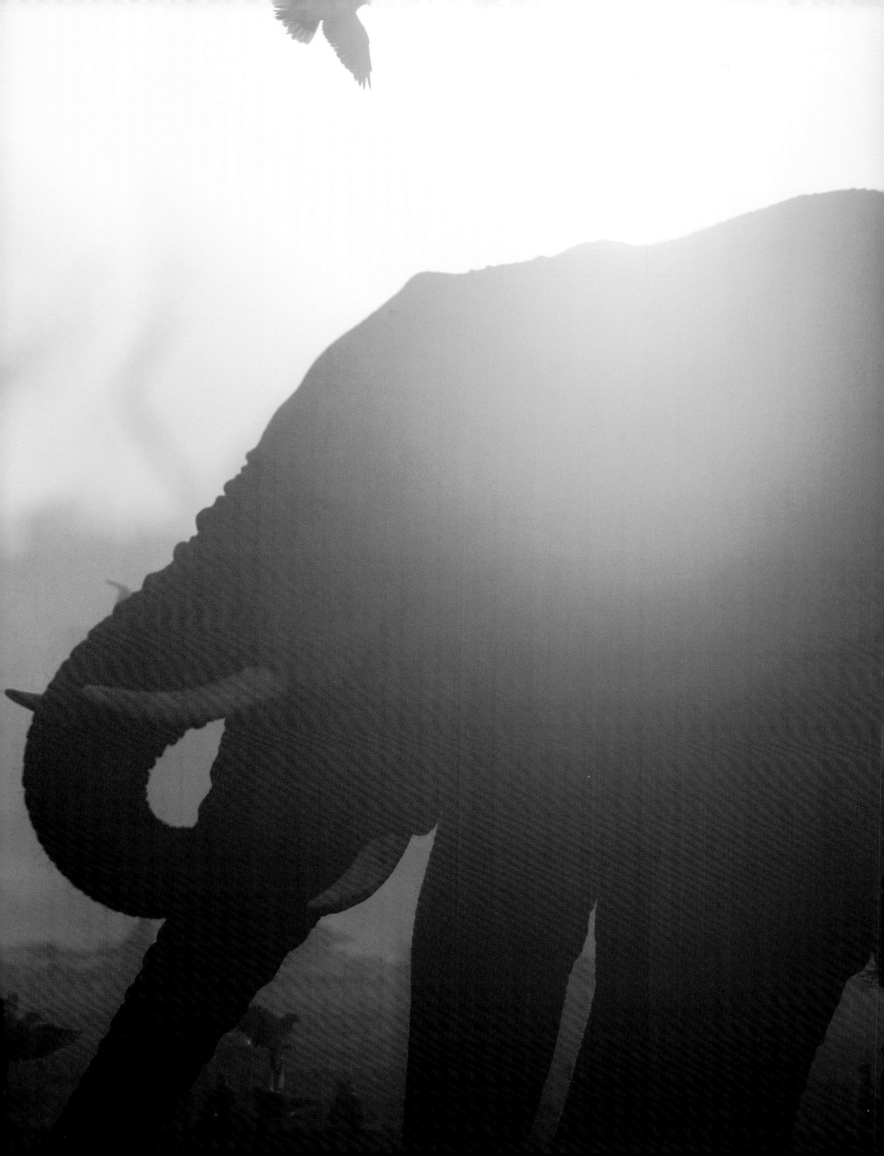

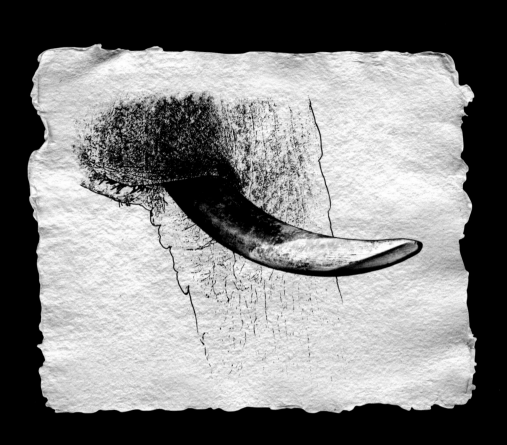

Sadly, our own myopic greed has almost driven them to extinction during recent decades. Though their numbers are recovering thanks to the restrictions on the ivory trade, the hunger for 'white gold' during the 1980s severely threatened their tenure on this planet. In the last century alone, their population has fallen from ten million to five hundred thousand. A couple of hundred years ago they were found in forty-six countries, a number now reduced to a mere handful. Local Africans were puzzled by early white hunters who built ships and organized expeditions to kill elephants on a grand scale, merely to make ivory trinkets and cutlery handles that could so easily be fashioned from wood. Once an object is perceived as being superior to its alternative, humans are reluctant to accept second-best, a psychological trait well exploited by the advertising industry. The fact that electric cars do not go as fast or as far as petrol-driven ones, seems sufficient grounds for us to choose far more environmentally destructive gas-guzzlers, recklessly behaving as if there were no tomorrow. Ivory was once thought of as the best material for piano keys. It felt special to the touch, and absorbed sweat from the fingers. How ironic it is that so many elephants were sacrificed to make those very instruments through which the human soul is expressed. Pianists would unleash their feelings and reach out to others through the physical medium of an elephant's tusk. These animals died for our music.

In Victorian times billiard balls were made from ivory, and it took the tusks of two bull elephants to make a single set for one table. This made the popular game of billiards the bloodiest of sports. Suitable alternatives such as Bakelite and plastic were later invented, so piano playing and billiards can now be considered to be somewhat less barbaric.

The scale of our abuse of elephants has been colossal. Elephants are very large, and the smell of a single dead elephant rotting in the African sun is totally overpowering. A small piece of rotting meat in the kitchen is obnoxious, so imagine a large decaying elephant emitting an acrid, pungent wave, so unbearable that you block your nostrils and it is virtually impossible to get close. Imagine the repugnant stench of two dead elephants burning your throat as you try desperately to breathe through your mouth; now double that to four, eight, a hundred, a hundred thousand. Imagine the industrial scale of the massacre of hundreds of thousands of elephants. The smell alone is beyond anything we can imagine. The slaughter of an elephant, a sensitive, deeply emotional, highly intelligent creature, is ultimately tantamount to killing a part of ourselves.

In Botswana one morning I came across a hefty chunk of tusk lying on the ground; the result, no doubt, of a heated argument between two elephants. I had stopped at that same spot for breakfast an hour earlier, and so the dust had barely settled. I picked it up and explored its texture with my fingers. A large, heavy piece, it weighed down on my arms as I raised it aloft. There was something about it that was deeply fascinating – an allure, a mystical exquisiteness. I marvelled at its density, and felt a sense of wonder at this extra weight that the elephant had until recently carried. It felt so very organic, with a life of its own, glowing in the sunlight with a lustre that seemed to emanate from within. It was as if I were holding the very spirit of an elephant in my hands, and at once I understood the intensity of the appeal of ivory. I imagined a slow-motion movie: dust flying, giant heads clashing, the gut-wrenching sound of bone cracking, a tusk spiralling through the air, landing with a resounding thud. I wondered how the elephant was coming to terms with his loss. I gently laid the tusk on the ground, back into its own imprint in the soft sand, exactly where I had found it. And then I thought of the beautifully carved ivory figurine, an unfortunate family inheritance from long ago, that sits in my dining room and serves as a constant reminder of the brutal lengths to which we are prepared to go for our aesthetic indulgences. As thinking, moral beings, if we allow elephants to become extinct, the legacy of deep and painful remorse will be carried like an open wound for generations to come.

When I watch a group of elephants splashing and enjoying the water, I feel like I am watching my own family at play at the seaside, or perhaps I am sensing something of the veneration strong among Hindu families when they joyously bathe in the Ganges. I stand in amazement, watching a kaleidoscope of frenetic activity: forms and shapes splashing about, exuding the very essence of life.

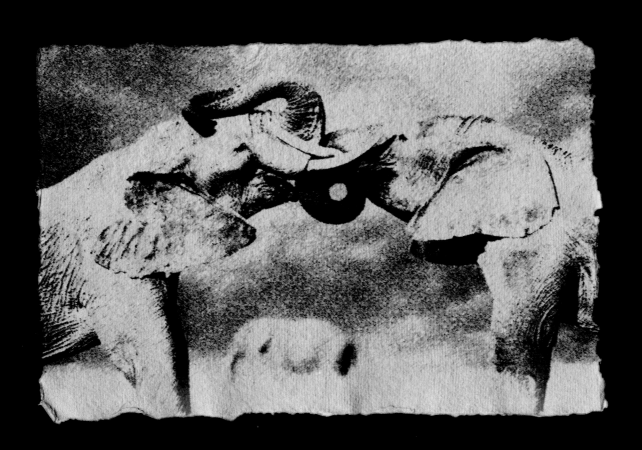

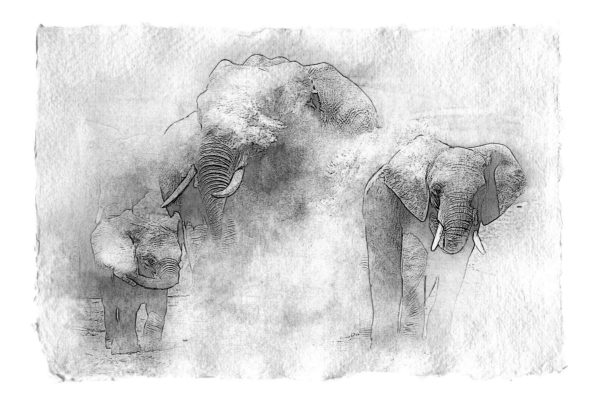

Their bodies may be different from ours, but the spirit feels so very human. The mothers keep watchful eyes on the children as they wallow, roll and spray water at each other. A mischievous baby ventures too deep, and is hauled out by an anxious matriarch. When mum decides to go, it is time for everyone to go, no arguments, and they all move off as collectively and quickly as they had arrived. An uneasy calm pervades the pool, until the vibrant, noisy arrival of the next family disturbs the air. The experience of seeing such activities helps to blur the line which separates the species, so enabling us to feel a greater affinity with the natural world. Just imagine a world without elephants.

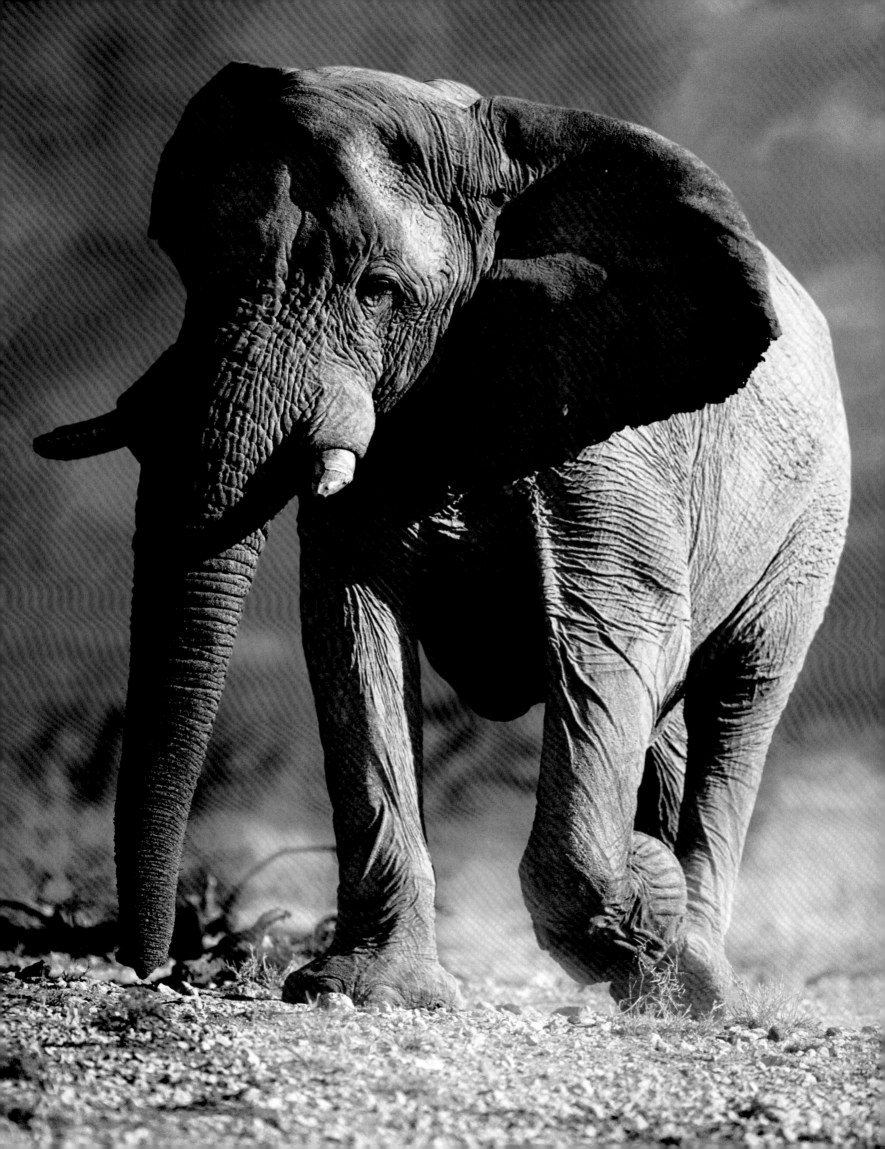

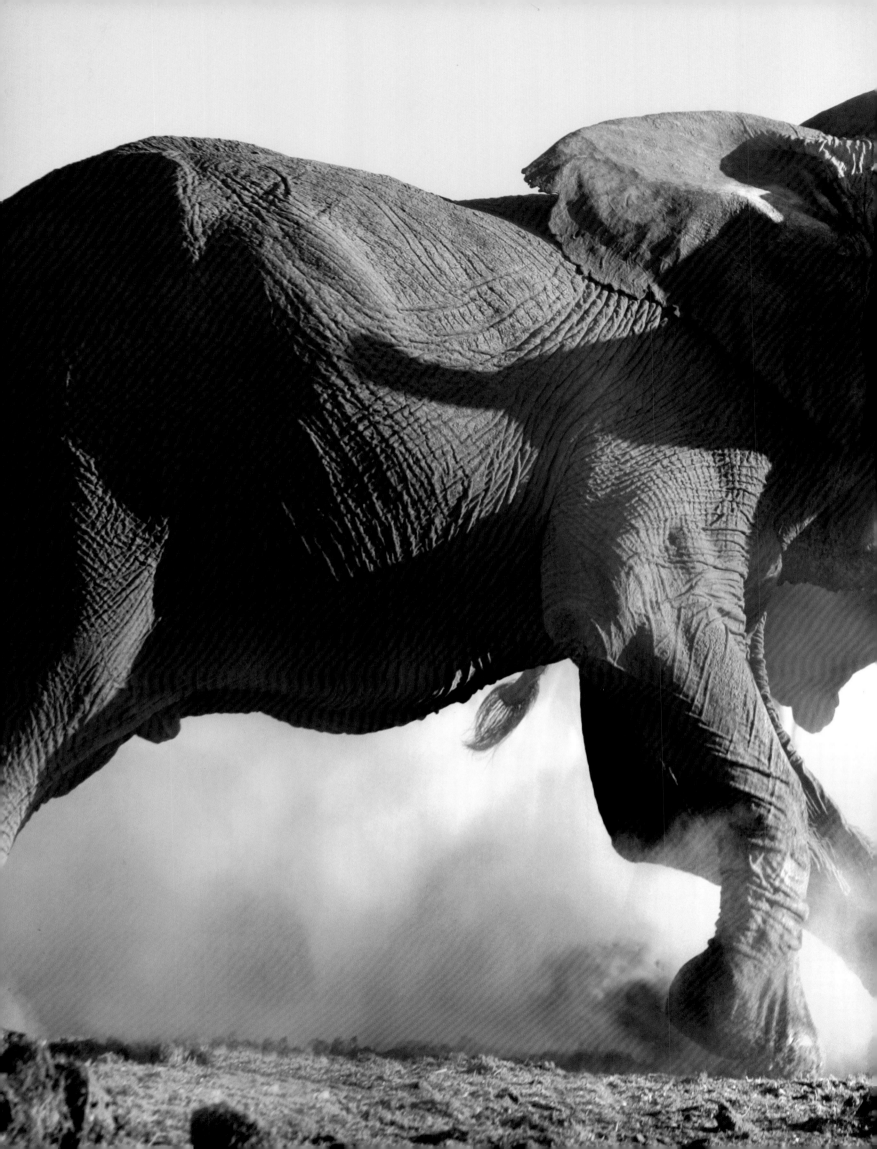

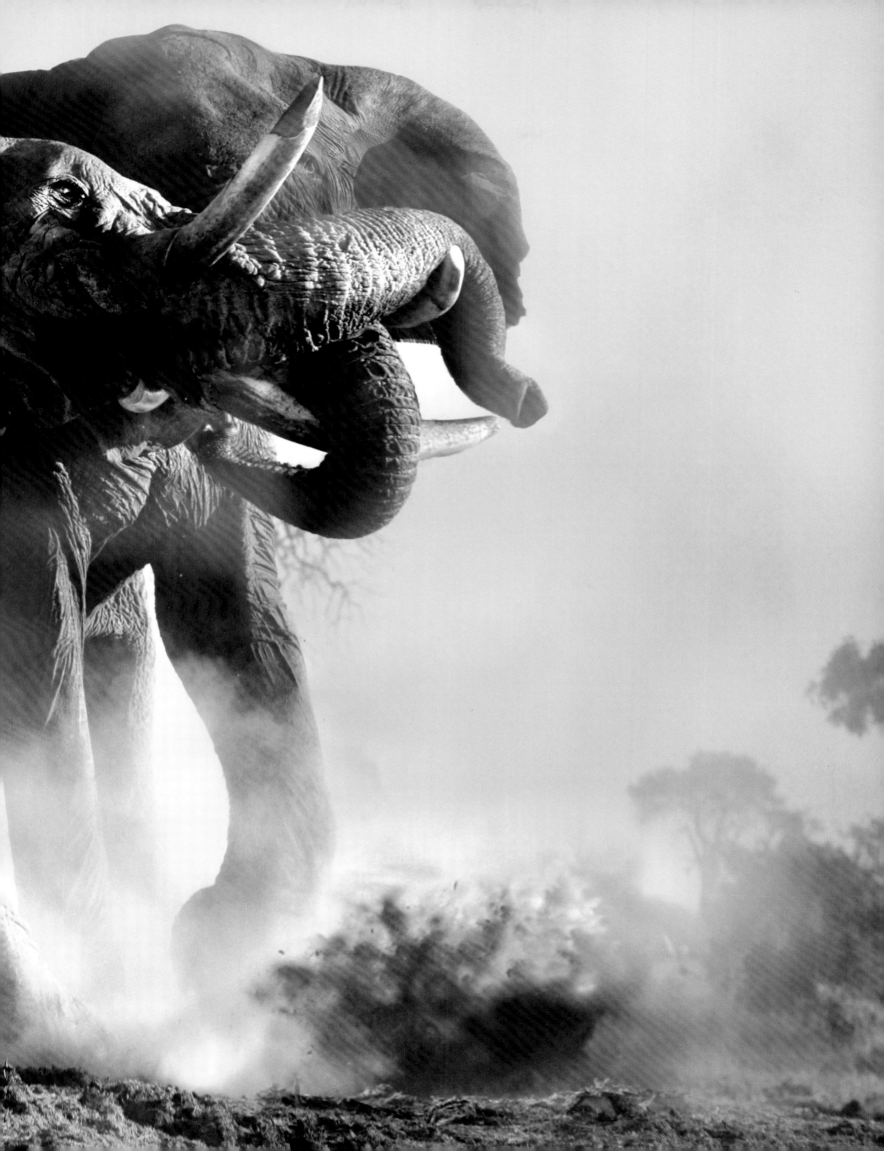

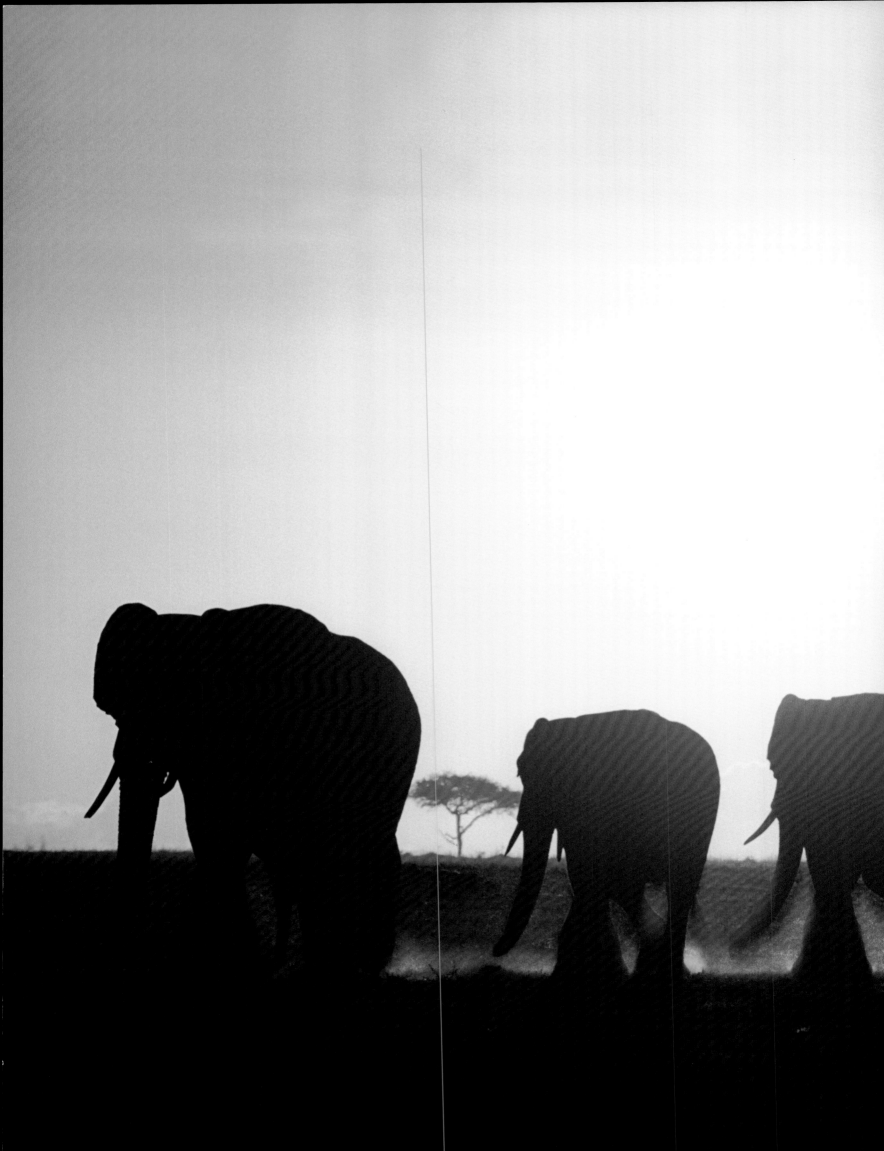

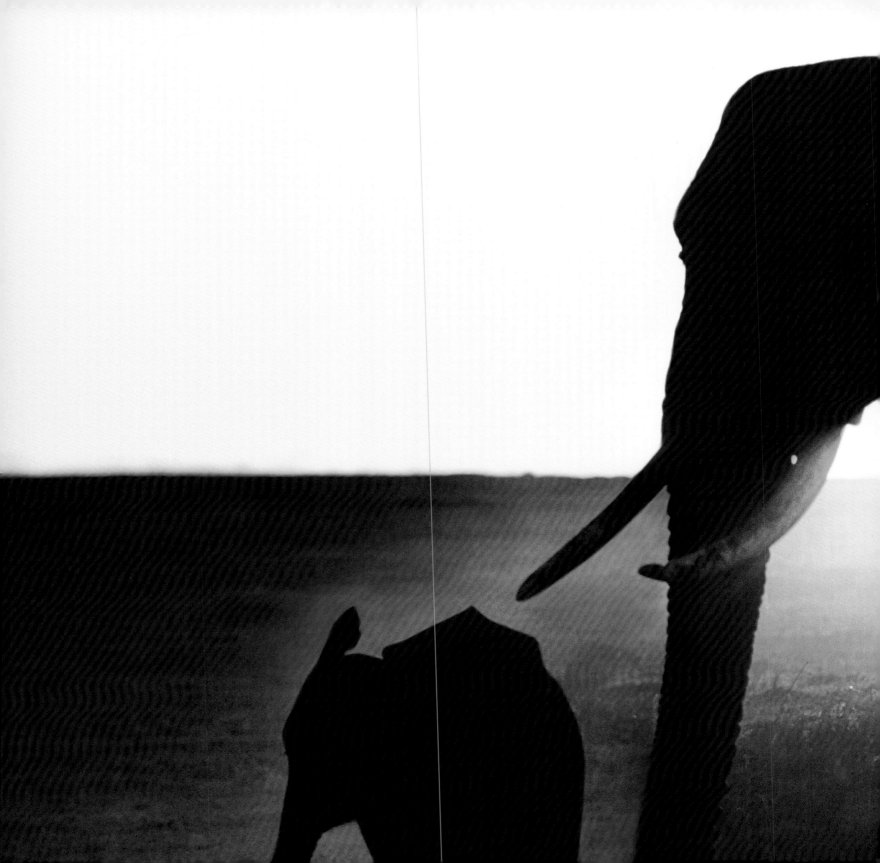

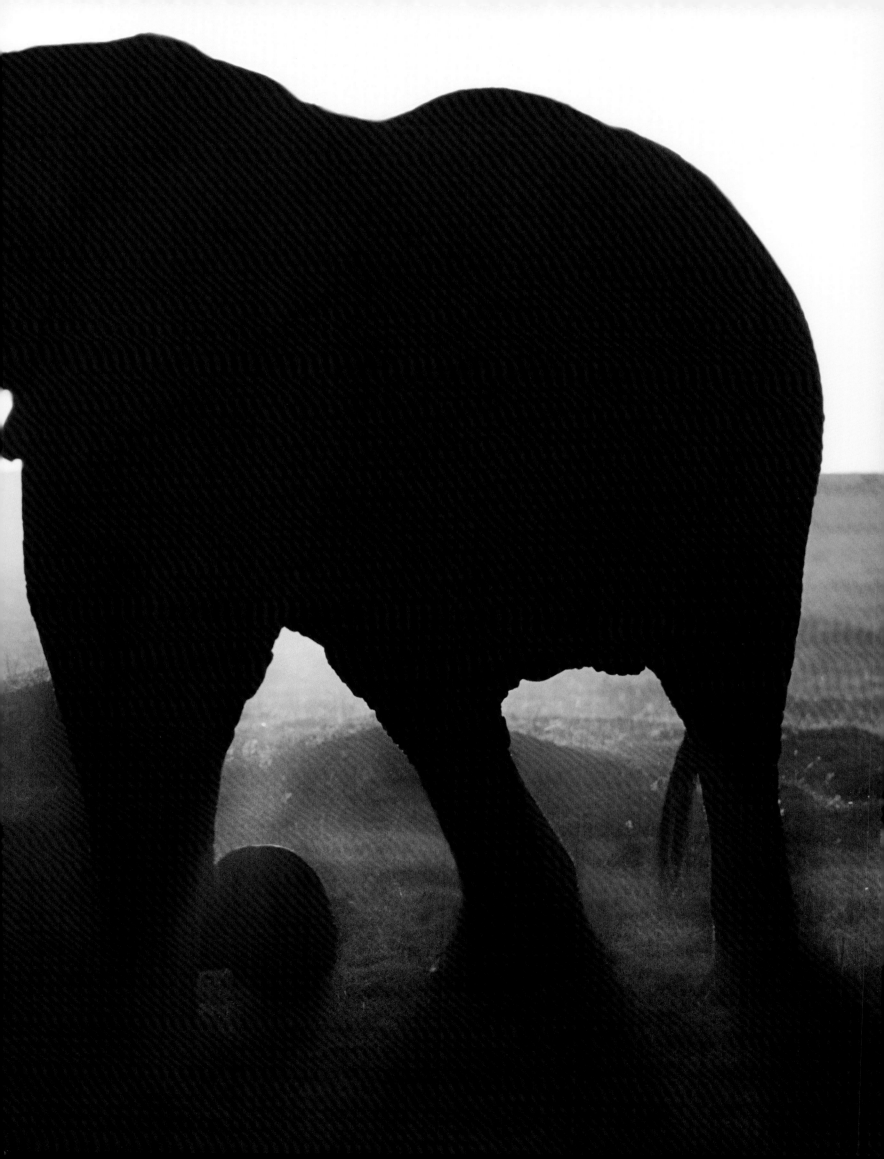

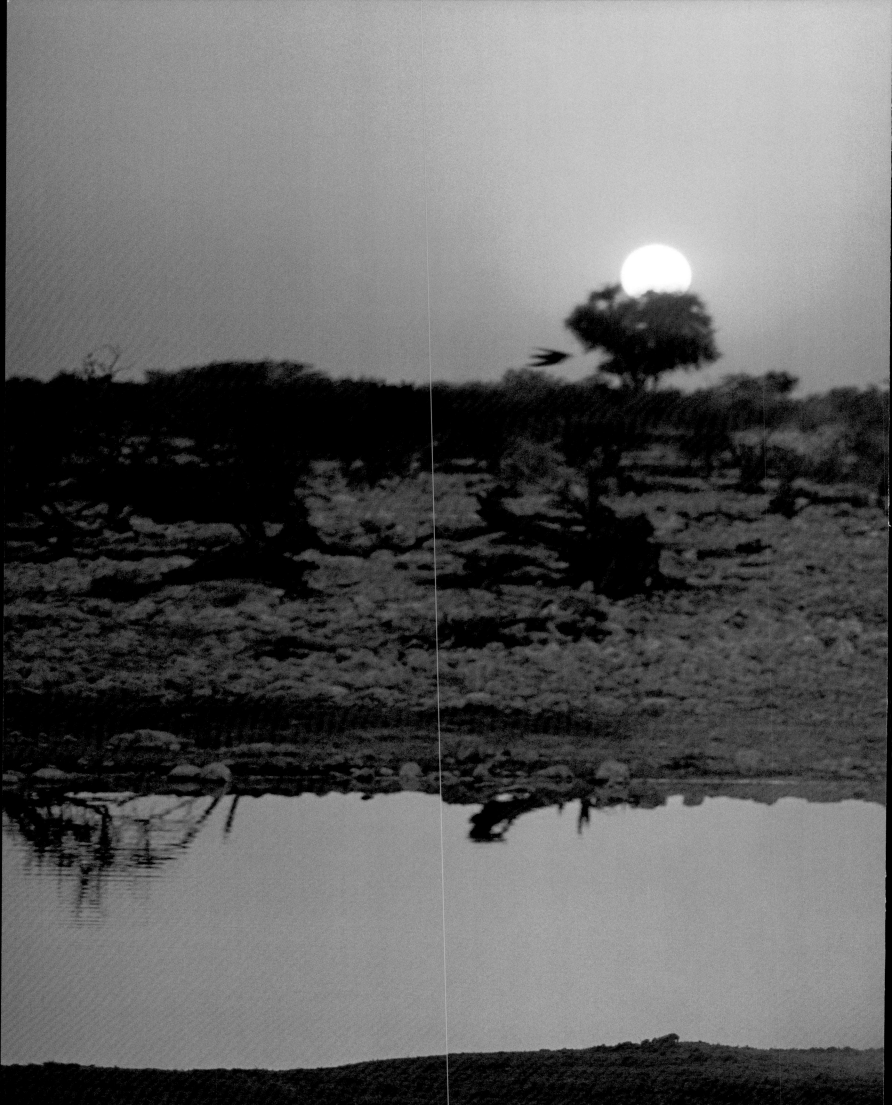

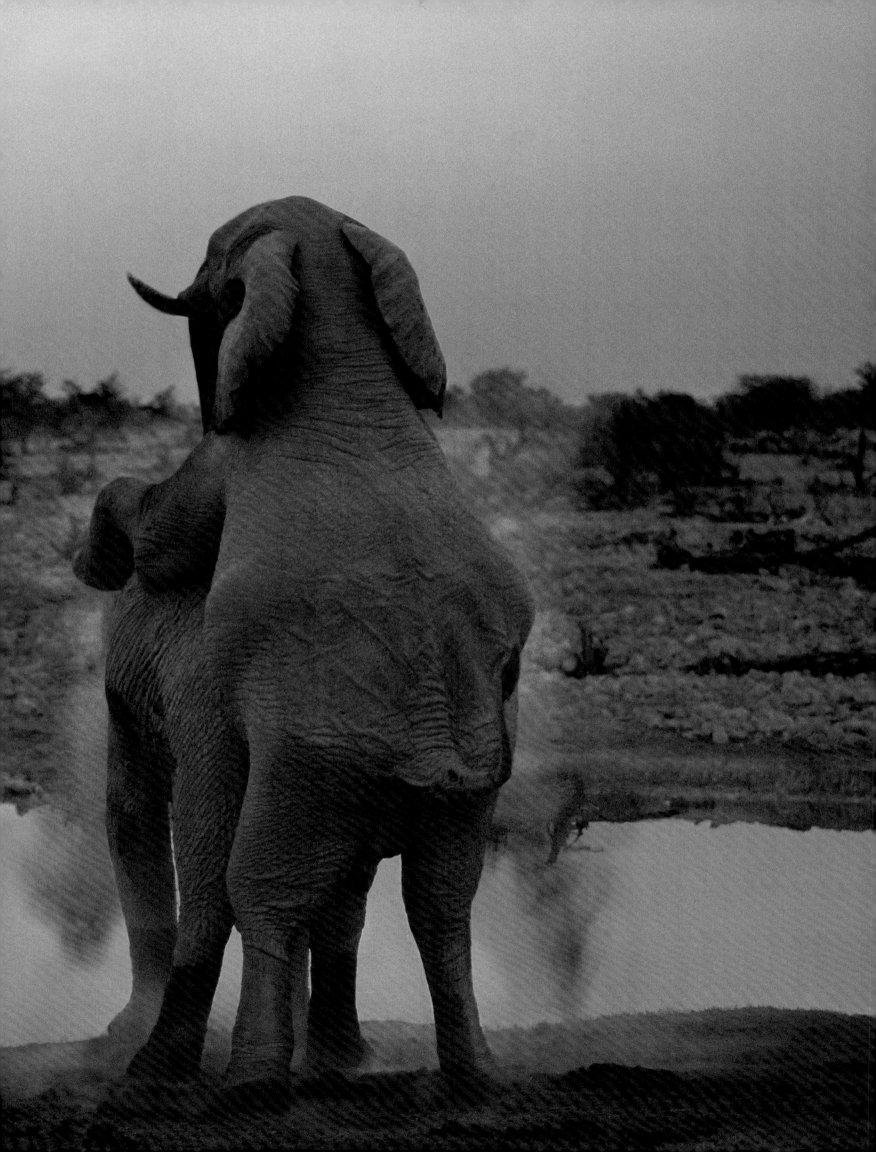

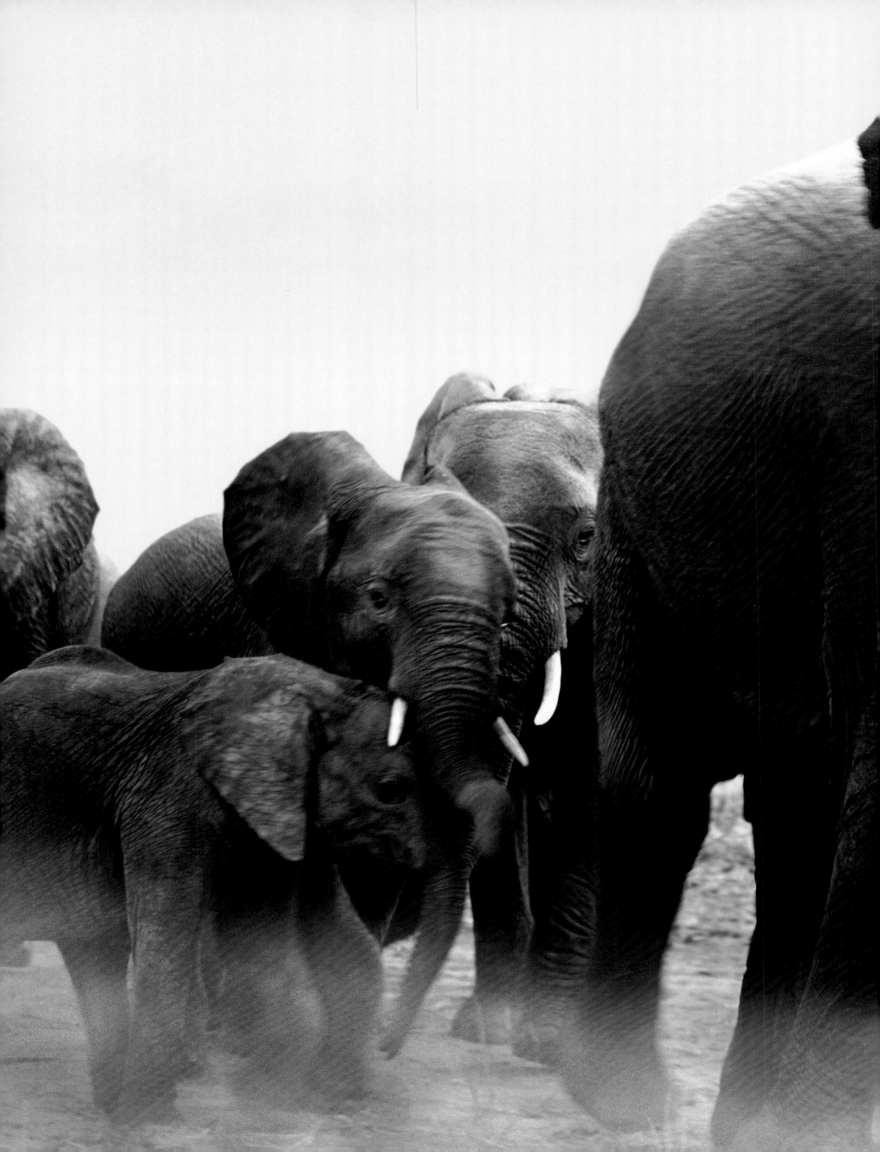

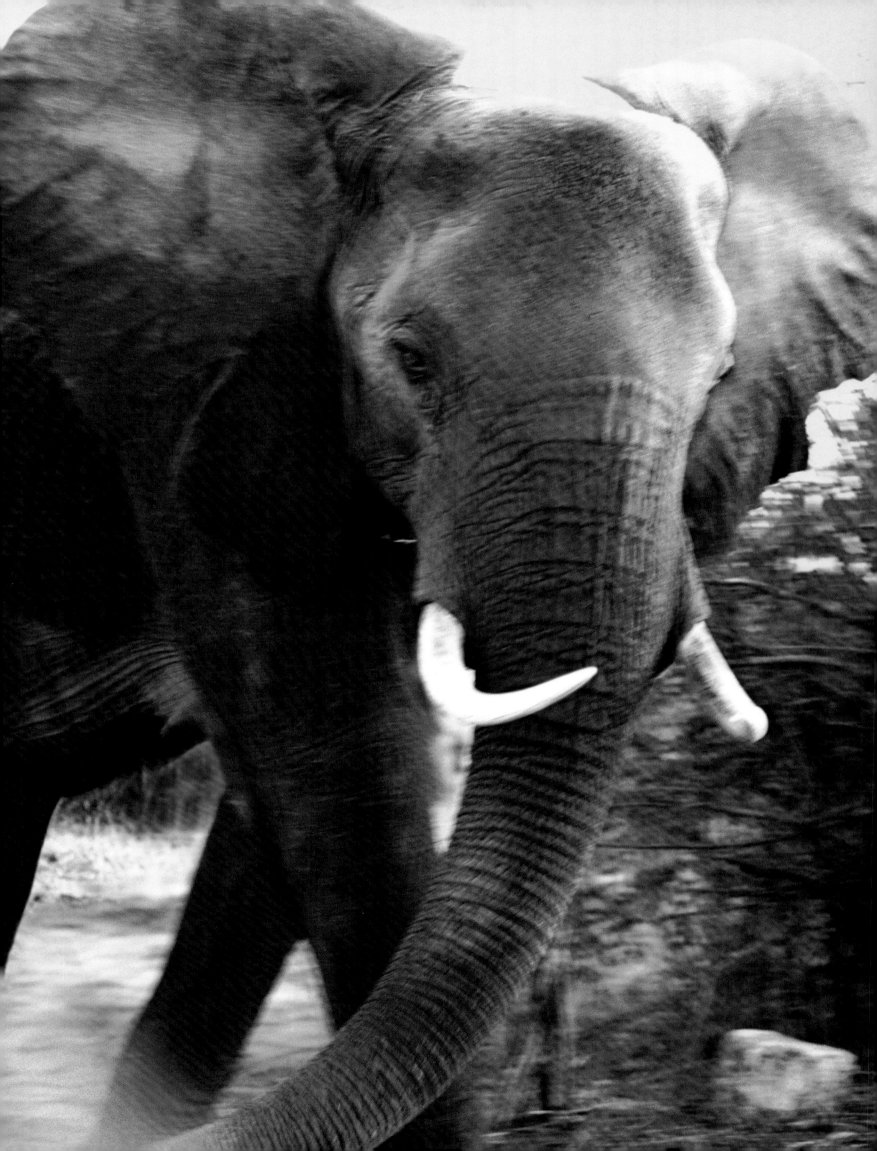

Imagine the wildest, most remote regions of Africa, with teeming masses of animals. Such a mental picture would be sadly lacking without the inclusion of elephants marching proudly across the plains.

They are certainly more entertaining to watch than lions, who, like most cats, lie around and sleep for much of the day. Many visitors to the reserves have a tendency to seek out big cats, and when a lion is sighted, herds of tourists will rush past elephants, as if demonically possessed. When they reach the lions, tour drivers jostle for position, forming a laager of four-by-fours which encircle the slumbering cats, surrounding them with the clattering rumble of diesel engines. The slightest twitch of a feline ear sends clouds of flies into the air, amid the collective rattle of clicking cameras. Lions, accustomed to the sounds of the mini city that surrounds them, lie low, watching the flurry through one eye, half-open. Clouds of monoxide gas give them a taste of the air of Los Angeles or Athens.

Elephants are spared this indignity, and would probably not put up with such nonsense anyway. For me they hold a greater interest, as the quintessential symbol of Africa's wildlife. Their ears even bear an uncanny resemblance to a map of Africa, as if we need reminding! Their diverse personalities and interpersonal relationships are endlessly fascinating to watch, especially at waterholes, where dramas unfold like soap operas. I once watched as a young male elephant, unable to push through the crowd to gain access to the water, deliberately poked his tusk into the backside of a large and rather menacing bull. Chaos erupted, with the large bull fighting everyone in sight, amid loud trumpeting and flying dust. For a moment, a brief moment, the waterhole was deserted, and the young protagonist seized his opportunity to drink alone while all the others were embroiled in a bar-room brawl. Elephants, I suspect, have a sense of humour.

There are places in Africa where elephants have sanctuary, and nowadays, thankfully, not every elephant with large tusks has a looming death sentence. In some areas, long tusks have, to an extent, been bred out due to selective killing of large tuskers for the ivory trade. Although the habitat of Africa's elephants has shrunk dramatically in recent centuries, it remains a pleasure to find them in areas as diverse as the deserts of Namibia and the rainforests of central Africa.

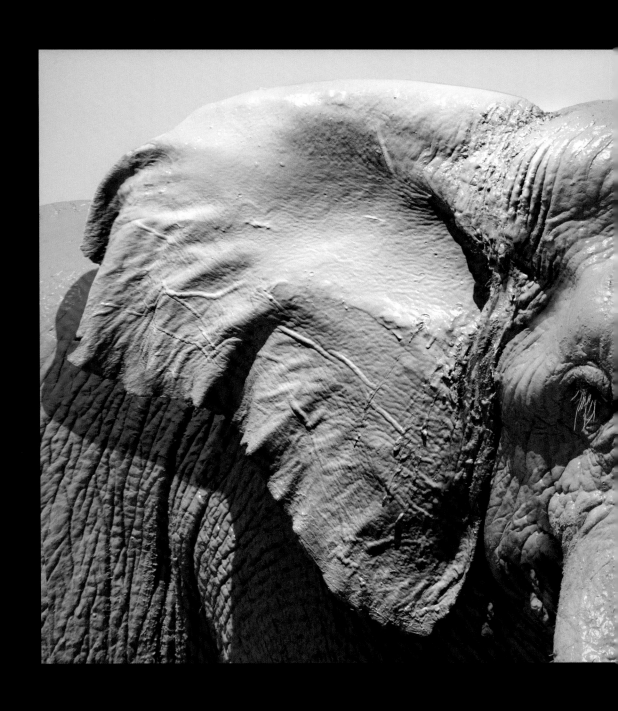

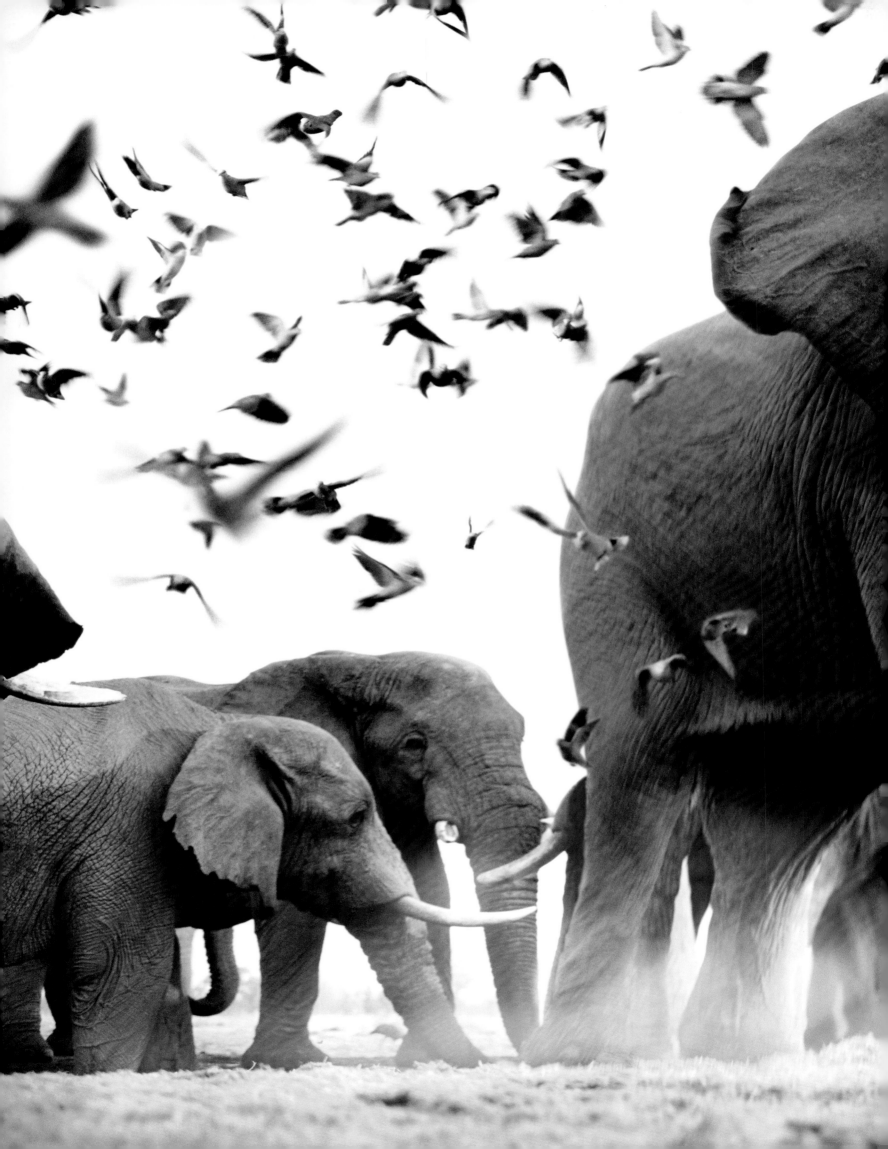

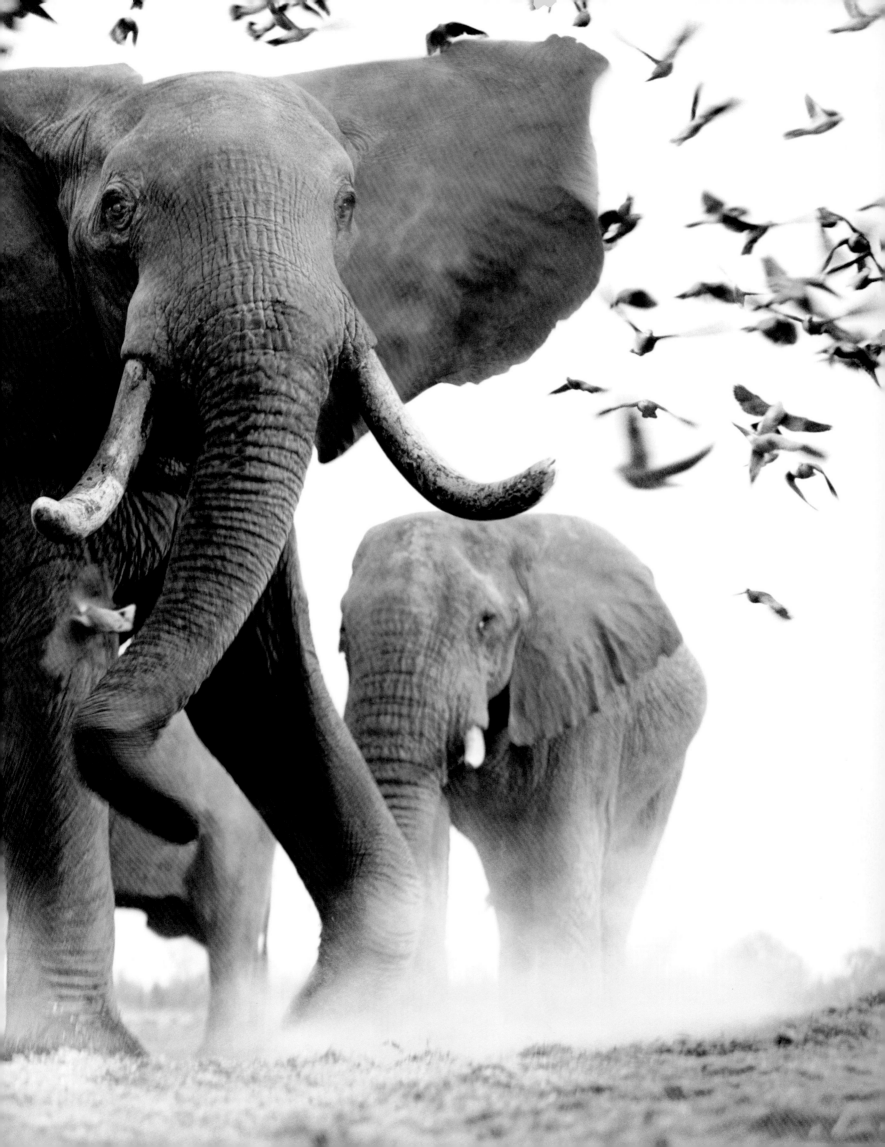

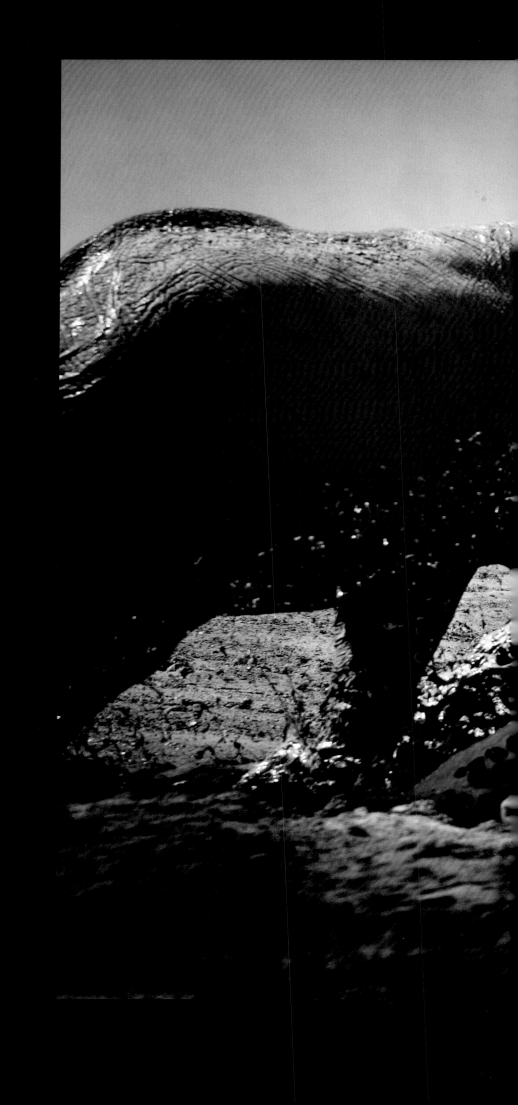

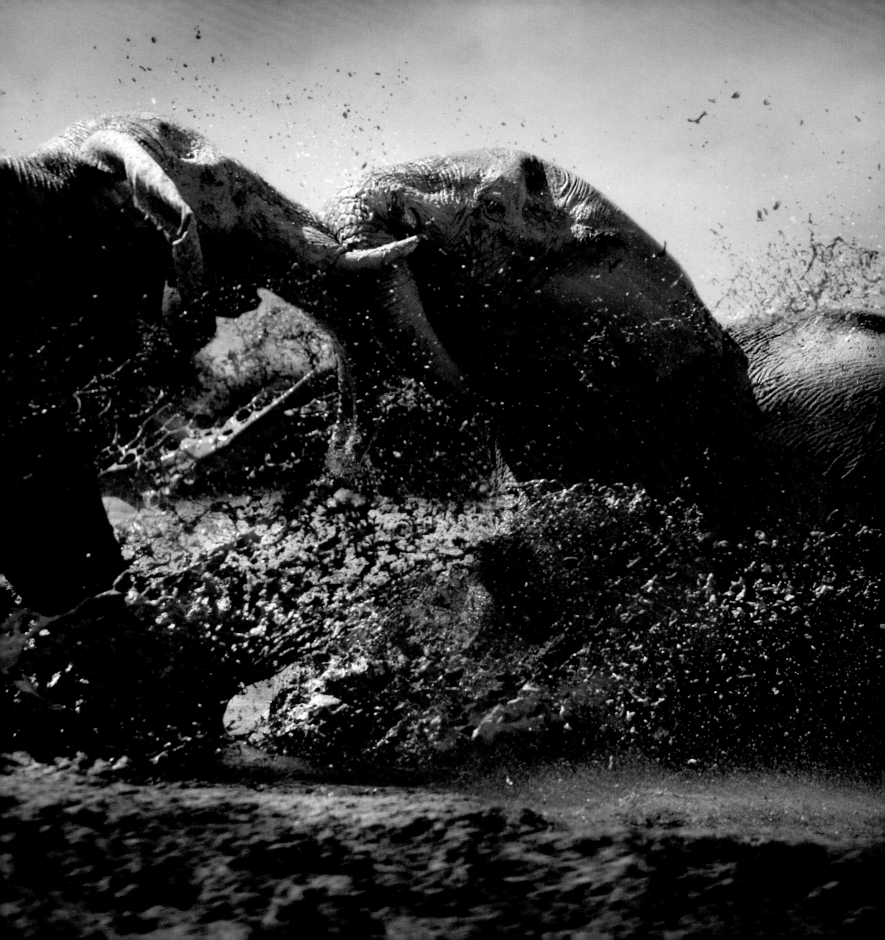

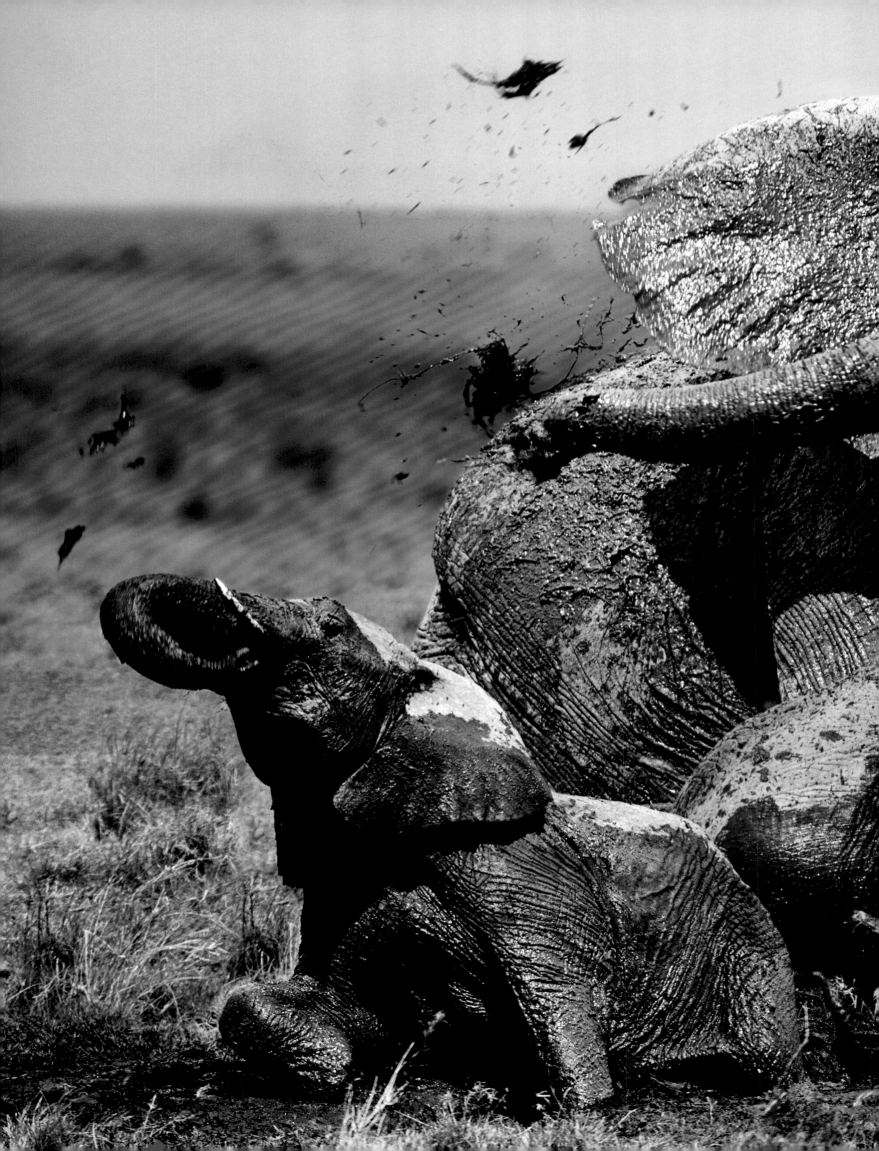

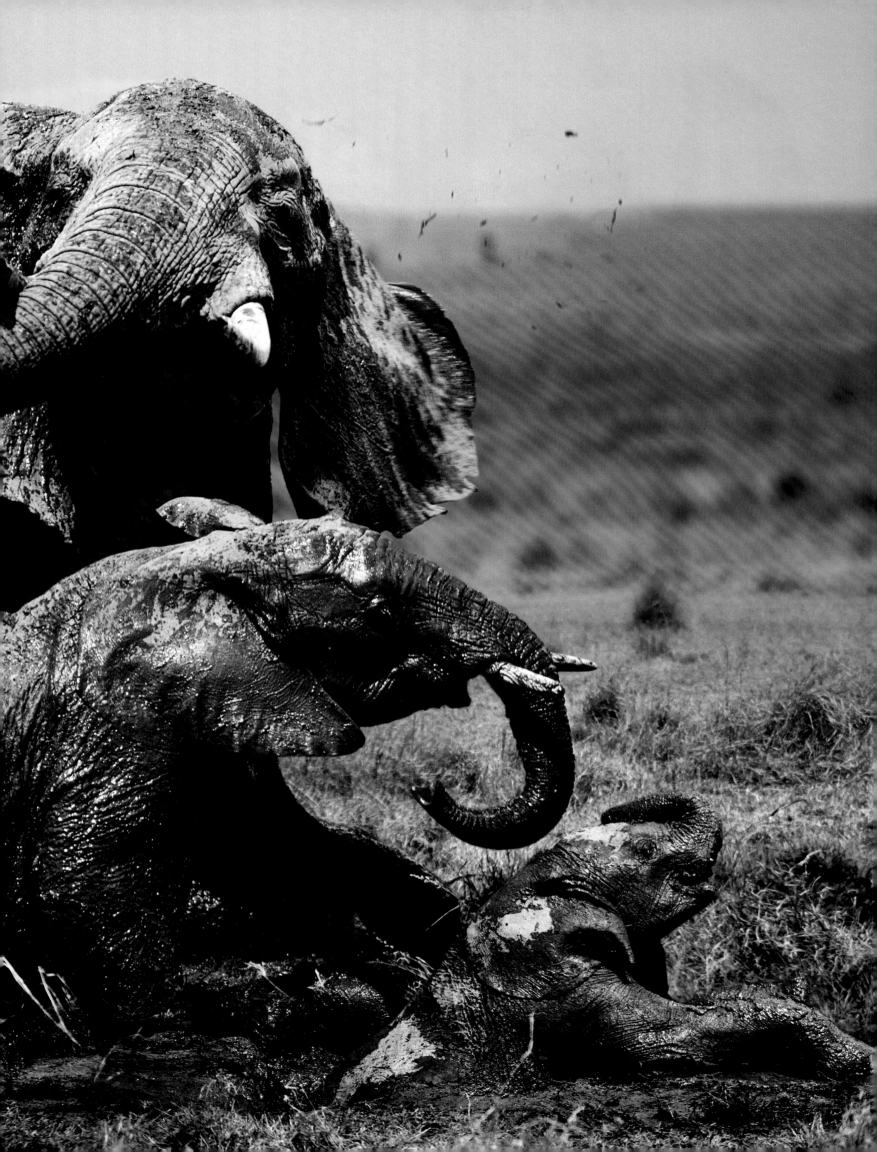

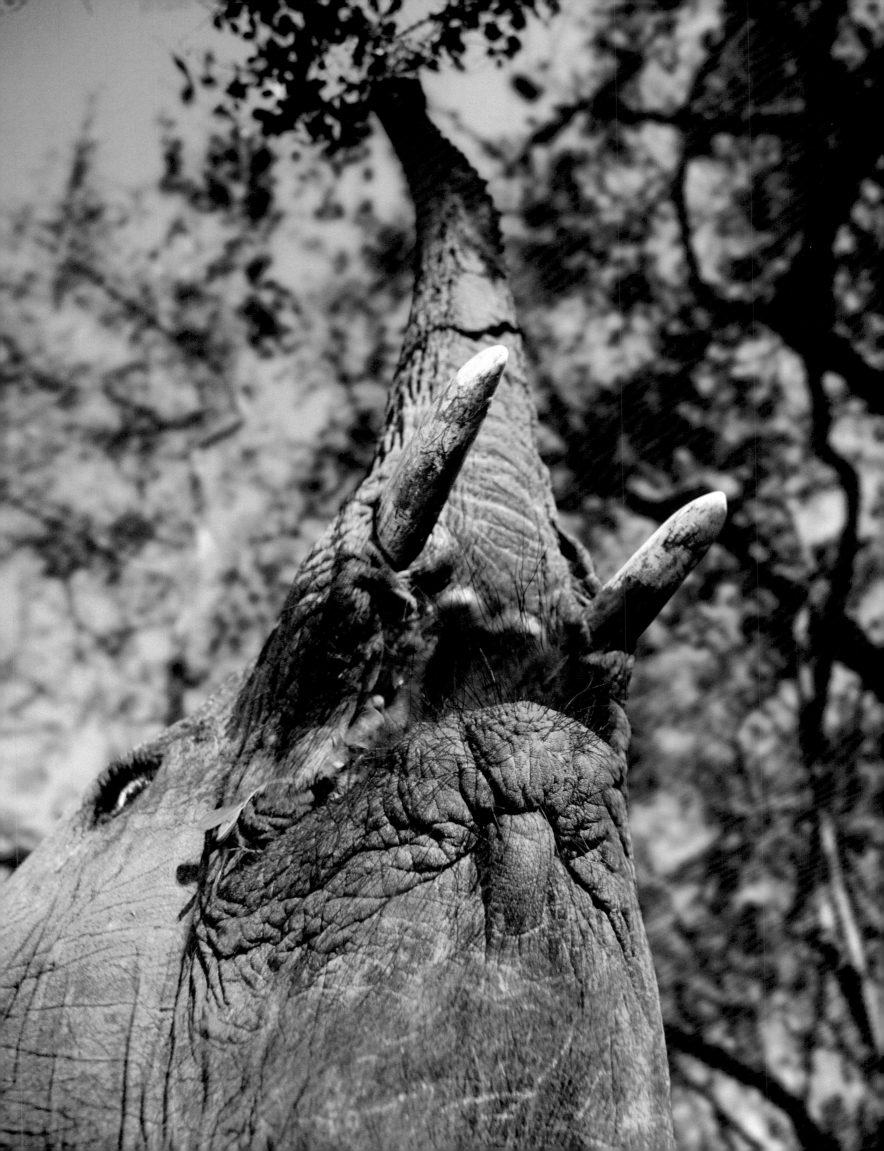

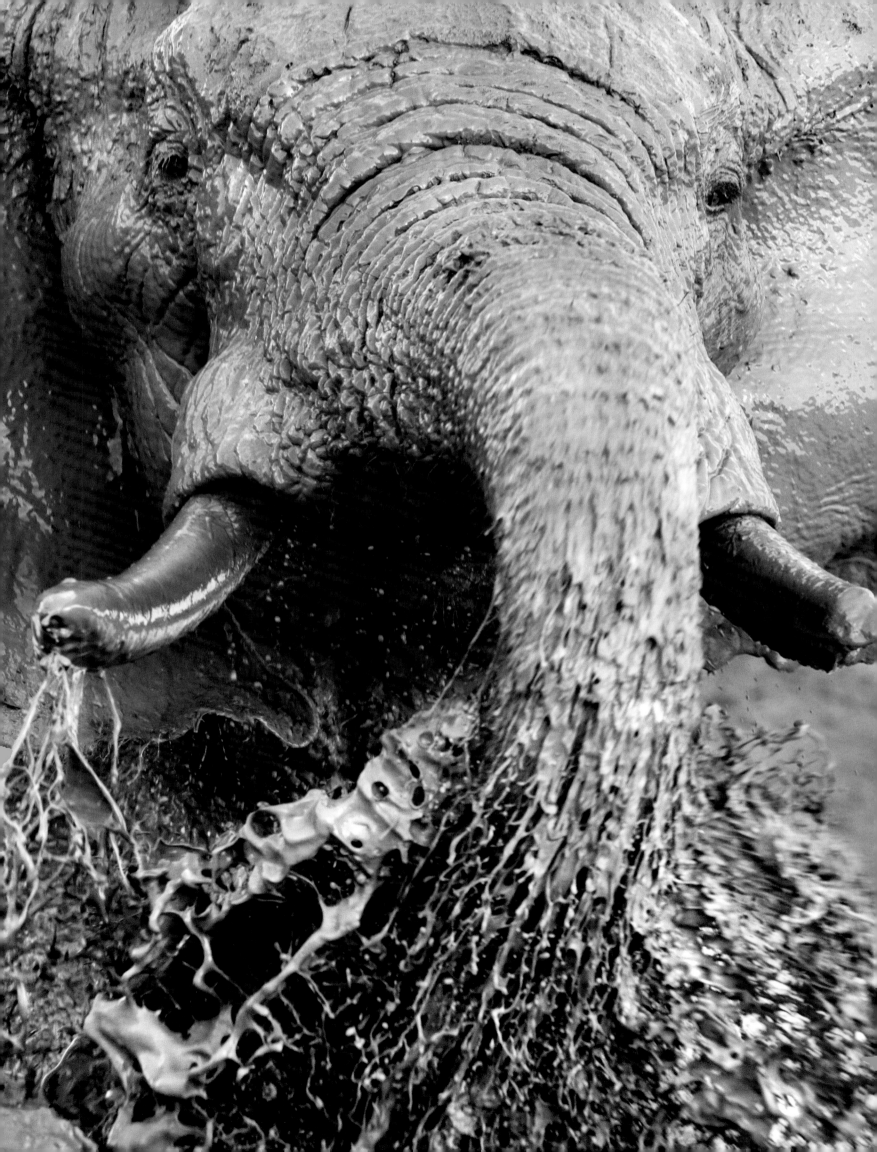

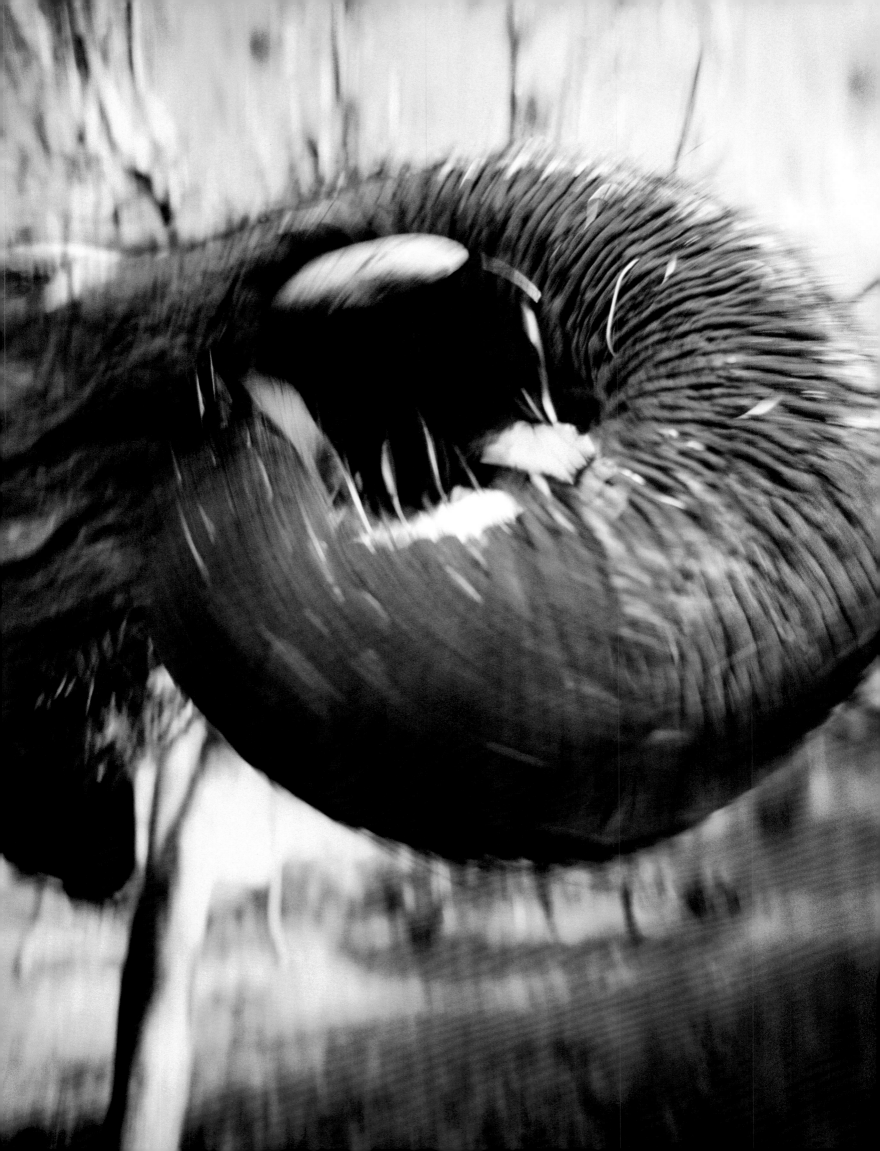

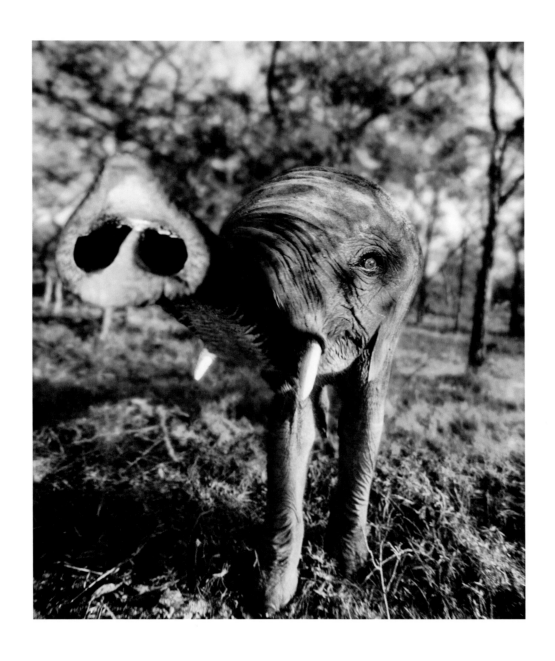

Elephants have their own built-in air-conditioning systems, and keep cool
by flapping each ear like a fan. As the day grows hotter, the tempo increases.
A draught is set up over the body which also cools the blood vessels in the ear.
When it is windy, they save energy by standing with their backs to the breeze
and spread out their ears to catch the moving air. The trunk is a masterpiece,
a complex fusion of hand, lip and nose with a multitude of functions.
It can fell trees, lift heavy logs, blow torrents of water, trumpet loudly,
or delicately pick up a single seed. A super-sensitive, telescopic antenna, it
rises high into the air to smell for danger, and can also be used as an effective
weapon. A trunk can reach seemingly impossible places, remove grit from the
eye, and be used to caress and give comfort. What better way for them to show
affection than to entwine trunks? An elephant with a crippled trunk is one
of nature's most tragic sights.

Elephants, despite their ungainly bulk and poor eyesight, tread with
a kind of quiet delicacy, avoiding small objects. Their soles spread to take
the weight, and built-in fibrous shock absorbers cushion the impact as they
touch the ground. I have experienced their surefootedness first-hand, whilst
searching for a wild tiger in the jungles of India. I rode on the back of an
elephant as he climbed a near-vertical slope. My heart was pounding as he
almost defied gravity, like a giant fly walking up a wall.

We may be unique in inventing the internet, one more progression in our
hunger to gain knowledge and expand our sophisticated communication
techniques. But we are not alone in the development of long-distance
communications. Elephants use infrasound, a deep rumbling which is inaudible
to human ears. The sounds travel over vast distances, as much as six miles
(ten kilometres). They appear to have a broad vocabulary, with many distinct
calls having specific meanings. There is much we still do not understand.
During a culling operation in Zimbabwe, a herd of elephants ninety miles
away (128 kilometres) ran off and were found several days later, huddled
together against the boundary fence of the reserve, as far from the slaughter
as possible. Shortly before the devastating South Asian tsunami in 2004,

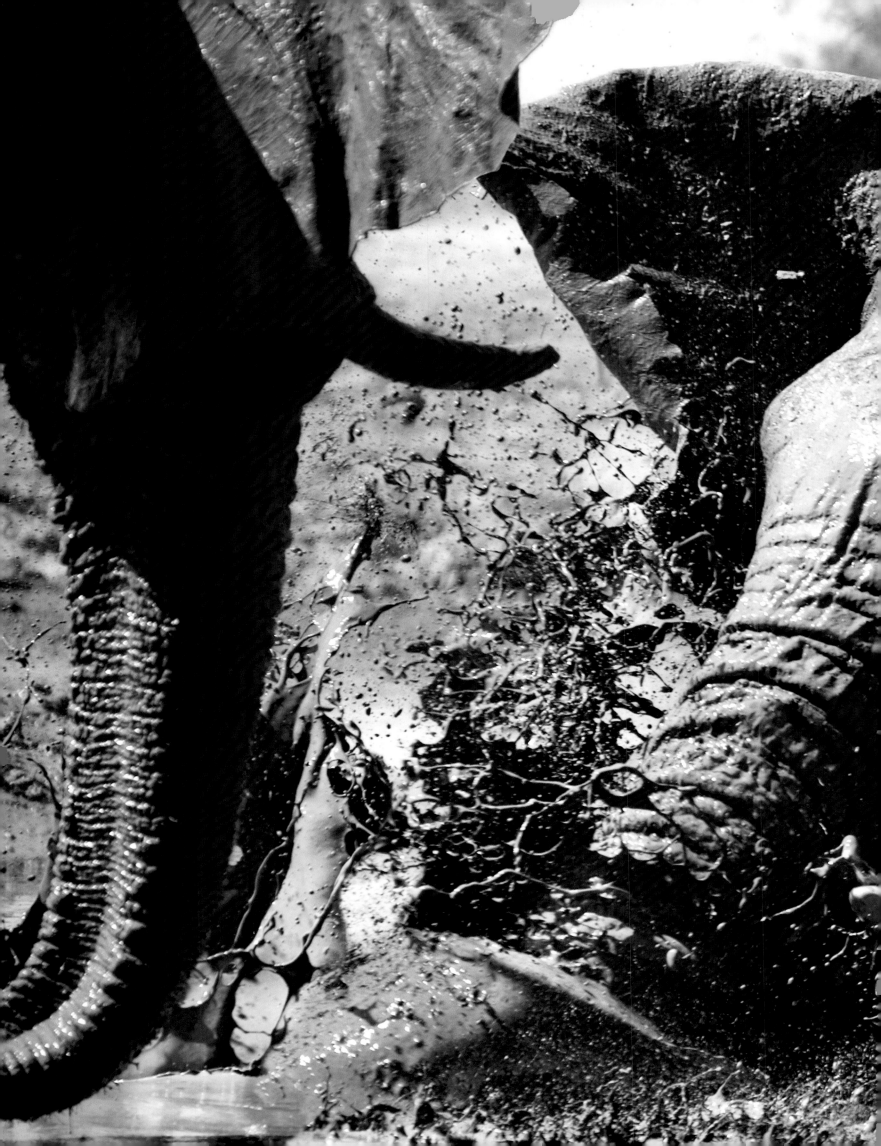

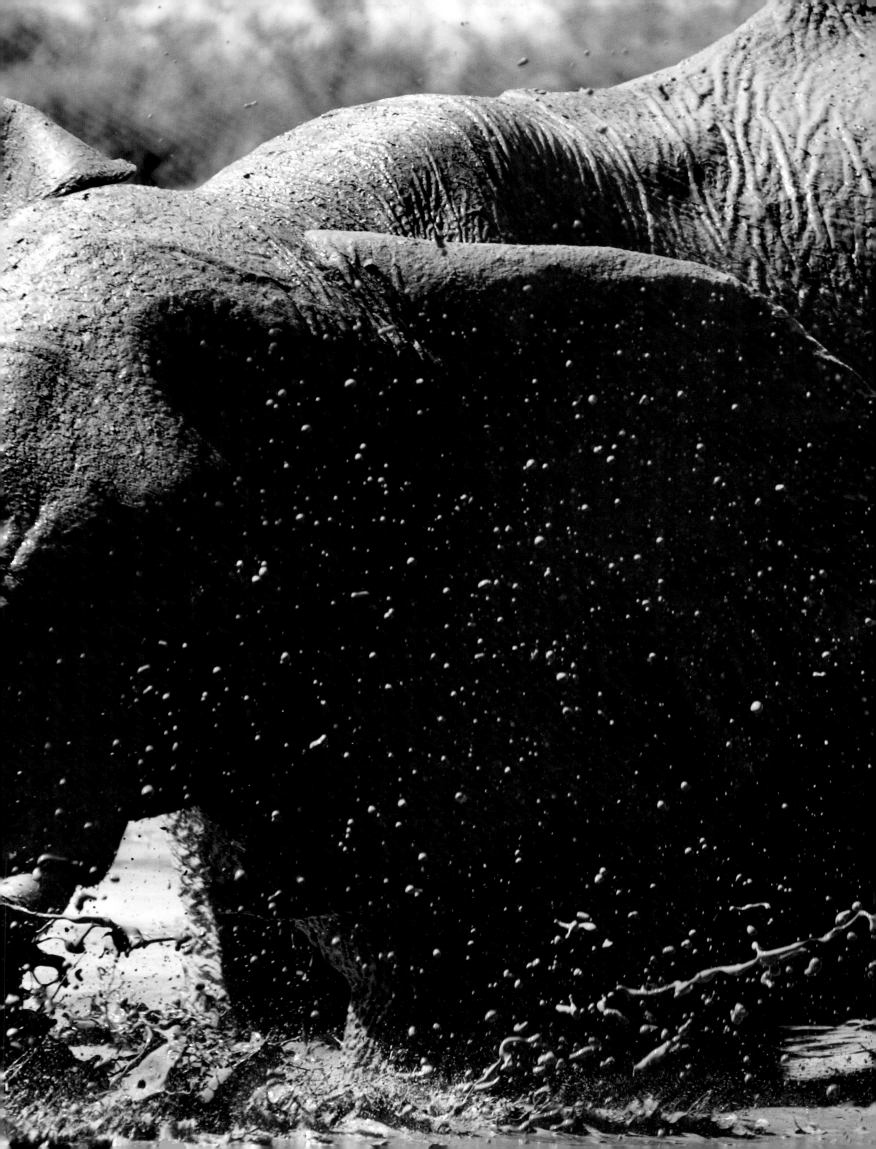

workers in Thailand were apparently woken by the sounds of wailing elephants. Concerned that the elephants may have been attacked, they rushed over, and found that the group was highly agitated. There are suggestions of elephants acting heroically, snatching up people and running to higher ground. Some locals I spoke to on the Andaman Islands are sceptical about these claims, which may indeed be apocryphal. The shockwave travelled faster than the water, so it is not impossible that, with their ability to detect infrasound, they may have sensed the disaster that was to follow. A reasoning mind is not a prerequisite for knowledge.

Wild elephants are under huge pressure from an expanding human population that has squeezed them into smaller and smaller reserves, encroaching on habitat and breaking up traditional migratory routes. Elephants fell trees in order to reach the more succulent leaves, and in doing so upset the balance for other animals. But life is cyclic, with elephant numbers reducing as the food supply declines, only to recover again naturally as the trees re-establish. Whenever I hear arguments in favour of culling African elephants on the grounds that they are 'destructive', I cannot help but think of the real environmental culprits, those who destroy the rainforests and pump greenhouse gases into the atmosphere. During culling operations whole families are usually killed by marksmen in helicopters. I am bewildered at how anyone can look down the barrel of a rifle, see a terrified baby elephant, and pull the trigger. On occasions when babies are not killed, they are captured and sent to safari parks and zoos. The terror they endure is unimaginable, as they crawl over their mothers' bodies, before being torn away and dispatched to life-long imprisonment. Our goal should be to interfere as little as possible, acknowledging that there is much we do not understand about the complexities of ecosystems in these reserves. They are certainly not within the gamut of our absolute control.

After seeing family groups in action, most people are left in no doubt that elephants experience many of the caring attributes also known to humans. If a baby becomes stuck in the mud, the group will rally together to rescue him. We should not regard such behaviour as extraordinary, but instead, view it as perfectly normal, just as we humans would react in similar circumstances. Elephants may be aware of the concept of death, and they apparently experience grief too. Stories about elephant graveyards may be mere legend, but sick and dying elephants do go to specific places where shade and water are abundant. I have seen a distressed mother mourn the death of her baby, staying with it by the river's edge for several days after her infant drowned, the extent of her grief clearly evident. They are well known for picking up and investigating elephant bones, while ignoring those of other animals. The death of an individual in a family may cause lethargy in the other members, and disrupt the harmony within the group.

Elephants have been observed making distinctive patterns on the ground, and these small but significant actions once again give weight to the idea of a link between us and them as sensitive, feeling creatures, capable of a degree of cognitive behaviour. There are elephant-rescue sanctuaries where the residents have learned to use their trunks to produce fanciful paintings which are sold to tourists. Not all elephants are willing to paint, but those that do are said to enjoy the pastime. In performing these acts, keepers usually choose the colours and position the paper on the easels. When watching such activities, we must remember that there is a line to be drawn between adaptive, yet natural behaviour, and the mechanical performance of human-taught tricks. Chimpanzees, for example, may be 98.6 per cent genetically similar to humans, but to dress them in human clothes and make them ride bicycles humiliates them. Such activities do nothing but line the pockets of the keepers, and alter our perception of chimpanzees from creatures who share many of our basic life experiences, to primitive objects for our amusement, mere things to be laughed at.

Periodically adult male elephants enter a state of heightened aggression, brought about by a condition known as *musth*, the result of a massive hormone surge. *Musth* is easily recognized by the dark oily secretion that oozes from the temporal glands on the sides of the head. The glands swell to the size of footballs, and press hard against the back of the eyes, causing considerable pain. The elephants will force their tusks into the ground to relieve pressure, and can sometimes be driven into a frenzy from the pain, attacking randomly. Body temperatures rise, and they flap their ears frequently to keep cool. Ketones flood the brain, altering their states of mind, which results in repetitive behaviour. Extra testosterone makes them more aggressive than usual, and limits their ability to function normally. They appear to want to dominate everything in sight, including humans, and the danger of such a state should never be underestimated. In the wild, *musth* helps the elephant to maintain his dominant position and mate with females who are in season. It is essential for an experienced mahout to recognize the early stages of *musth*, particularly in crowded Asian cities where the elephants are confined, and often have to stand still for many hours.

By interfering with nature, we can sometimes unwittingly set in motion a chain of events which creates catastrophic problems further down the line. In South Africa, for example, elephants began attacking and killing rhinos in a reserve, much to the horror of conservationists and park managers whose breeding programmes were helping to save the highly endangered rhino. Even though they were not competing for food or water, the elephants were gratuitously killing rhinos. In their search for the cause of this aberrant behaviour, conservationists came to the understanding that this was the result of earlier decisions and events. The young elephants originated from a herd in which all the adults had been culled, and these orphaned babies were then transported to the reserve where the rhinos were resident. In normal elephant society, a matriarch is in control of the group, passing on survival skills to the young. Juvenile males are taught how to deal with a range of situations, and stay with the herd until adolescence. At this stage, they generally leave the herd and attach themselves to older bulls who, by example, guide them into the ways of adulthood. *Musth* may appear in younger bulls for short periods, but it is suppressed in the presence of older, more dominant males. Without these dominant males, *musth* may become uncontrollable and completely take over the behaviour of young bulls.

Like humans, elephants, when orphaned in tragic circumstances, often grow up with severe emotional problems. The culling operation had targeted adult elephants, leaving the young orphans to deal with the trauma of loss of

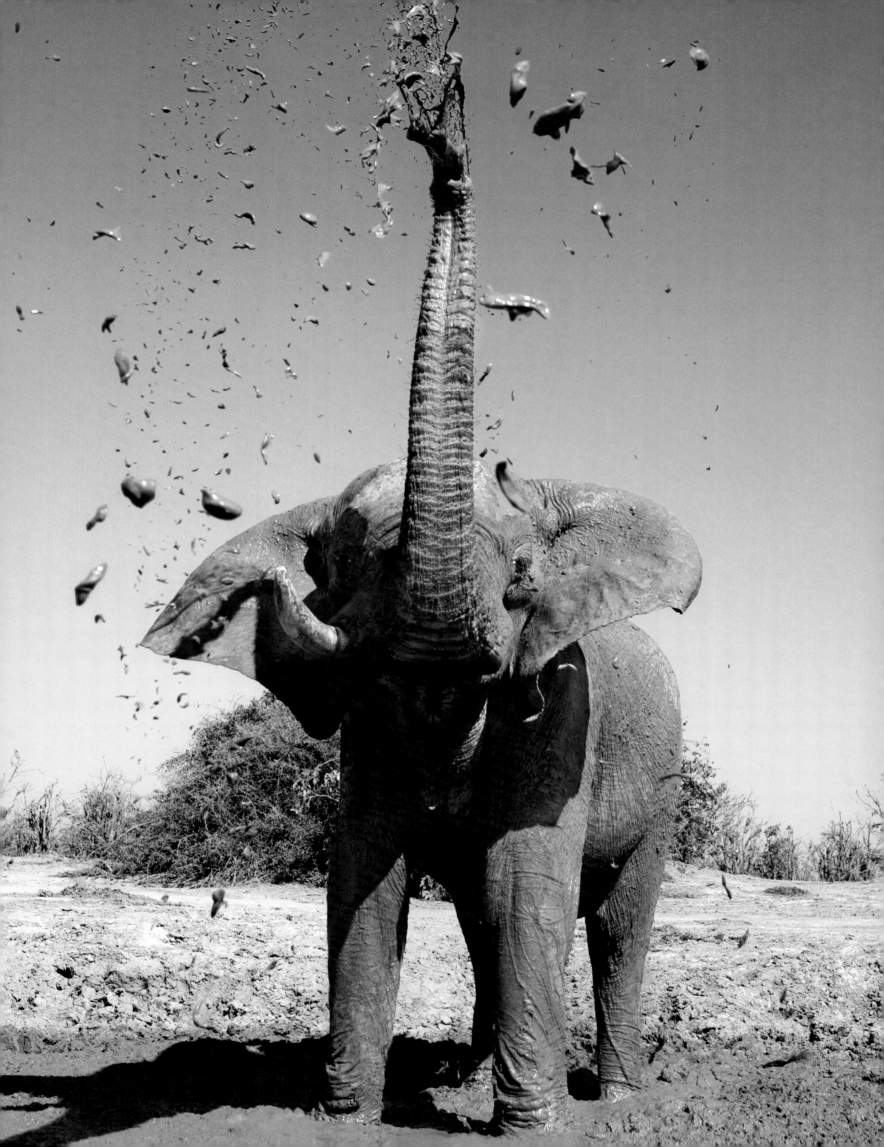

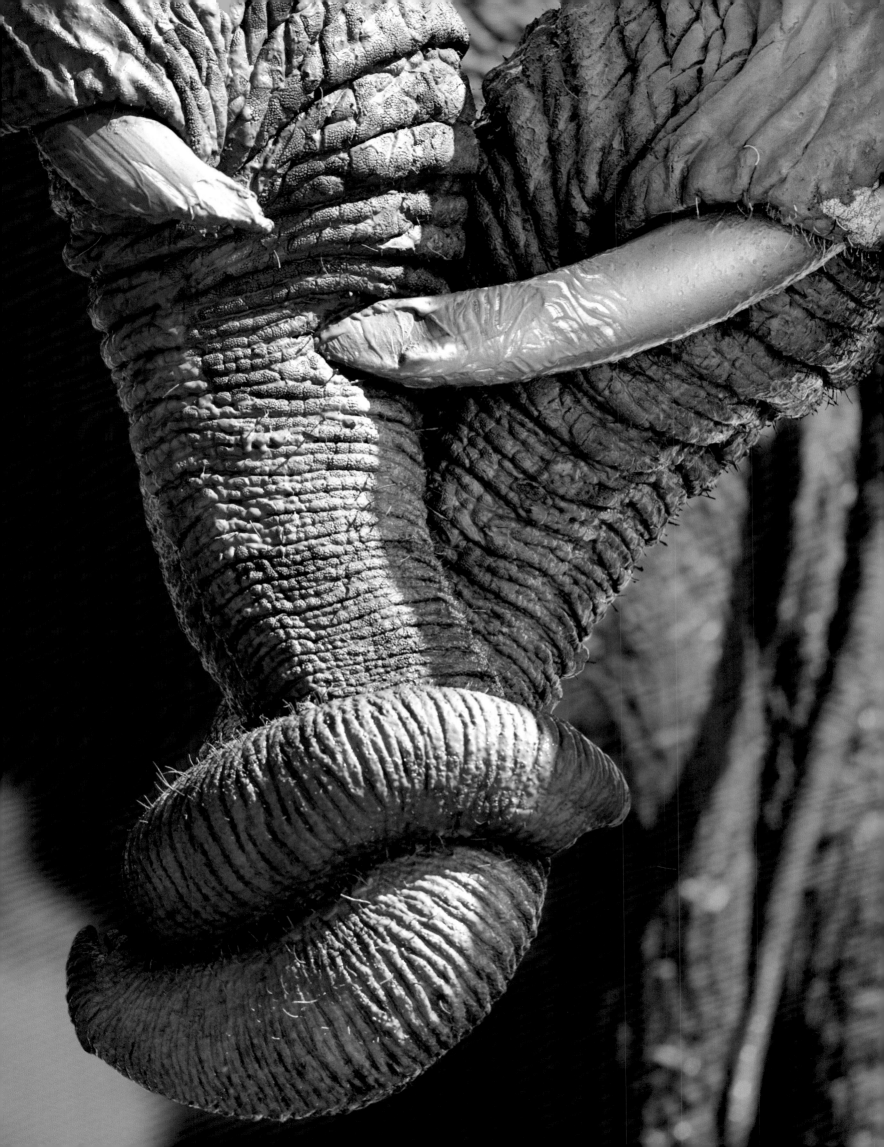

their elders and largely to fend for themselves. The early onset of excessive *musth* brought on unnaturally high levels of aggression in the young males, and they consequently attacked the rhinos. In an attempt to solve the problem, mature bulls were brought into the reserve from hundreds of miles away. It was hoped that their presence would suppress the adolescents' *musth* and inspire normal behaviour. However, a further question arises: what is the long term consequence if we take fully mature elephants out of their familiar domain, tranquilize them and transport them by lorry to a strange area, then leave them dazed and confused, in the vague hope that they will bond with young delinquents and teach them normal behaviour? We need to tread with great delicacy in those areas we do not fully understand.

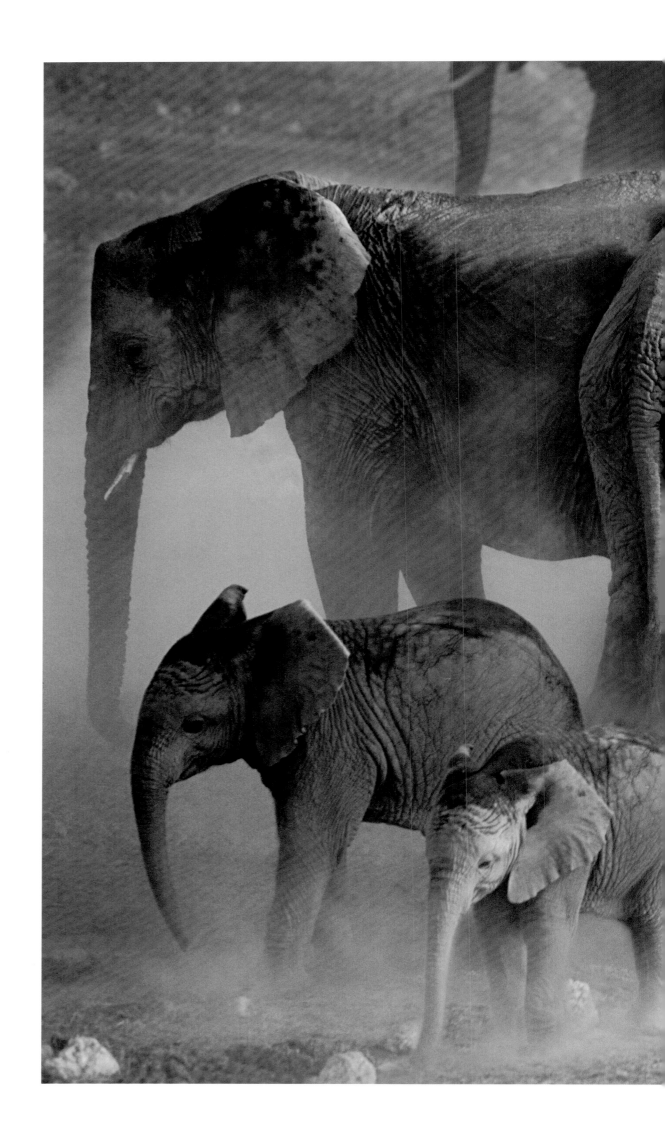

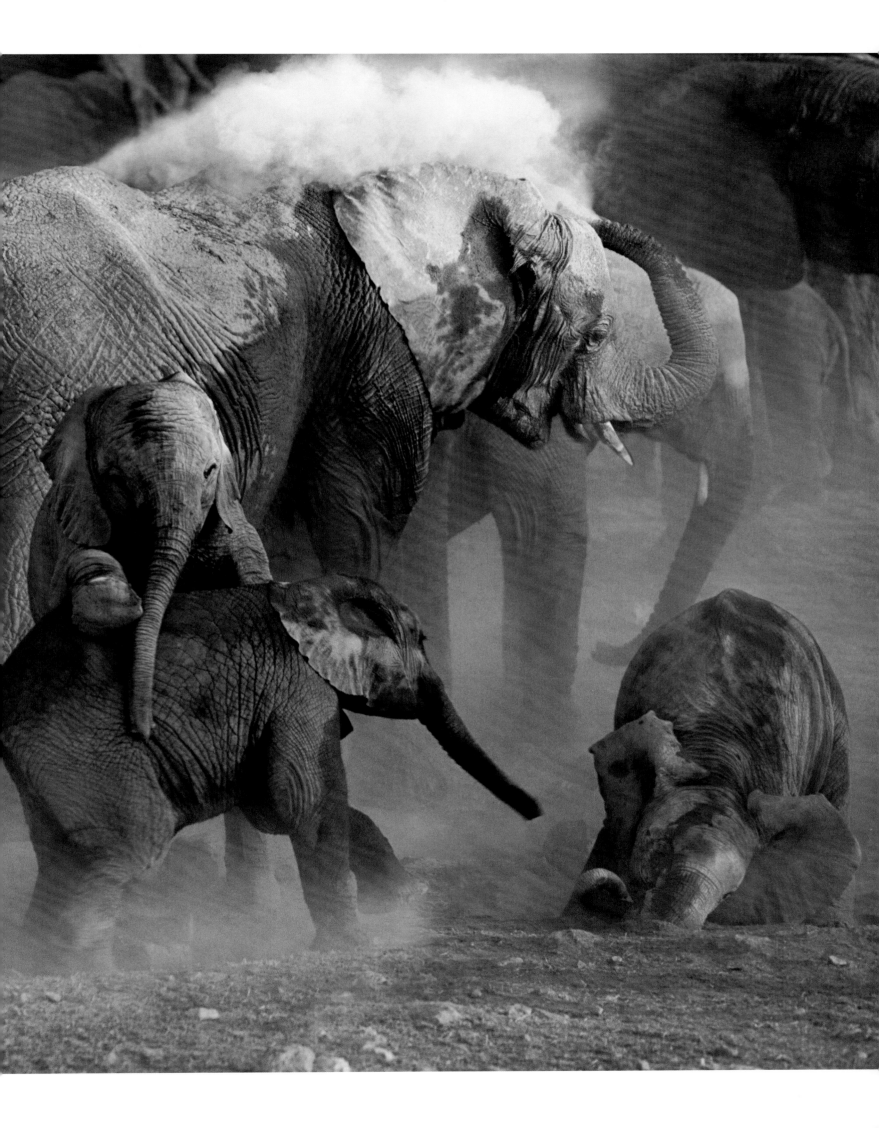

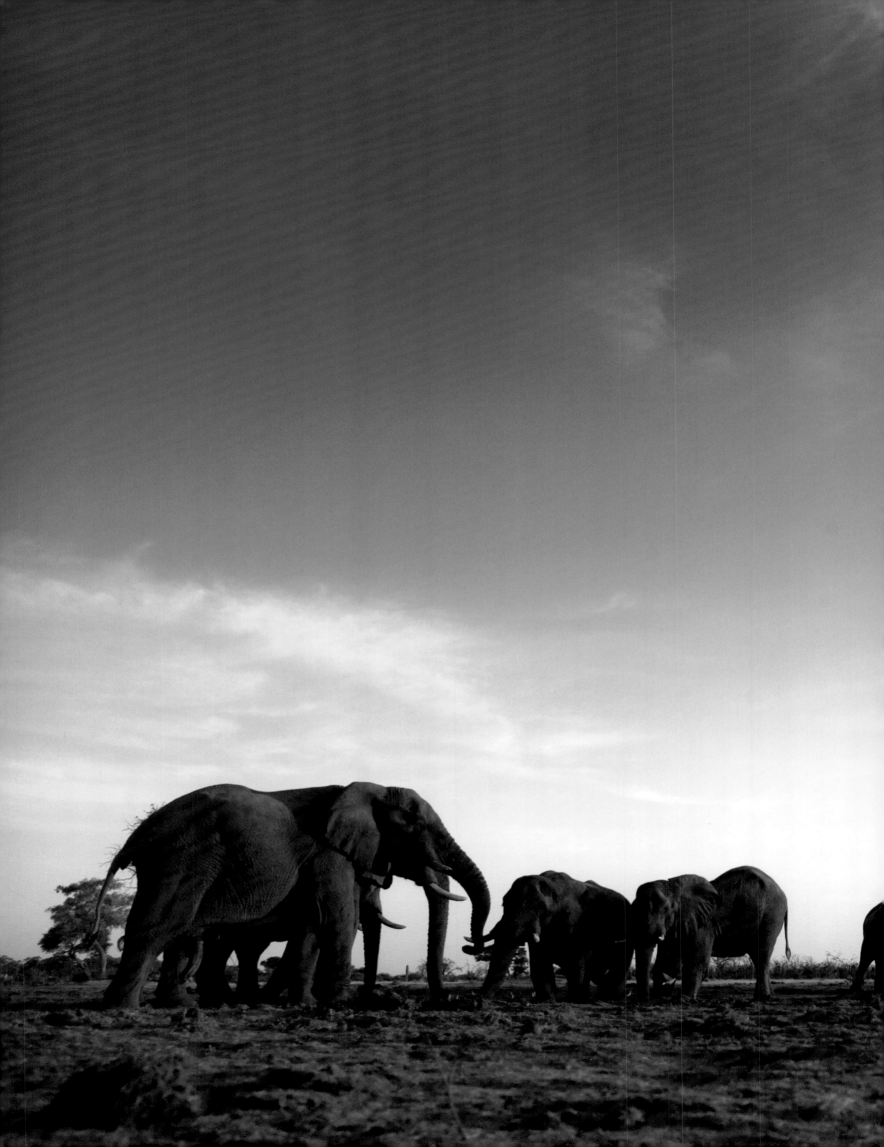

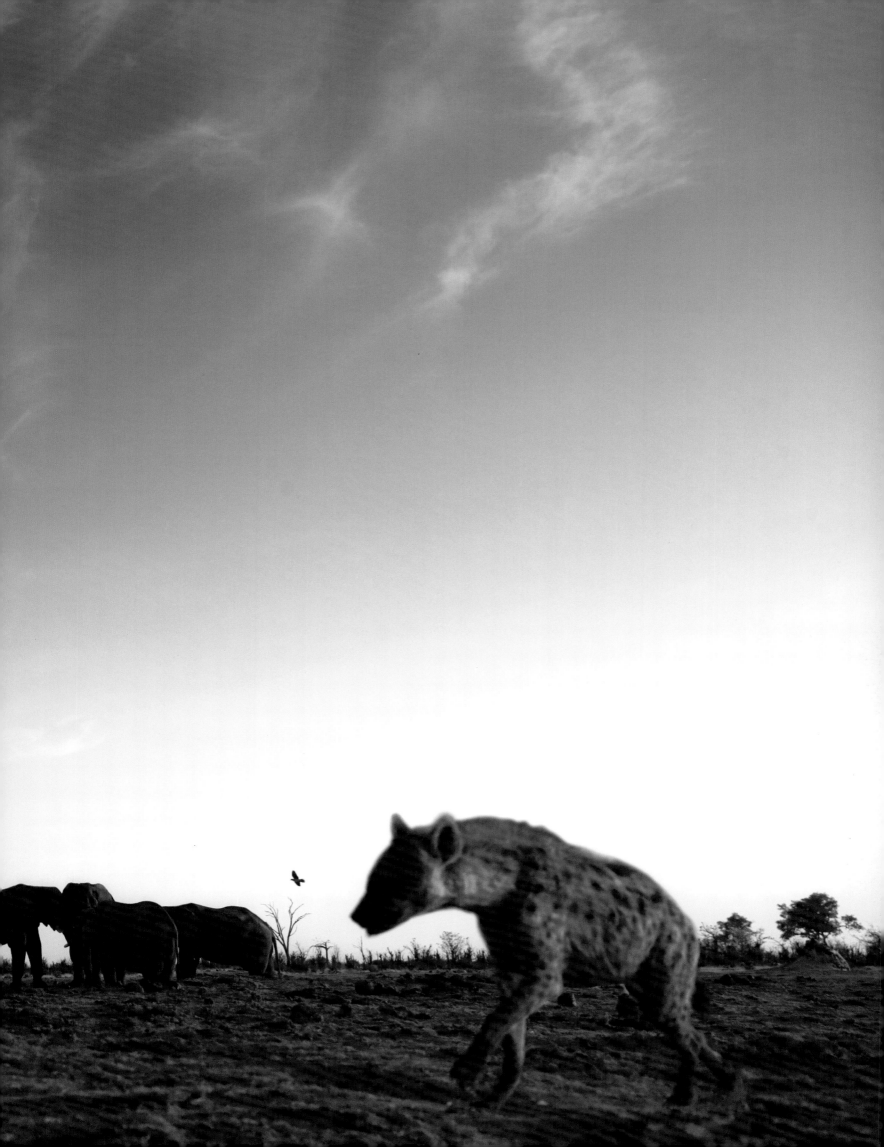

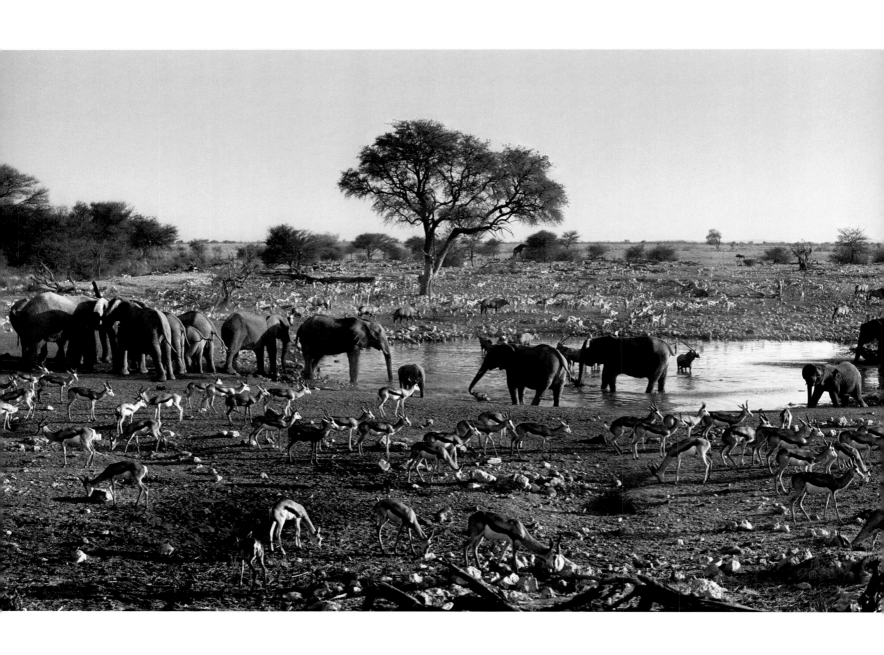

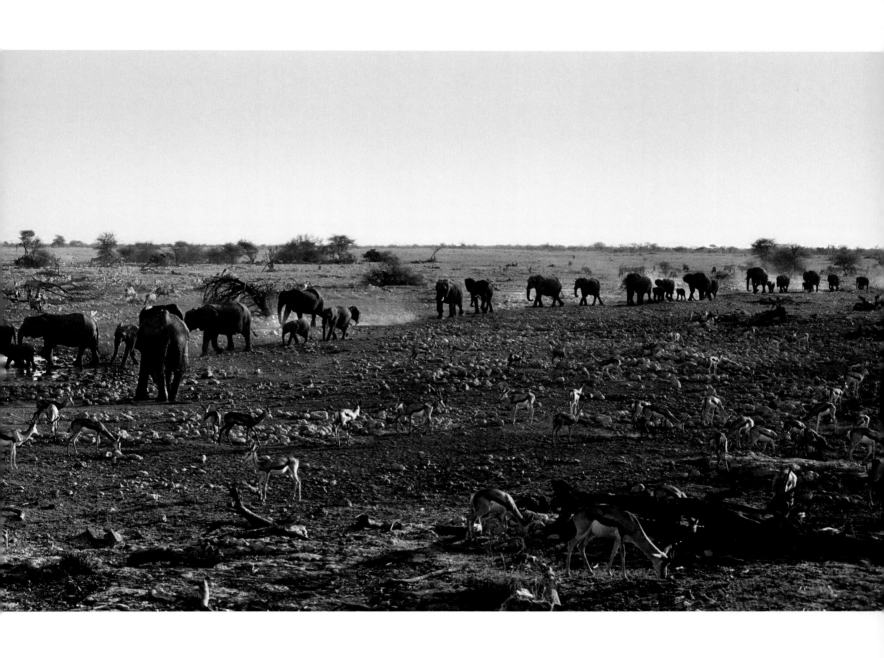

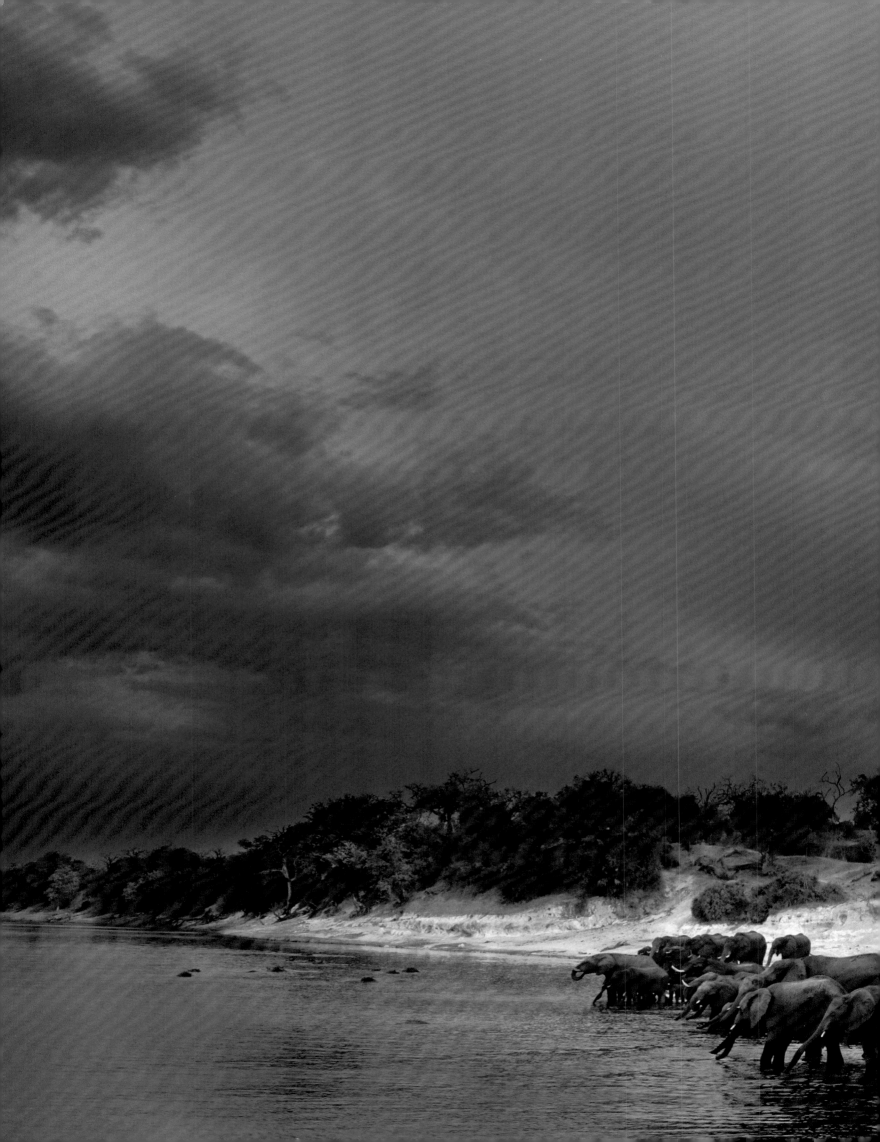

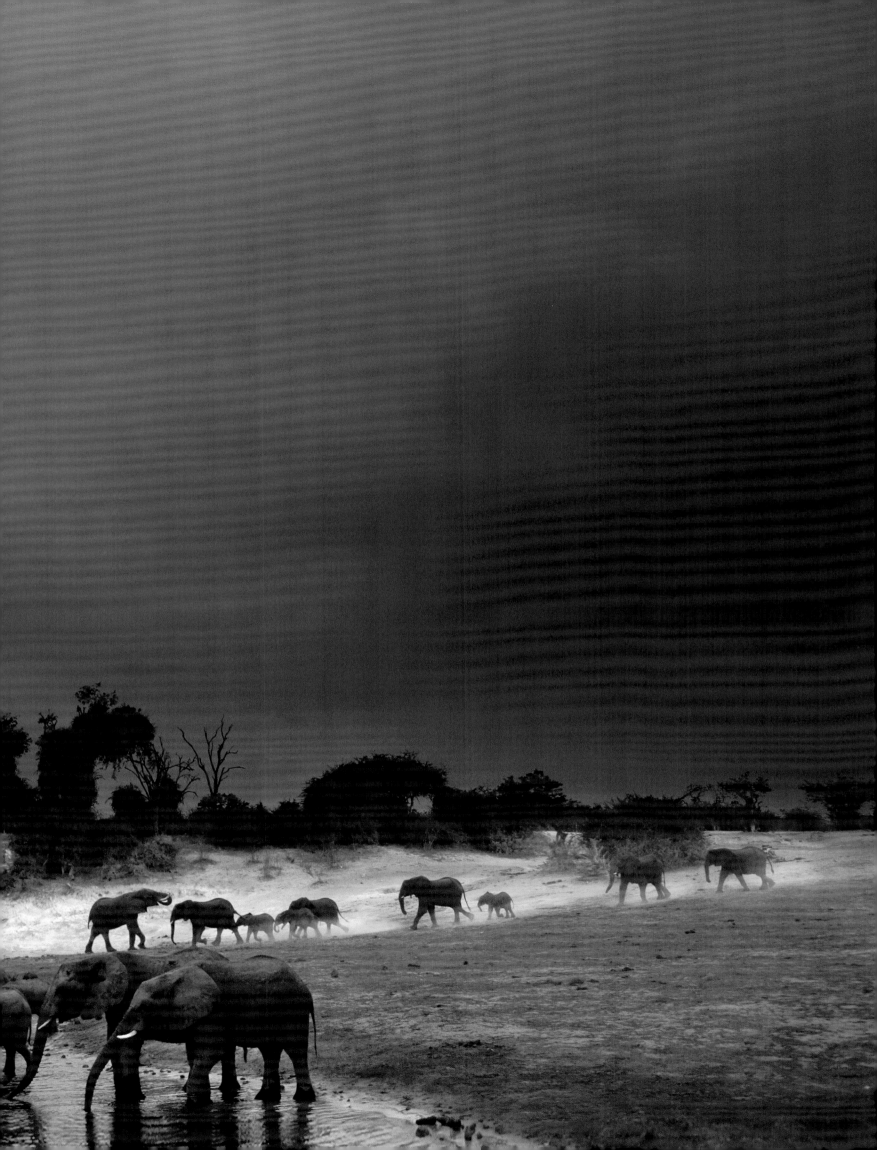

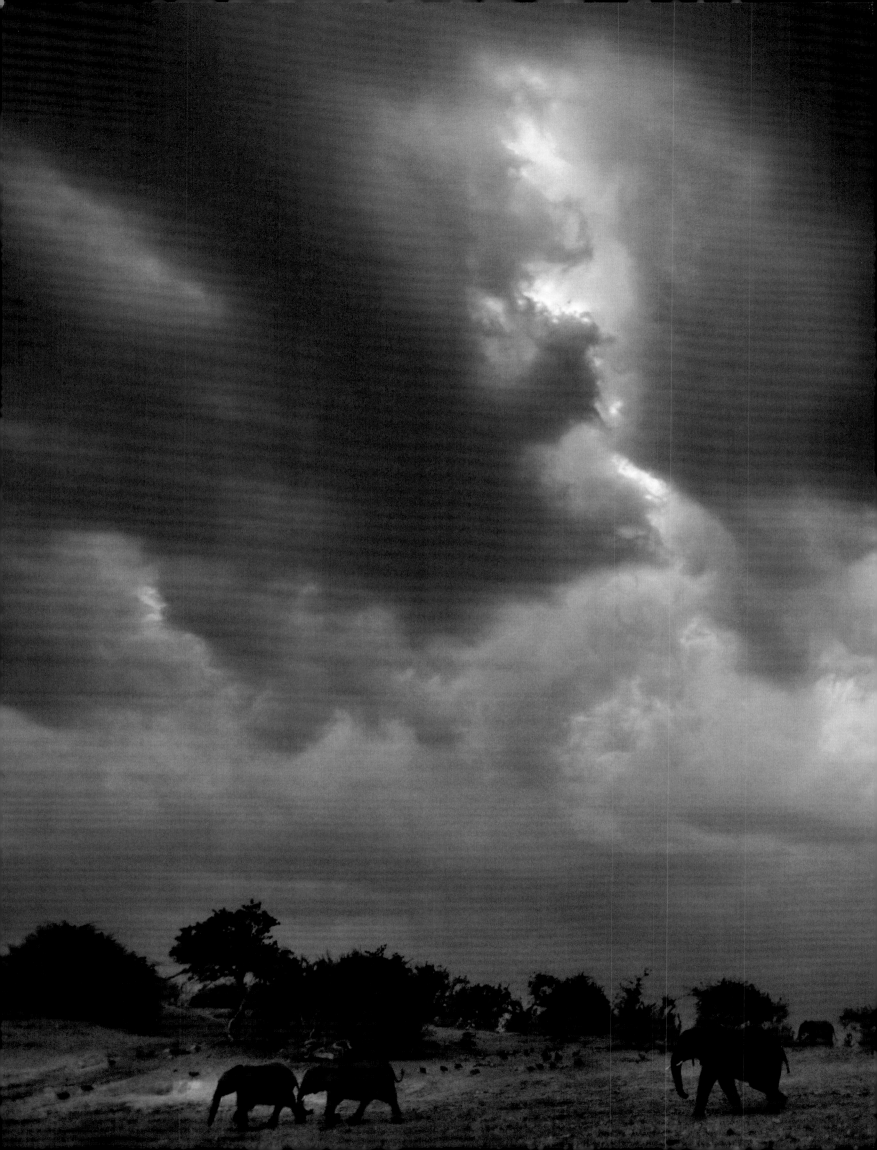

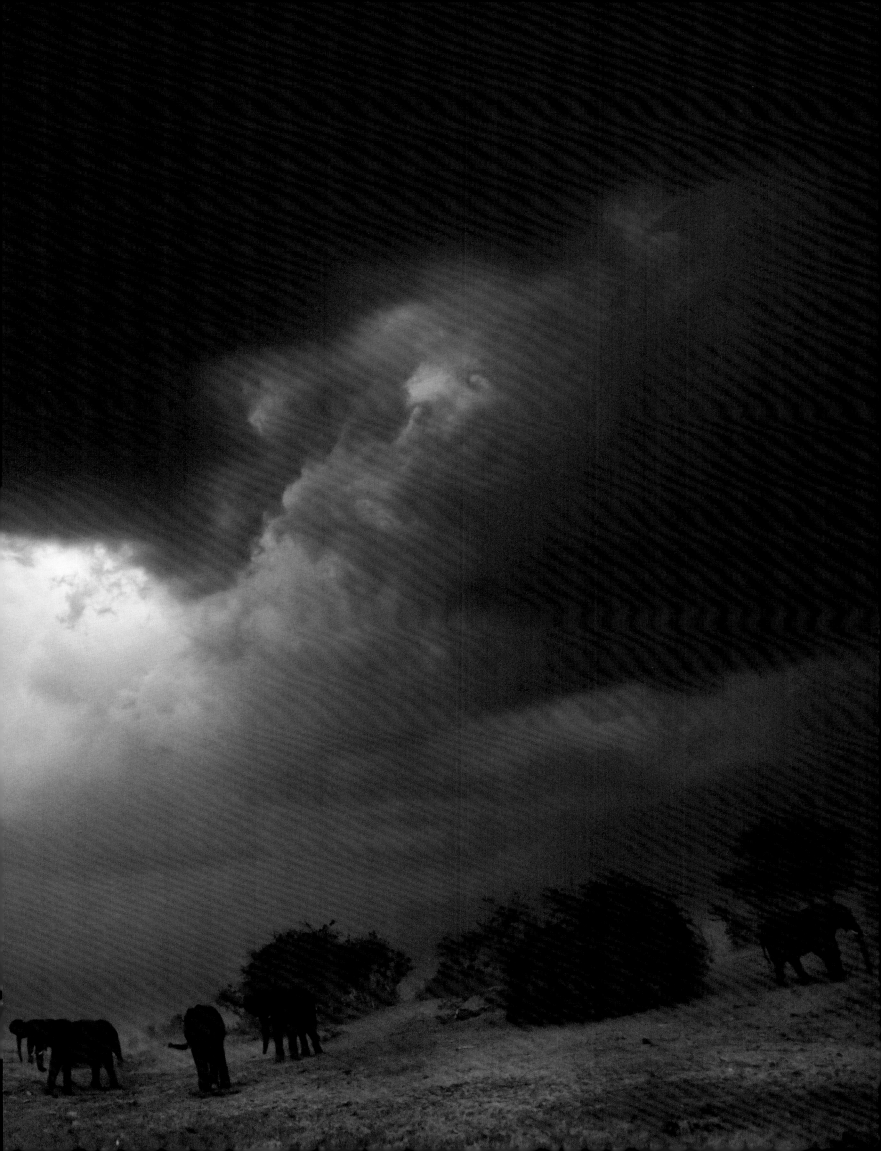

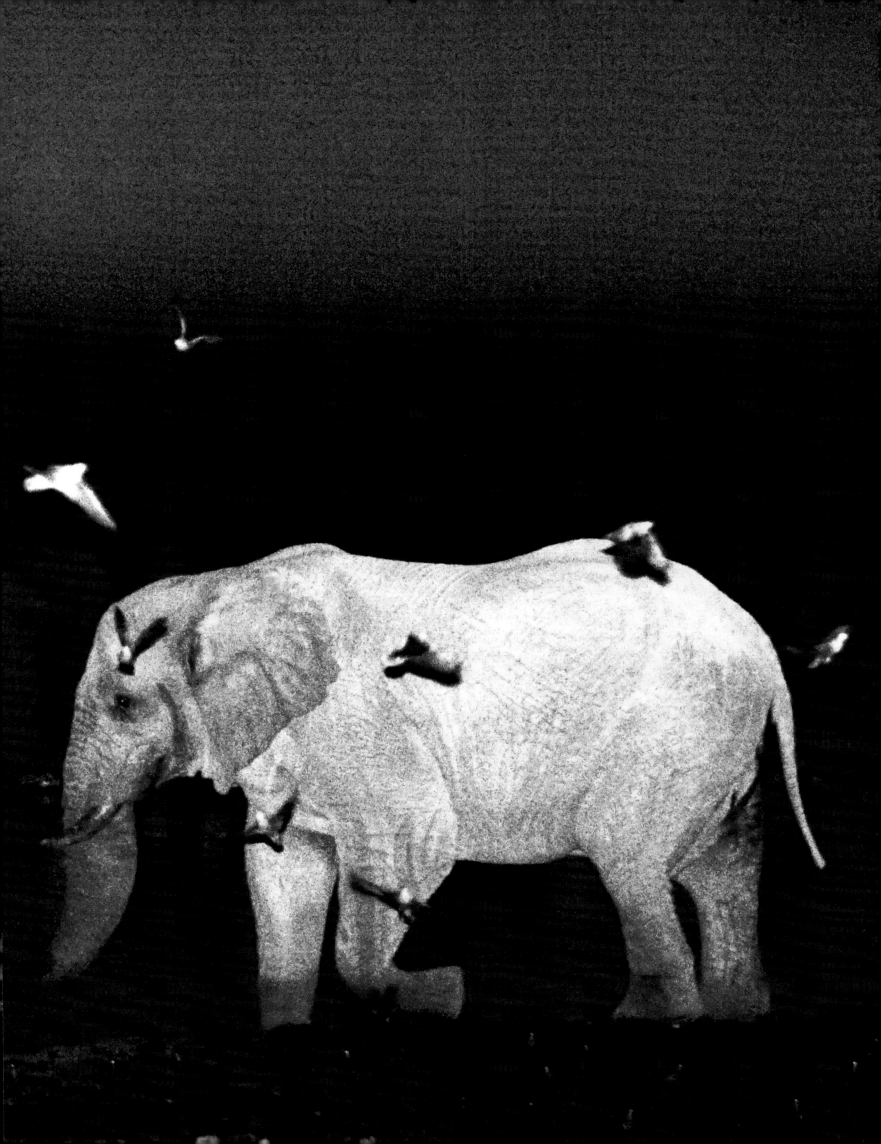

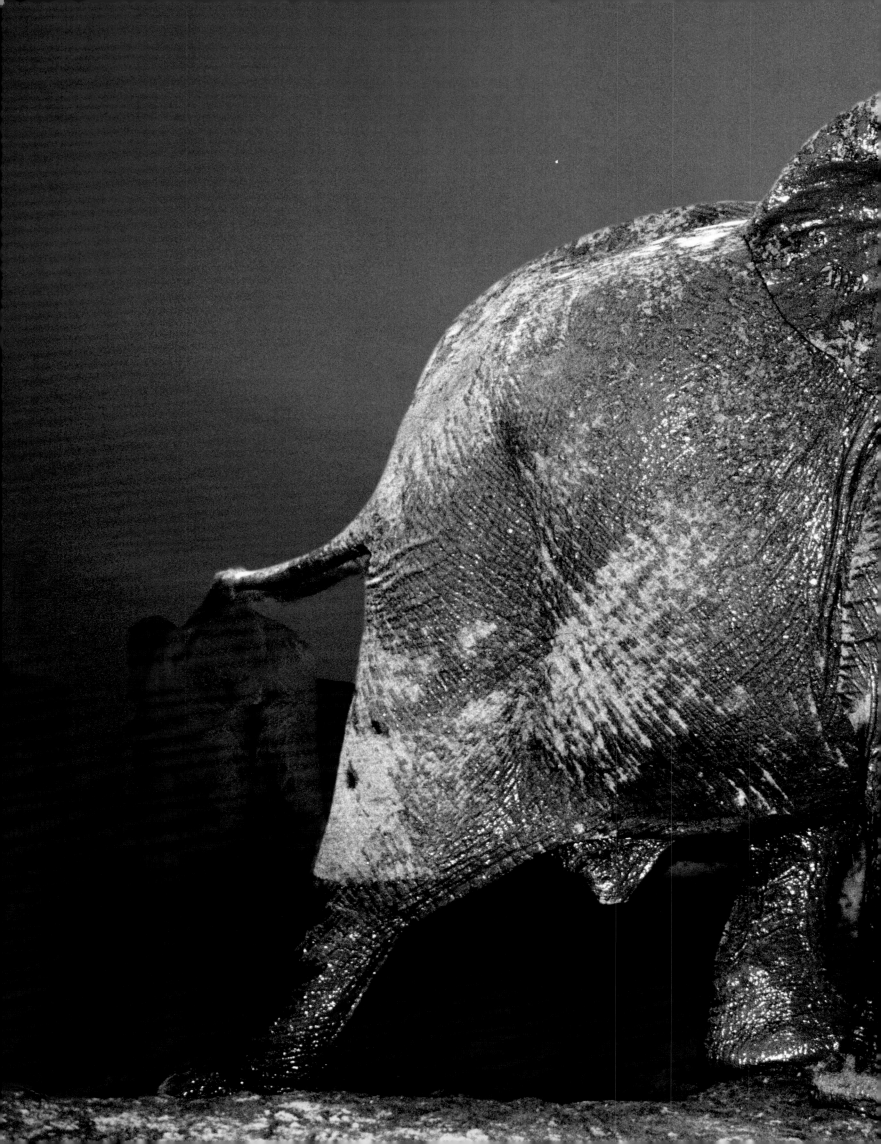

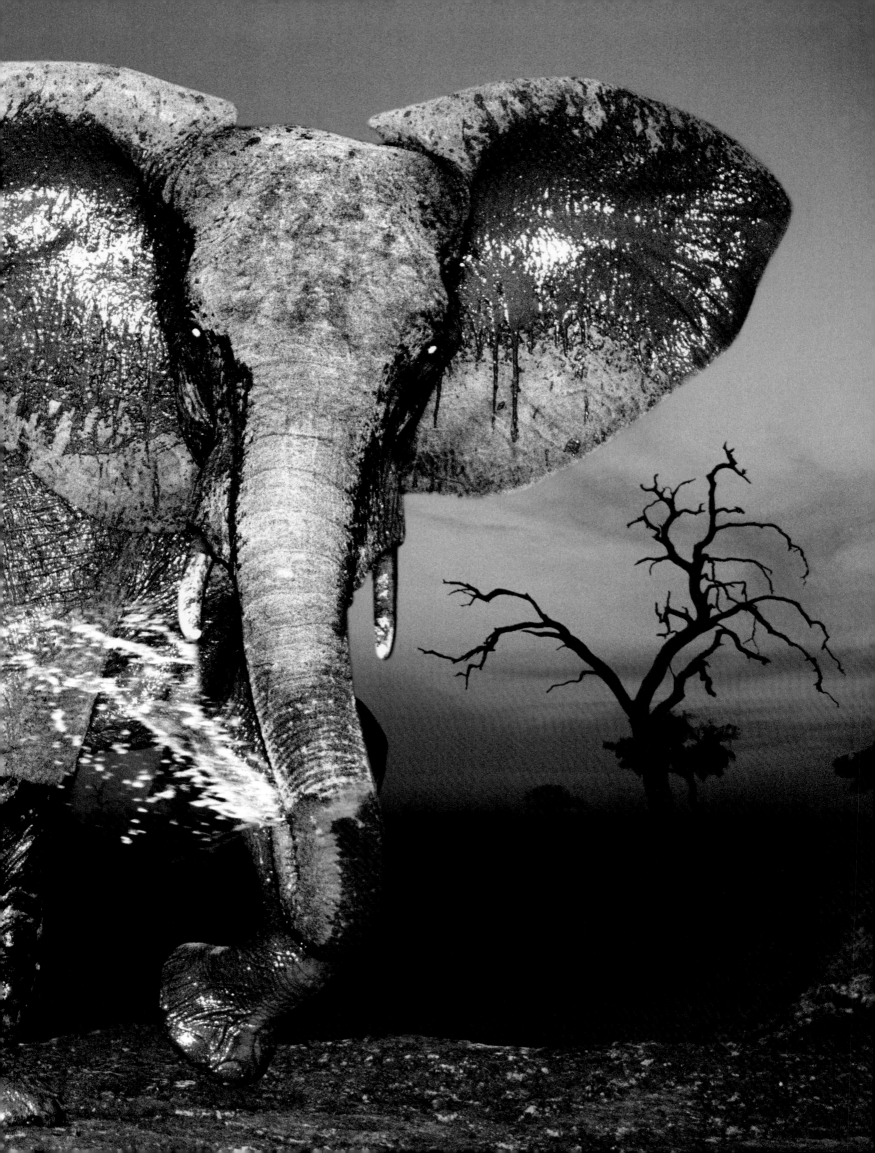

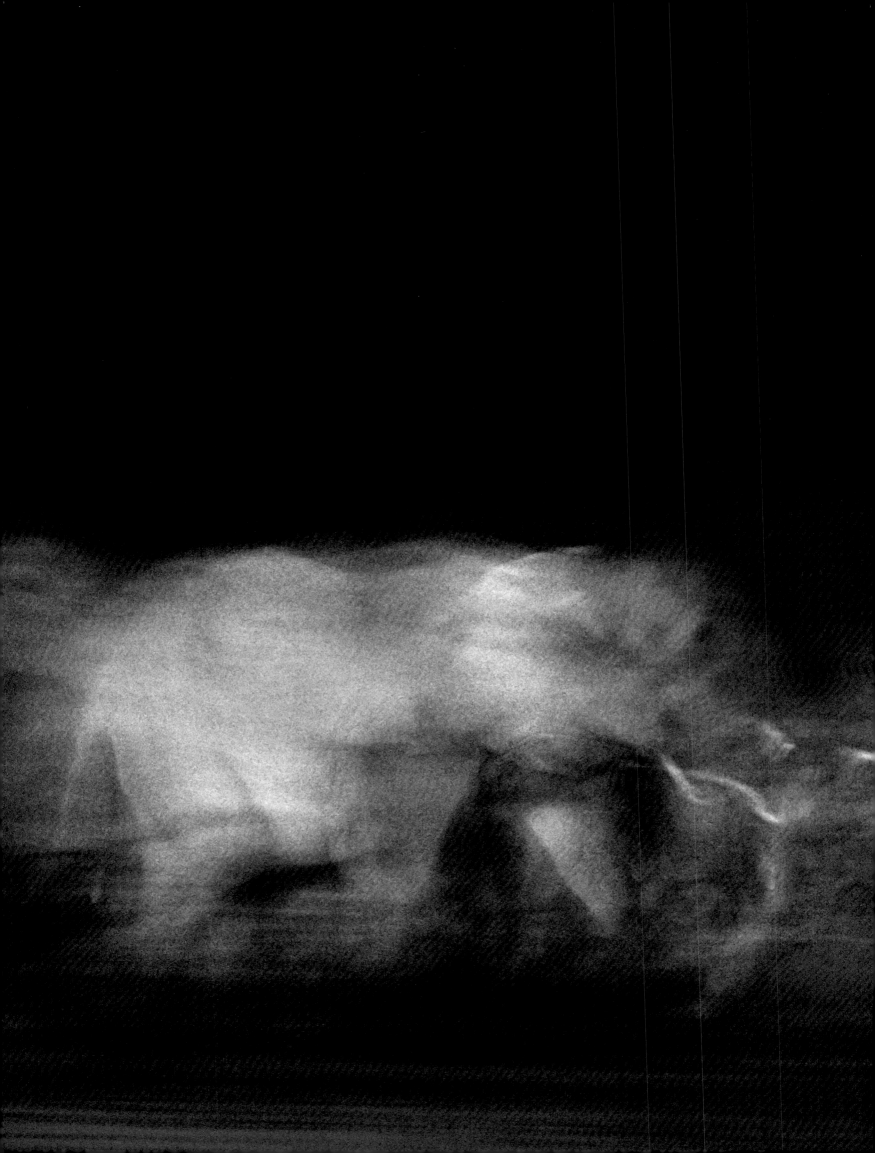

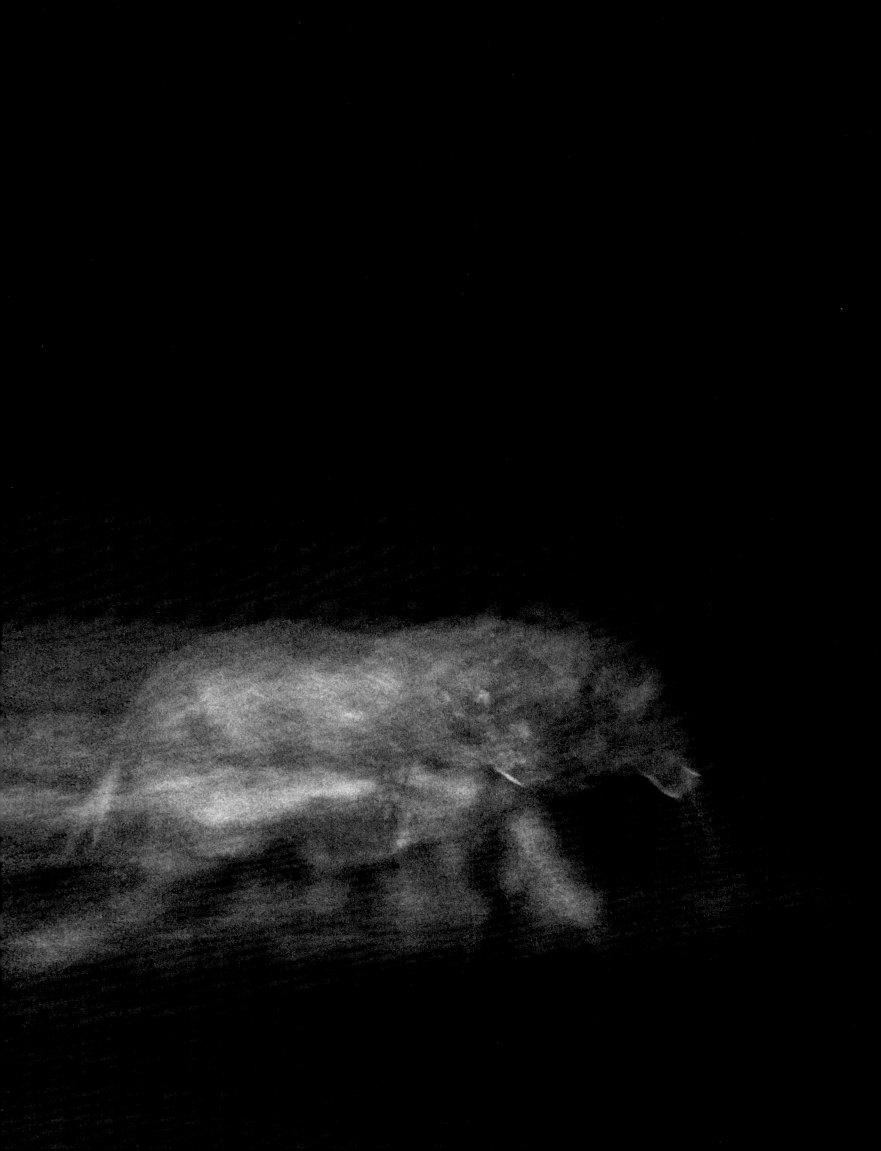

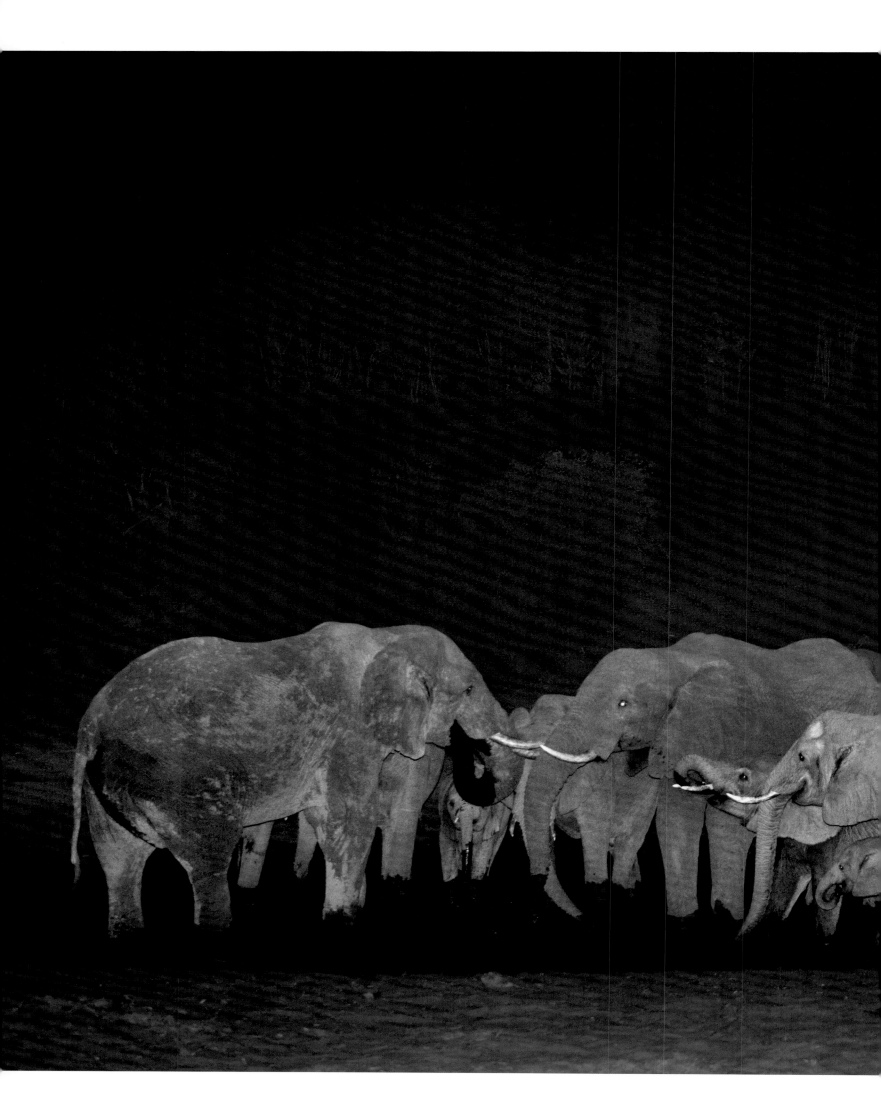

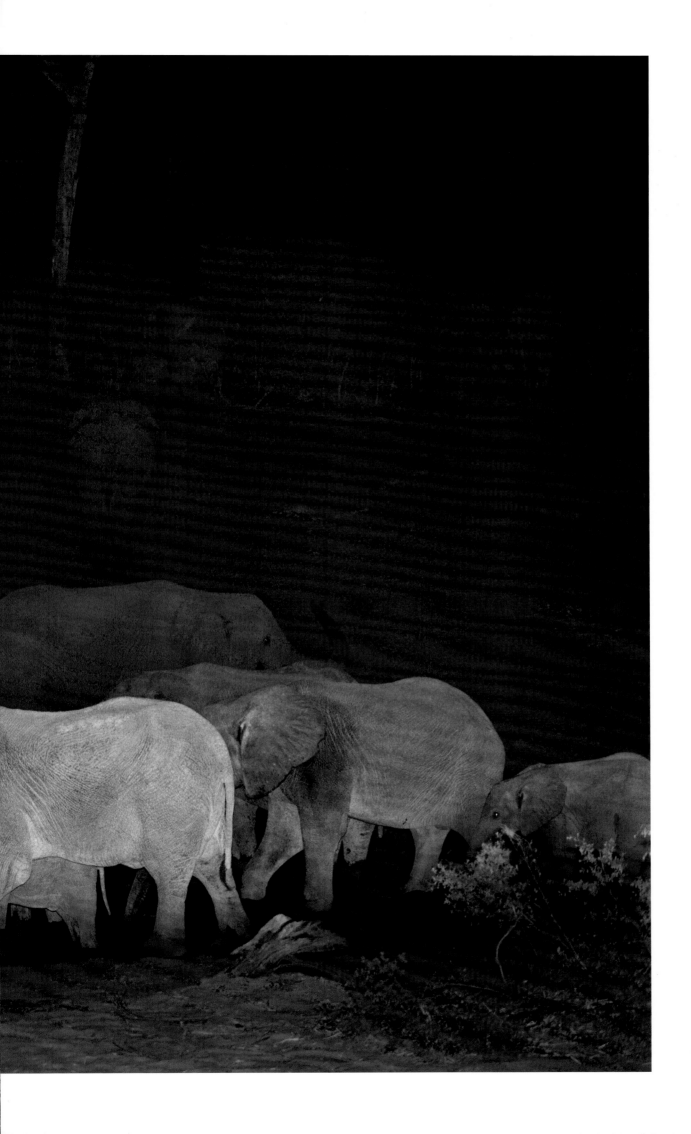

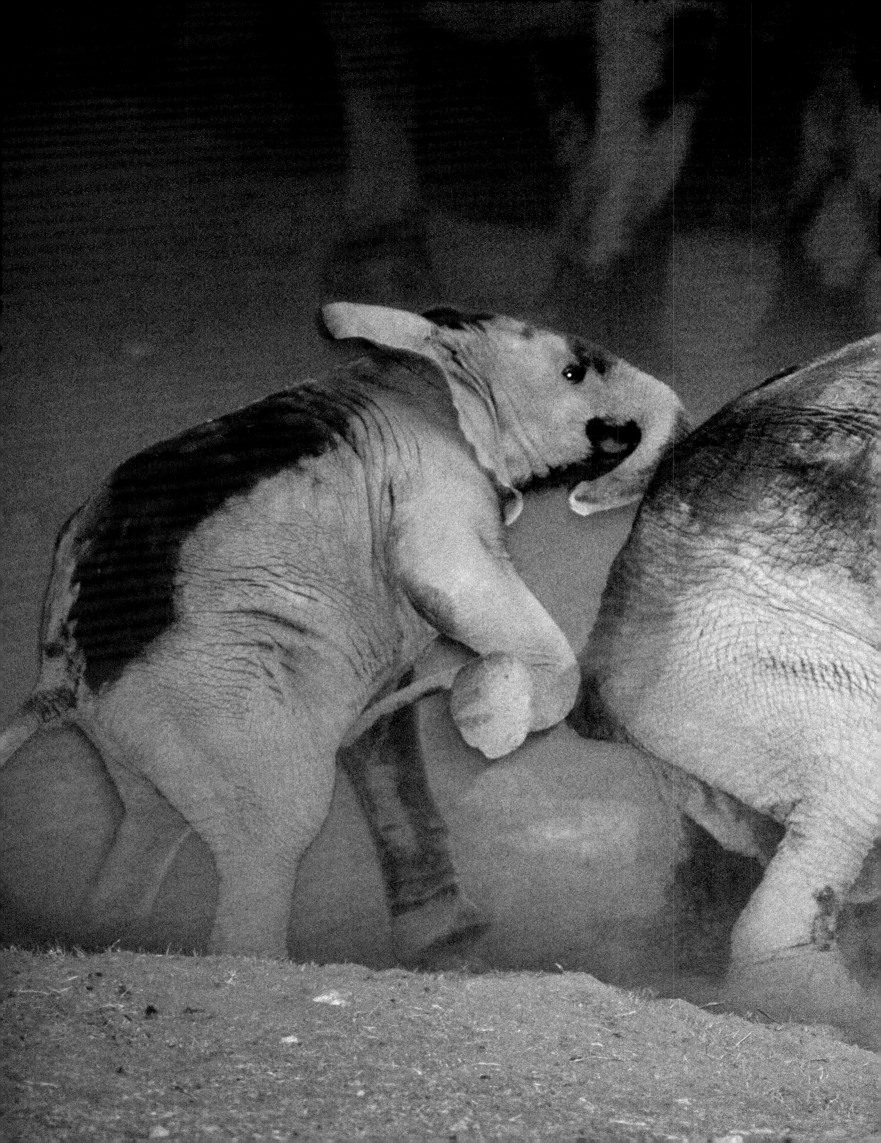

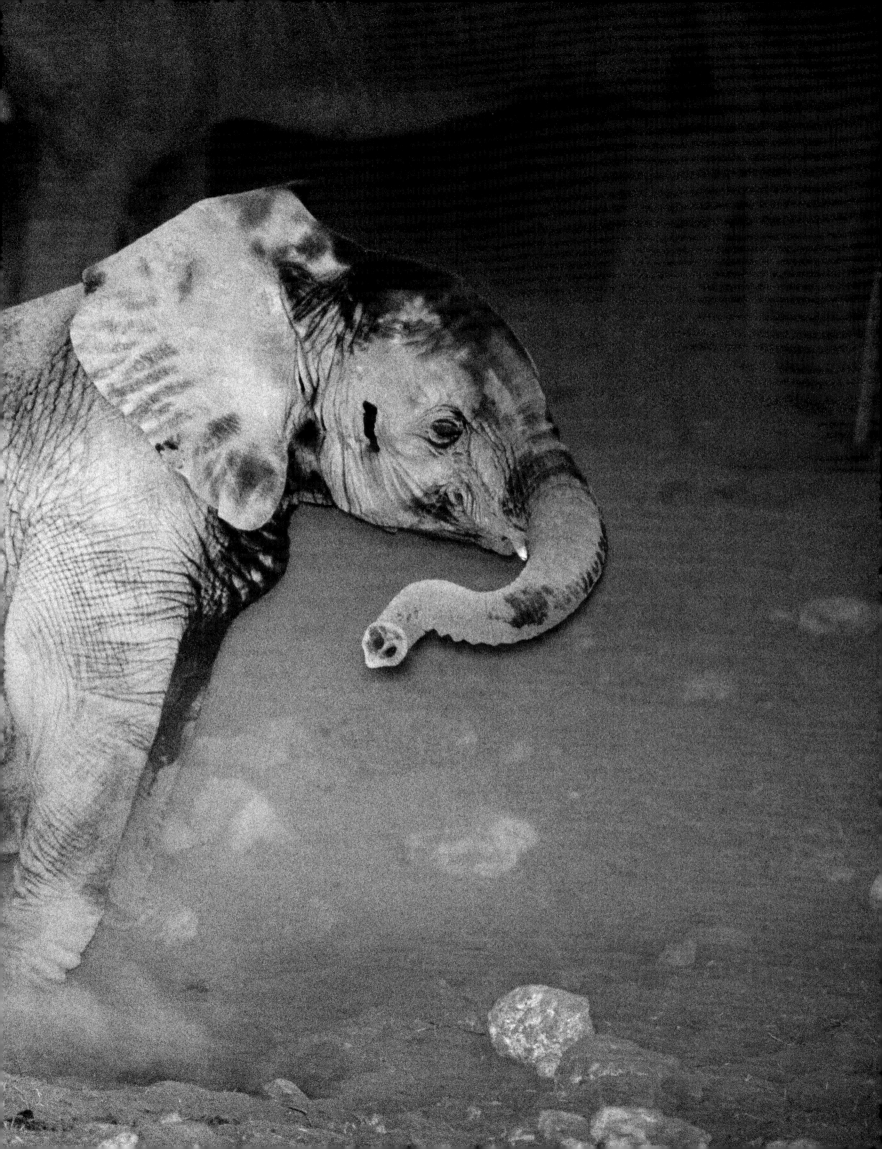

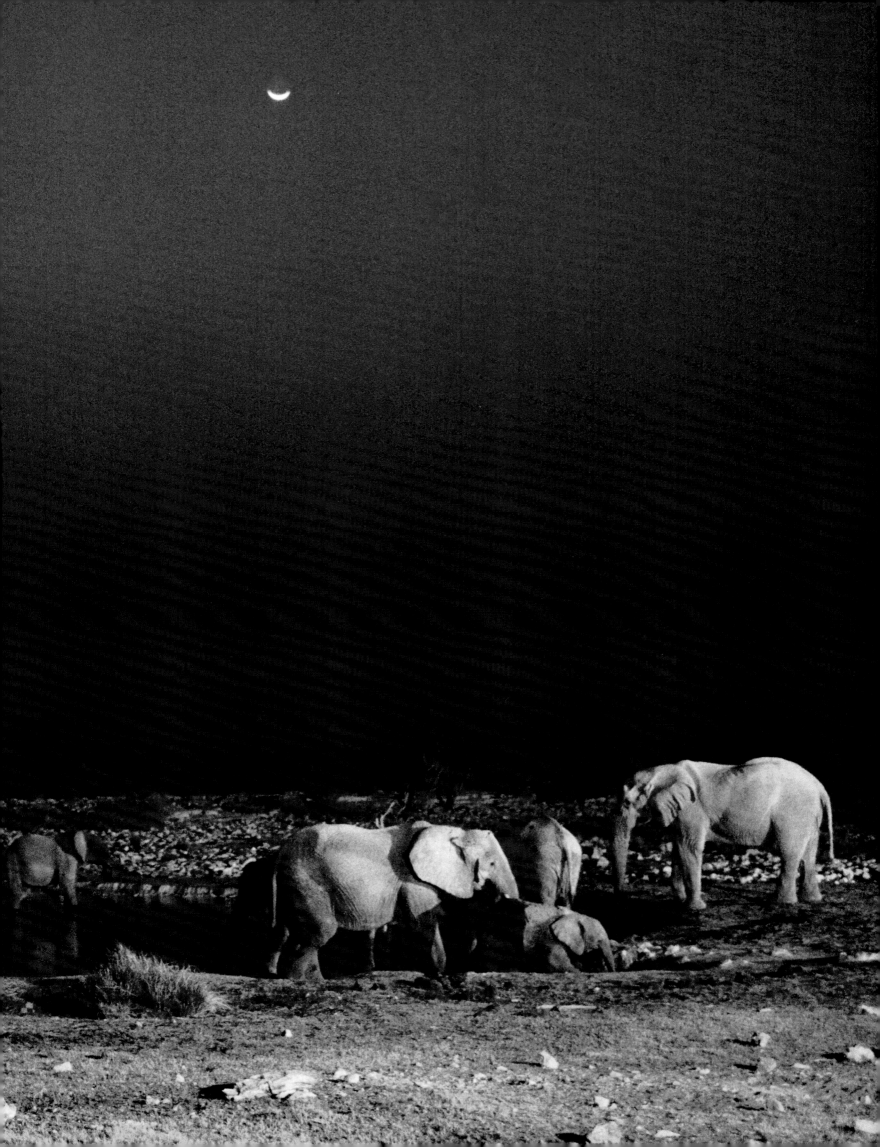

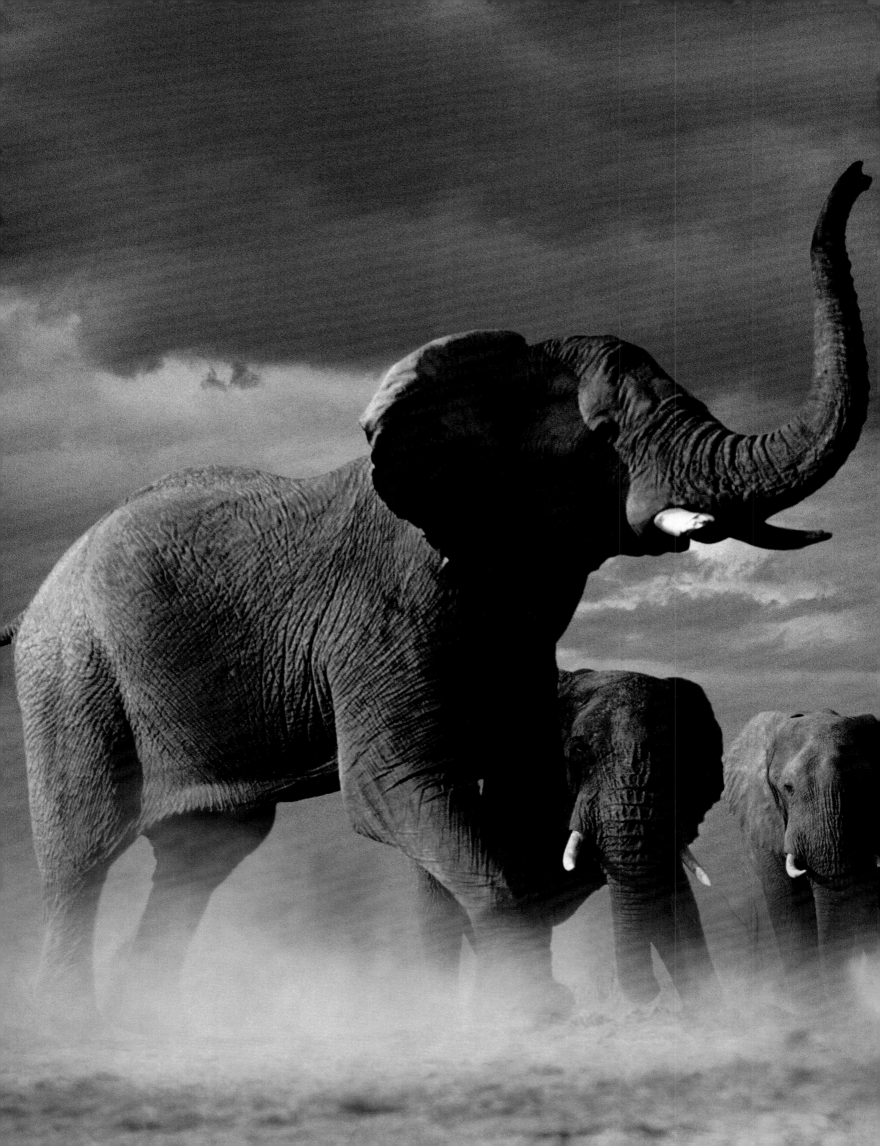

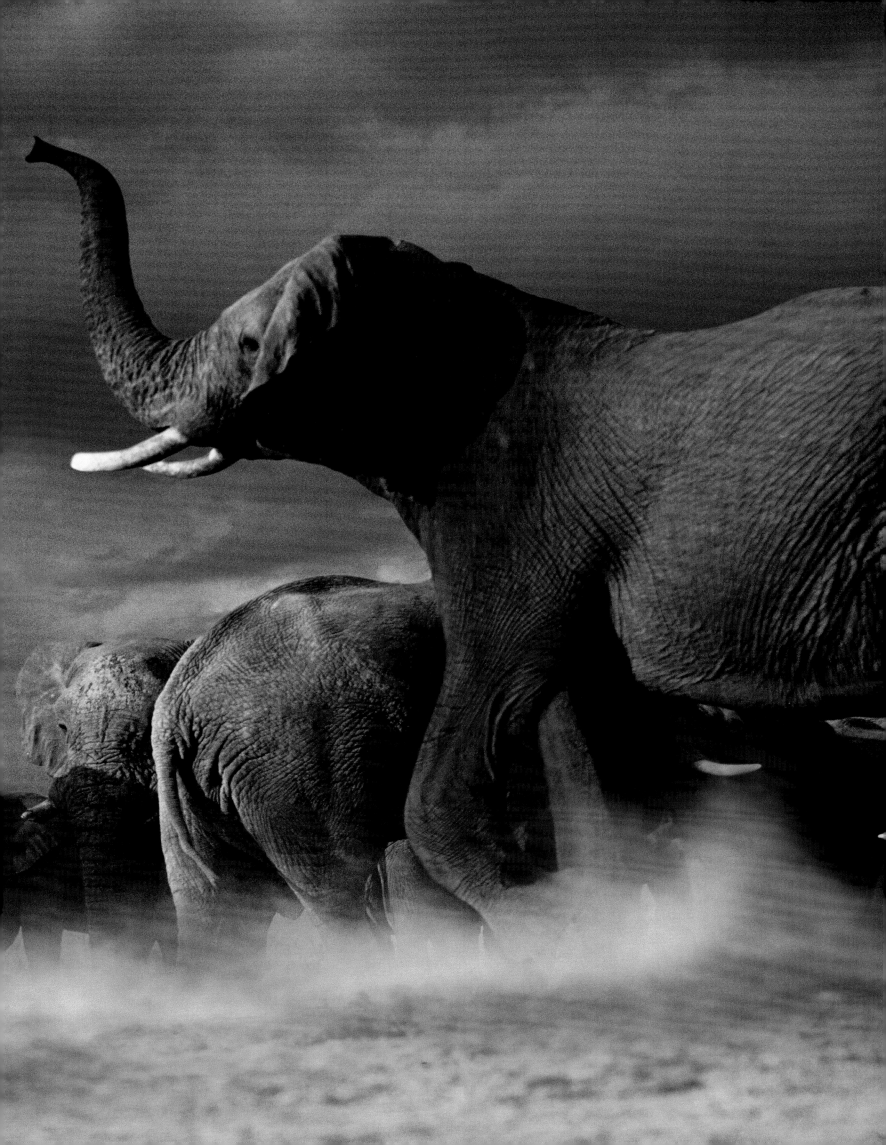

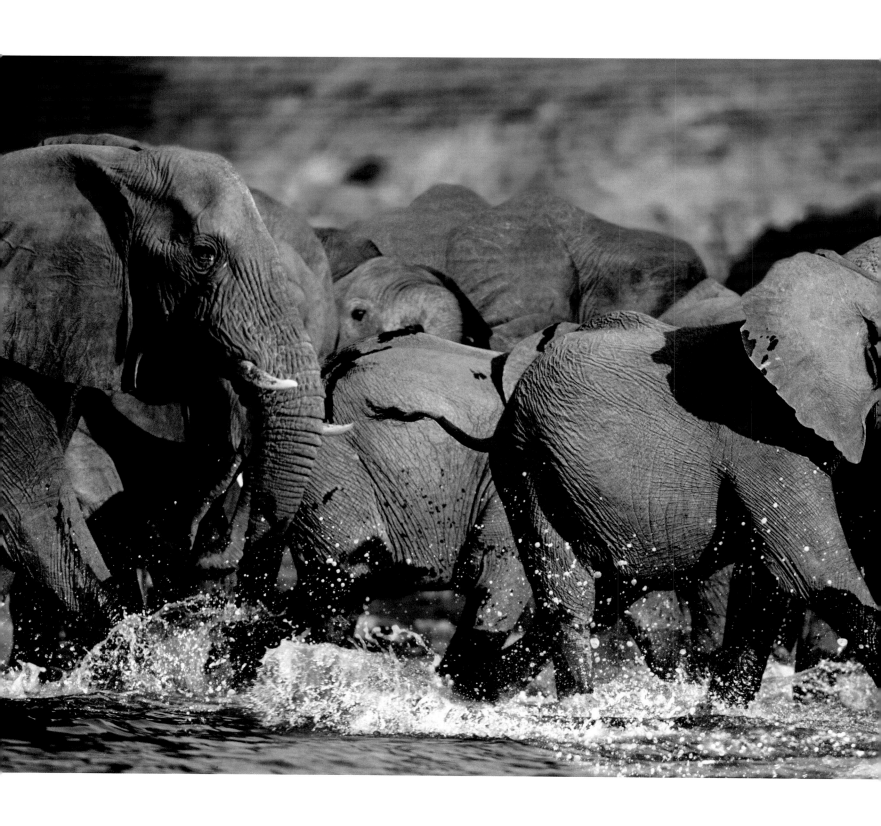

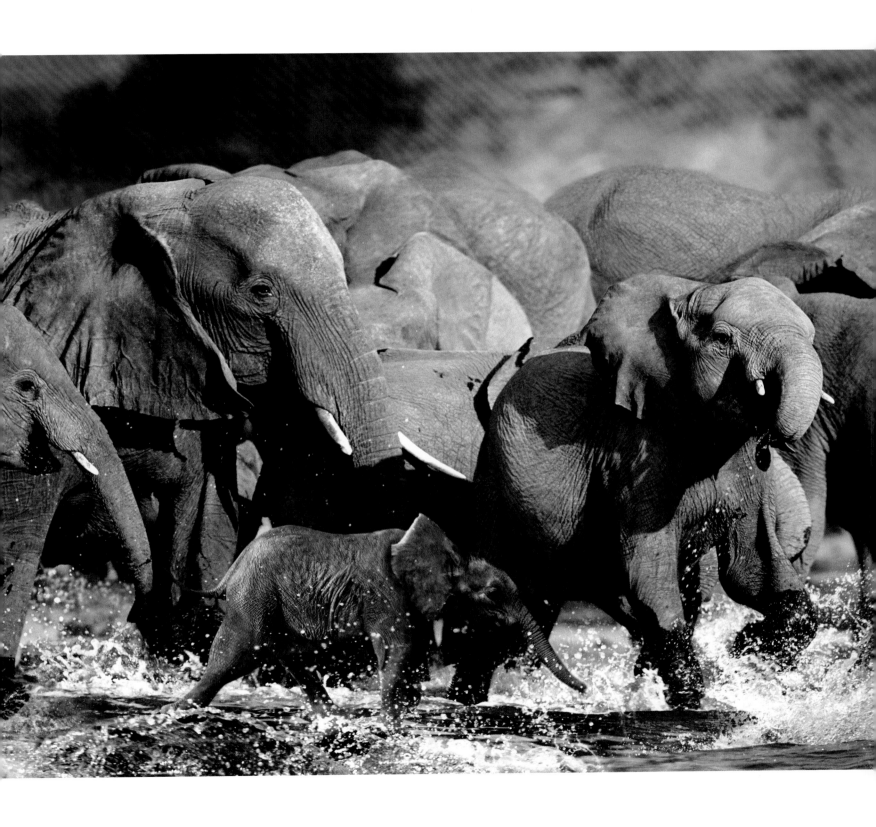

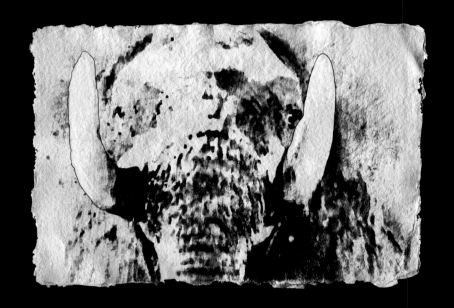

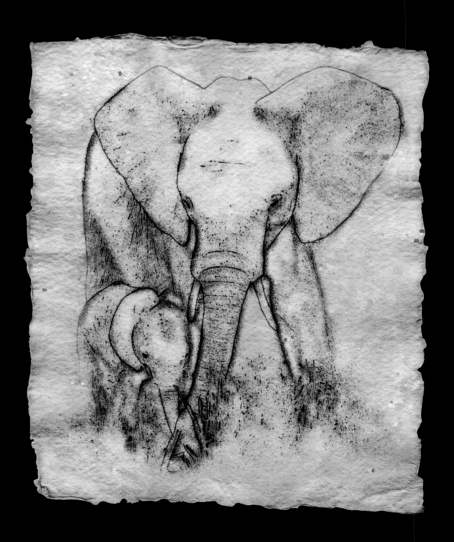

We may be moral beings, but we are also capable of immense cruelty. I have early childhood memories of visiting the circus, where an integral part of the excitement was the thrill of seeing animals in their cramped cages, cooped up behind the Big Top. The performing elephants amazed us with their tricks as they balanced on giant balls. We gasped in terror as an elephant suspended his front foot above the head of the recumbent ringmaster. We never spared a thought for the confines in which they were kept, and the suffering they undoubtedly endured during transportation. Elephants are prone to arthritis, and the difficult manoeuvres placed unnecessary strain on their joints. What child thinks about arthritis while watching a trick? There are also reports of an elephant who, slow to learn her circus routine, had been beaten as a consequence, and was subsequently seen practicing her act alone at night. Not all elephants cope in equal measure. A retired neighbour recalls how, in his youth, he chained up circus elephants in railway trucks. Each foot was anchored, severely restricting movement to a point where it was almost impossible. When the elephants, locked in their suffering, began to rock to and fro, the workers wrongly believed that the elephants were encountering an inner peace. The workers did not recognize the extent of suffering the elephants must have endured, nor acknowledge the existence of some kind of sentient spirit within. Awareness of others is a learned skill.

Growing up surrounded by images of Dumbo in his utopian cartoon circus, the real animal circus of our childhood was also perceived as a place of fun and excitement. We were blissfully unaware of the animals' suffering. Historically, early circuses merely displayed the elephants, but as the public became more accustomed to seeing them, the demand for stunts of greater complexity grew, and exploitation was pushed to extremes. Such circuses are thankfully disappearing, and my own children have grown up in an atmosphere of greater awareness, in which they find such places of animal torture appalling.

I spent my childhood in apartheid South Africa, a brutal society that made racial prejudice compulsory and went to great lengths to control and withhold the information we received. It is not surprising that, as children, we were

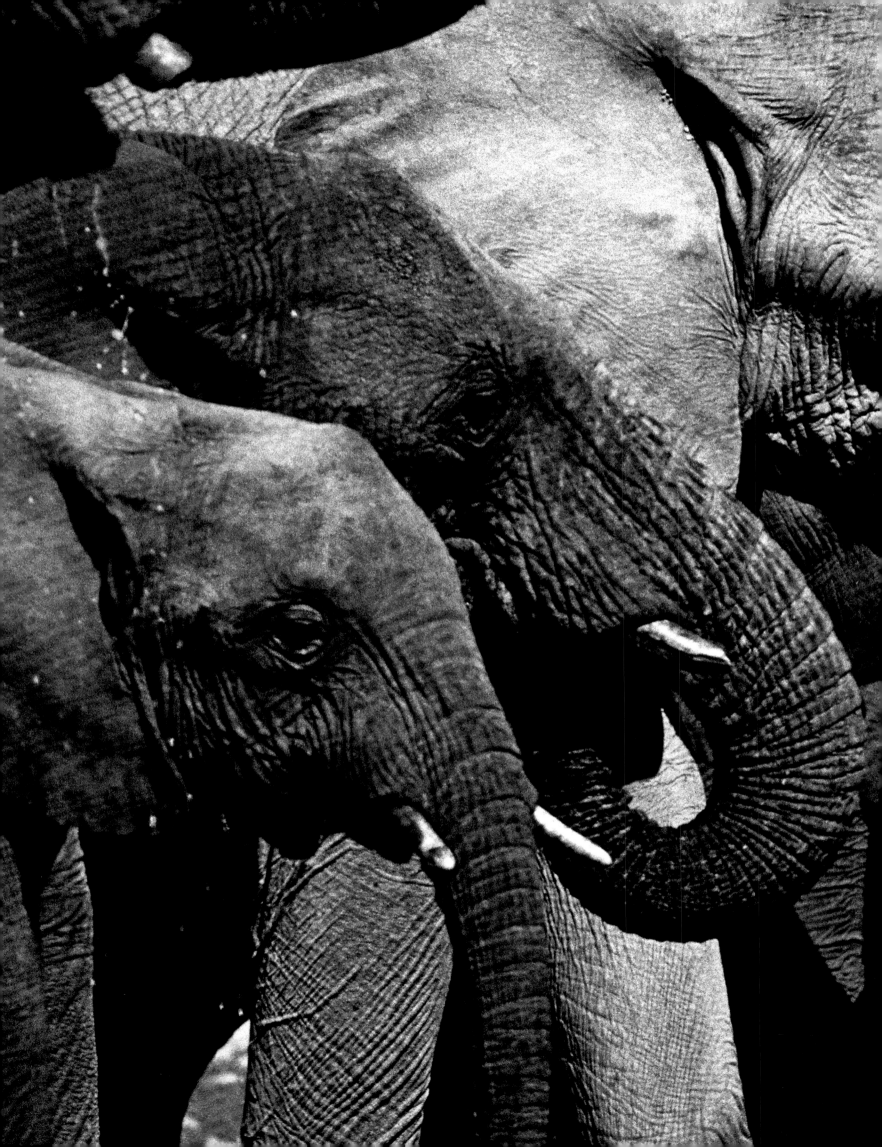

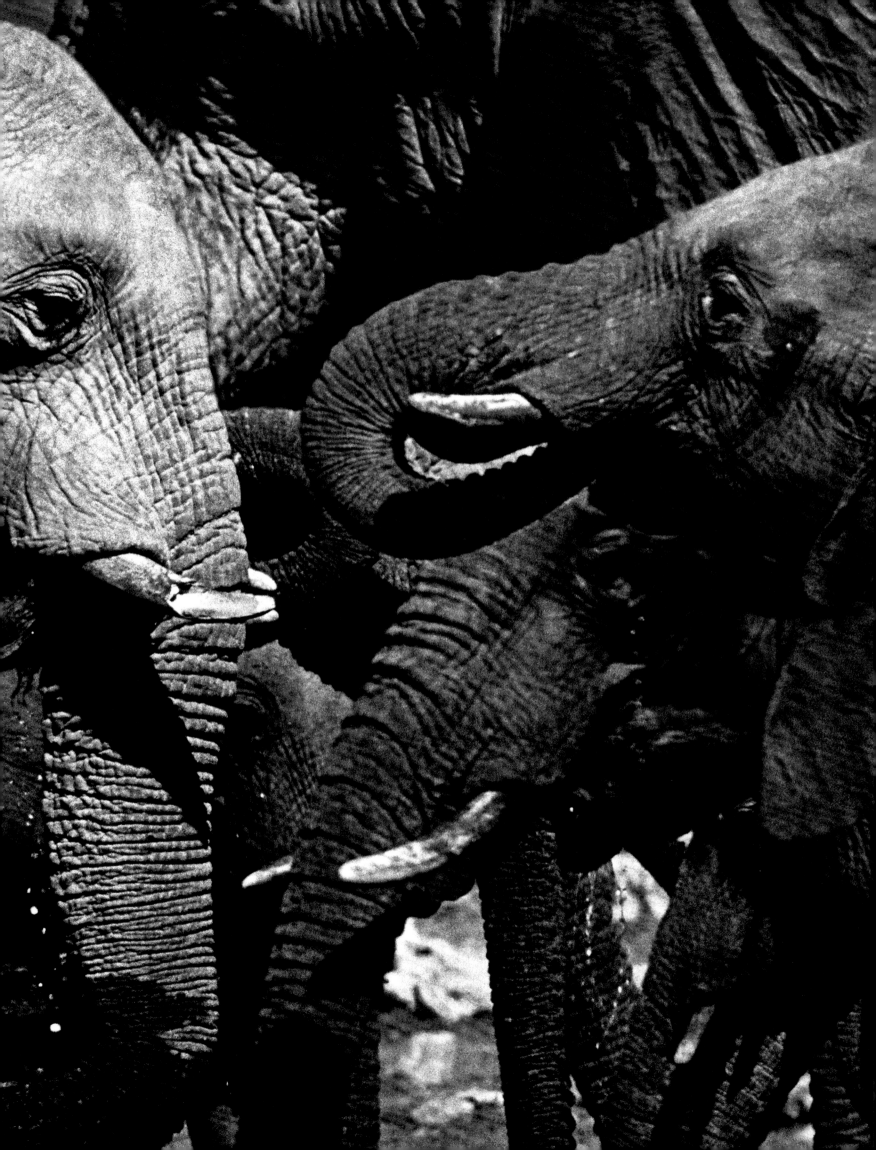

shielded from issues relating to human rights, with animal rights taking a back seat. Official doctrine was driven by irrational fear, with the brutal suppression of those who displayed inter-racial compassion and empathy. Although my own family had openly opposed apartheid throughout the era and endured the consequences, the denial of access to information was difficult to bear. The very process of dividing people into separate groups objectifies them, creating an environment in which empathy is absent and cruelty can flourish. It is all too easy to lose sight of the individual and be blinded by complacency. In creating this book, each of the many journeys I have made has been an inspirational learning process, with each experience building up a more complete picture of the essence of the elephant.

I wonder how many details we all inadvertently miss with regard to the rights of other people. Life is a continuous journey of discovery, and when the thirst for awareness of others prevails in the human spirit, it helps us affirm our own sense of identity. Within us all is an innate desire for freedom, which we can transfer to animals. When a captive wallaby called Wesley escaped from his pen near the English village where I live, he became something of a local hero. For many months he was spotted in the countryside and clearly demonstrated his ability to survive on his own. His determination and free spirit was hailed in the local press, and he evaded all attempts to recapture him. Similarly, a cow who escaped from a New York slaughterhouse became something of a national heroine, and after being caught, had her life spared. Sadly, elephants have not always been treated so sympathetically when they have escaped from captivity. Easily startled, a frightened elephant running amok is difficult to catch, and poses a great danger. In Sri Lanka during the late 1950s, an elephant was accidentally burned by a flaming torch during a religious ceremony. In the ensuing panic fourteen people were killed, most of whom were trampled to death by other people trying to get out of the way. The elephant was eventually caught and tied to a post, but when he broke free again, he was shot. In an Hawaiian circus, an elephant cracked under the strain of the constant performance, mauled her trainer and rampaged through the streets of Honolulu, attacking everyone and everything in sight. The police fired eighty rounds of ammunition at her. It took several more bullets and a lethal injection to end her suffering.

During the Second World War the authorities in Tokyo were worried that the city's zoo would be bombed and the animals would escape, causing danger to the population. A decree was signed stipulating that all the animals were to be poisoned, but the elephants refused to eat the poisoned food. Slowly, they starved to death. They performed tricks and did all they could to persuade their keepers to feed them. Traumatized by the decree he felt forced to obey, one keeper eventually smuggled food to an elephant, but it was too little, and came too late. They all suffered an agonising death from starvation. The harrowing pictures of Kabul zoo during the Afghanistan war in 2002 are a further example of the impact of war on captive animals.

In 1903, Topsy, a captive elephant at Coney Island near New York, killed a drunken keeper who had fed her a lit cigarette. The authorities decided that she must die. At a time when the electric chair had recently been invented, Thomas Edison, determined to prove to his commercial advantage that AC current was more dangerous to use than DC, sent a team of technicians, who wired her up to AC current. Topsy died after ten seconds. Perhaps Edison became haunted by his actions, because he later wrote: 'Non-violence leads to the highest ethics, which is the goal of all evolution. Until we stop harming all other living beings, we are still savages.'

Elephants have been known to shed tears, and have been seen crying in captivity. Charles Darwin commented on observations of the capture and tethering of Indian elephants. After initial resistance, the elephants gradually descended into total submission. It was noticed that one individual, though lying motionless, gave out muffled cries, his cheeks wet with tears. There have been reports of circus elephants who, tormented by the frustrations of training, lay down and cried. I remember hearing the cry of a baby elephant in Kenya's Masai Mara reserve. He was playing in the long grass, and became separated from his mother for a short time. When he noticed her absence, he wailed uncontrollably and she quickly rushed to his side. As she reassured him with her trunk, he sobbed gently. The cry of a lost infant elephant has a resonance that reaches out to all of us, transcending species. My local guide turned to me and exclaimed, 'They are human, I tell you, they are human.'

The world of the elephant has inspired much of our folklore. There is a story about a group of blind people, each of whom was given a single part of an elephant to explore, and then asked to describe what they found. One person described a foot, another an ear, and so on, until the air was filled with a confusion of diverse descriptions of the various parts they were touching. The core elephant is made up of many parts; our understanding of these creatures revealing but a small part of the whole. Likewise, my photographs are but one dedicated aspect of a multitude of viewpoints. In my observations I make no scientific claim, choosing instead to use the medium of photographic art: an approach that has the potential to touch the heart with a spark of an eye, a captured moment, a balanced composition and the intense interplay of shapes and colours. As a photographer I am influenced by the way an elephant's trunk feels when I touch it, and so I aim to create images that express my own personal feelings. After all, a photograph is essentially a tiny slice of frozen time, a photographer's subjective interpretation, a jigsaw piece of his or her own person. Photographs stimulate laterally. When I listen to my son play the saxophone, the haunting beauty of the sound he creates touches me deeply, though I wouldn't have a clue how to play the instrument. It is beautiful to listen to and look at, but only a few have the ability to release its power. You don't have to understand the science of acoustics to feel the music, nor do you need to dissect an elephant in order to acknowledge the common experience of sentience.

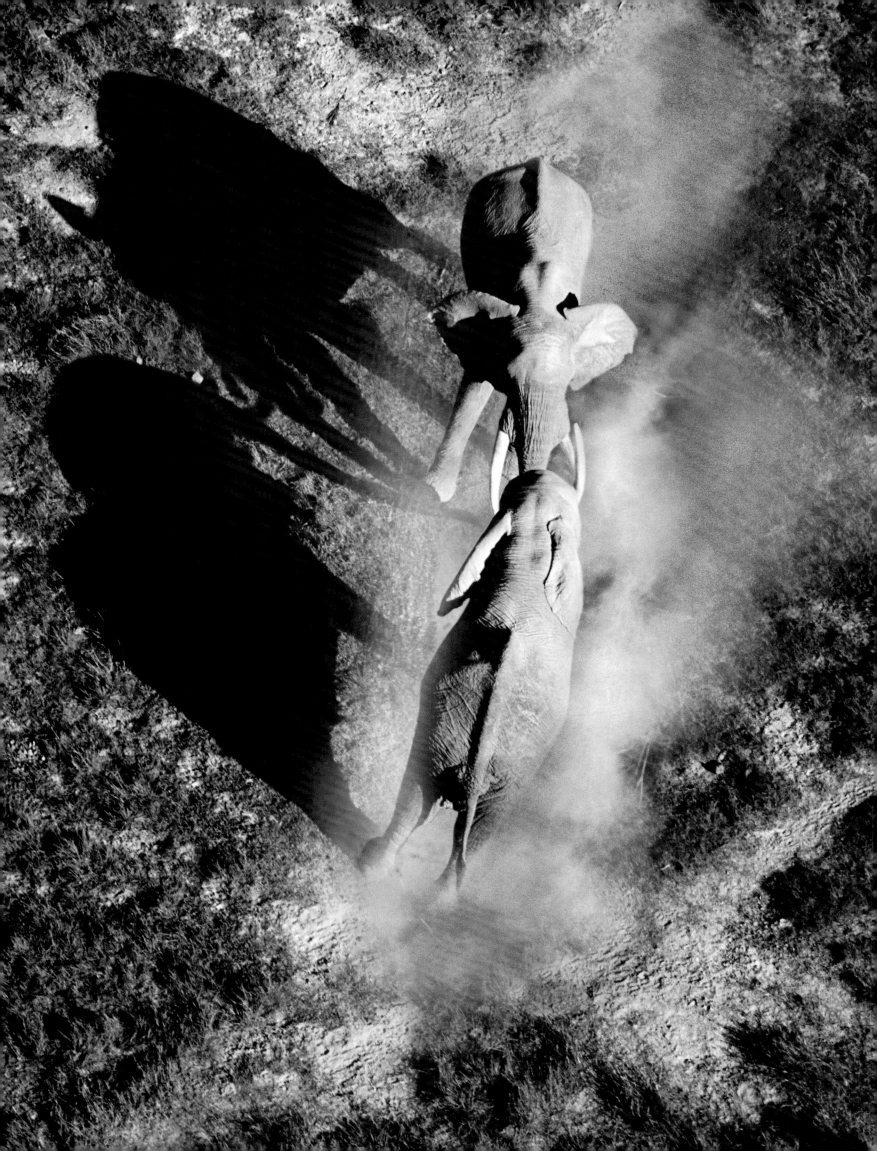

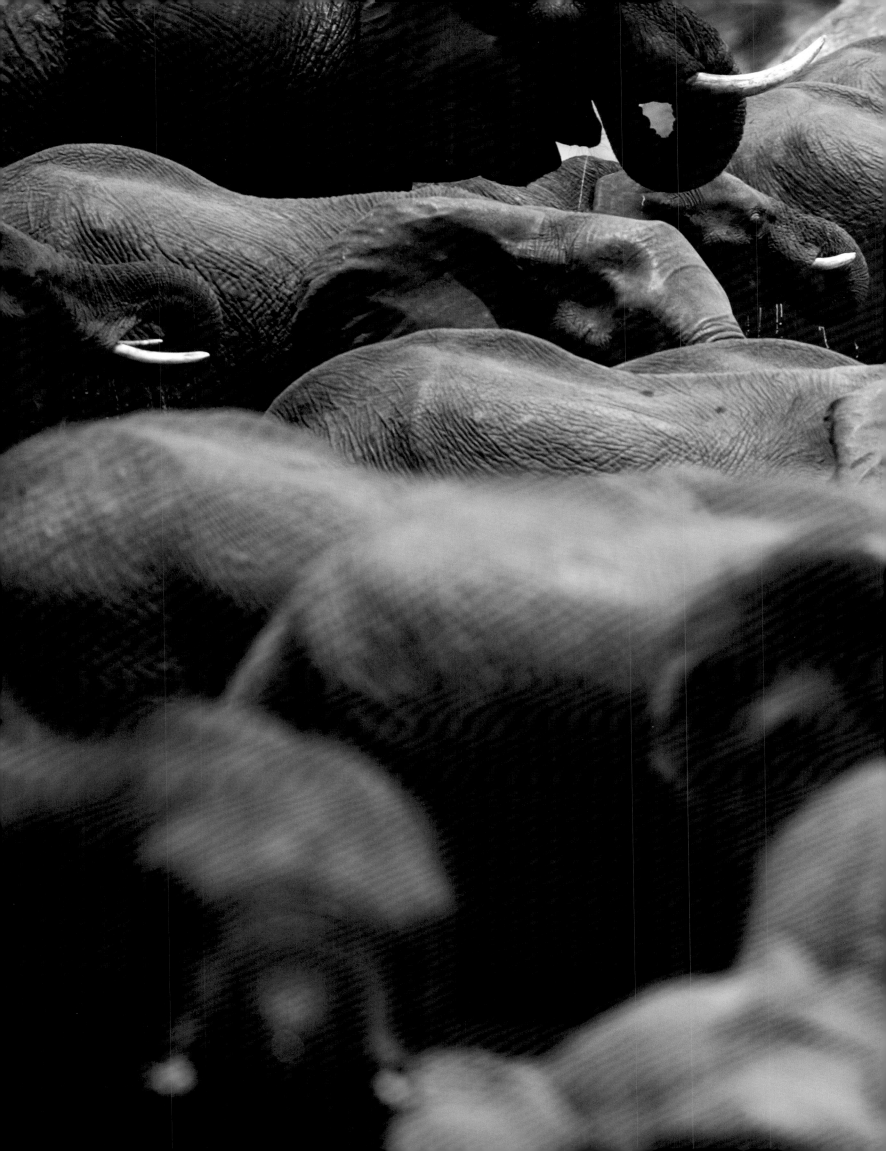

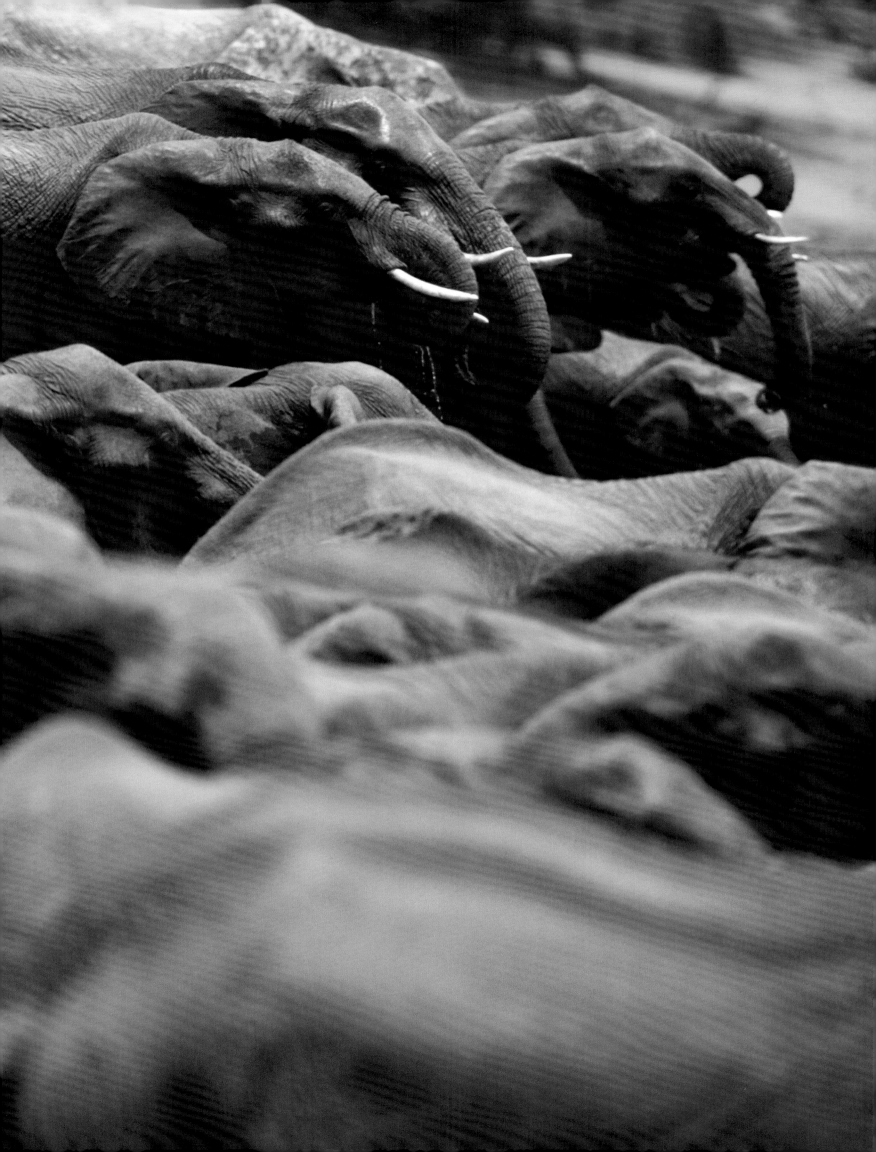

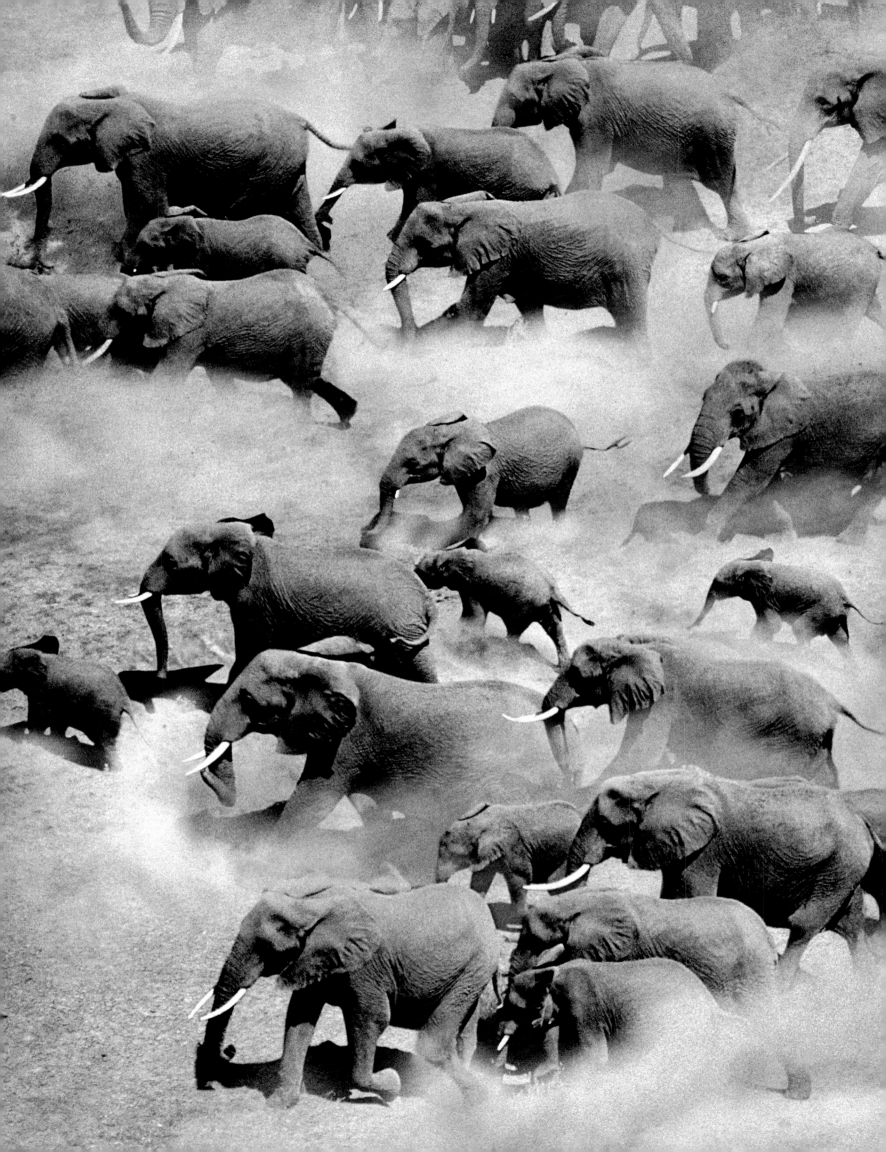

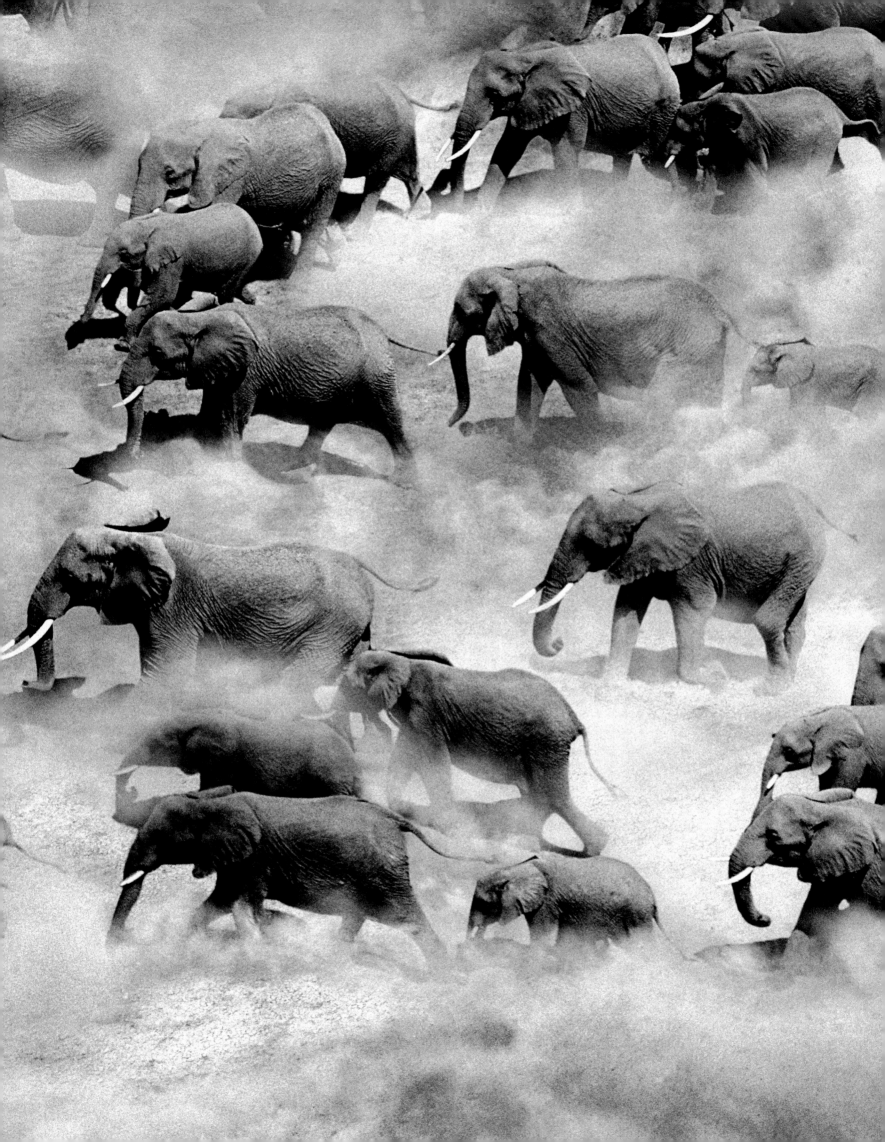

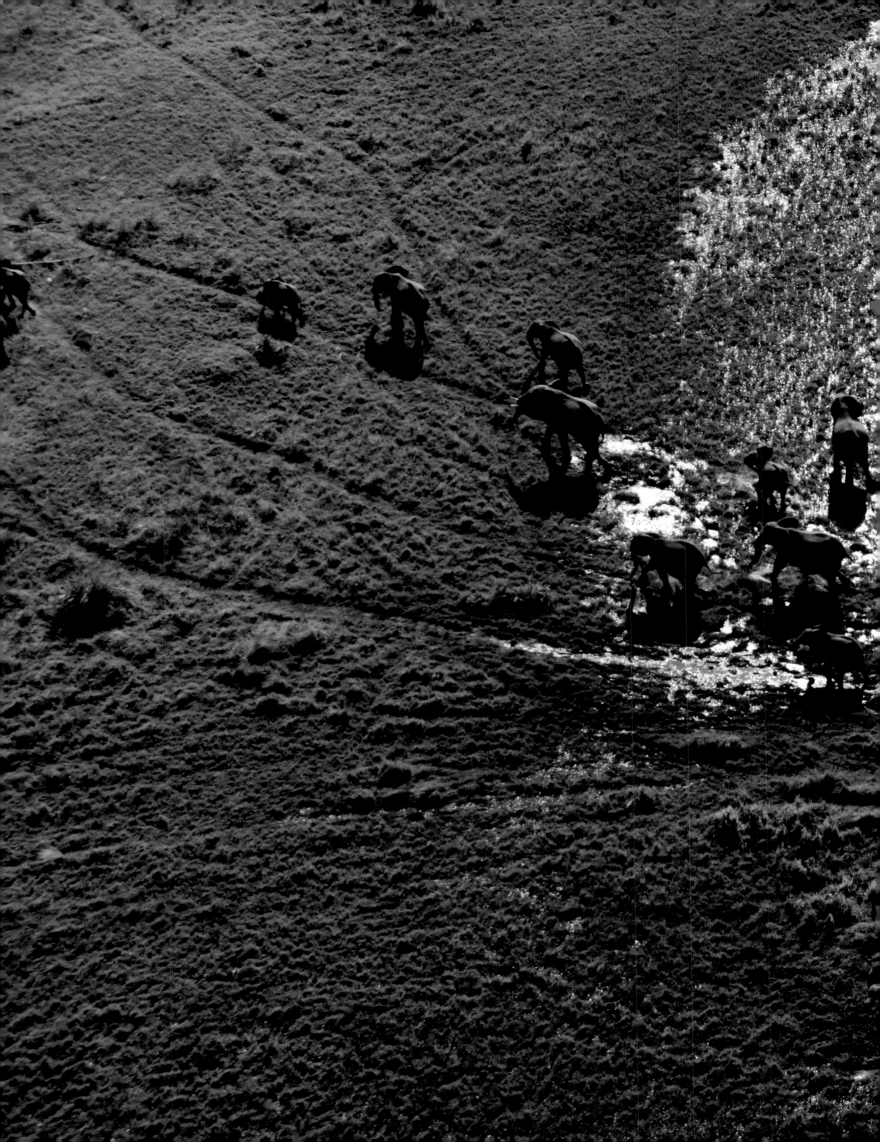

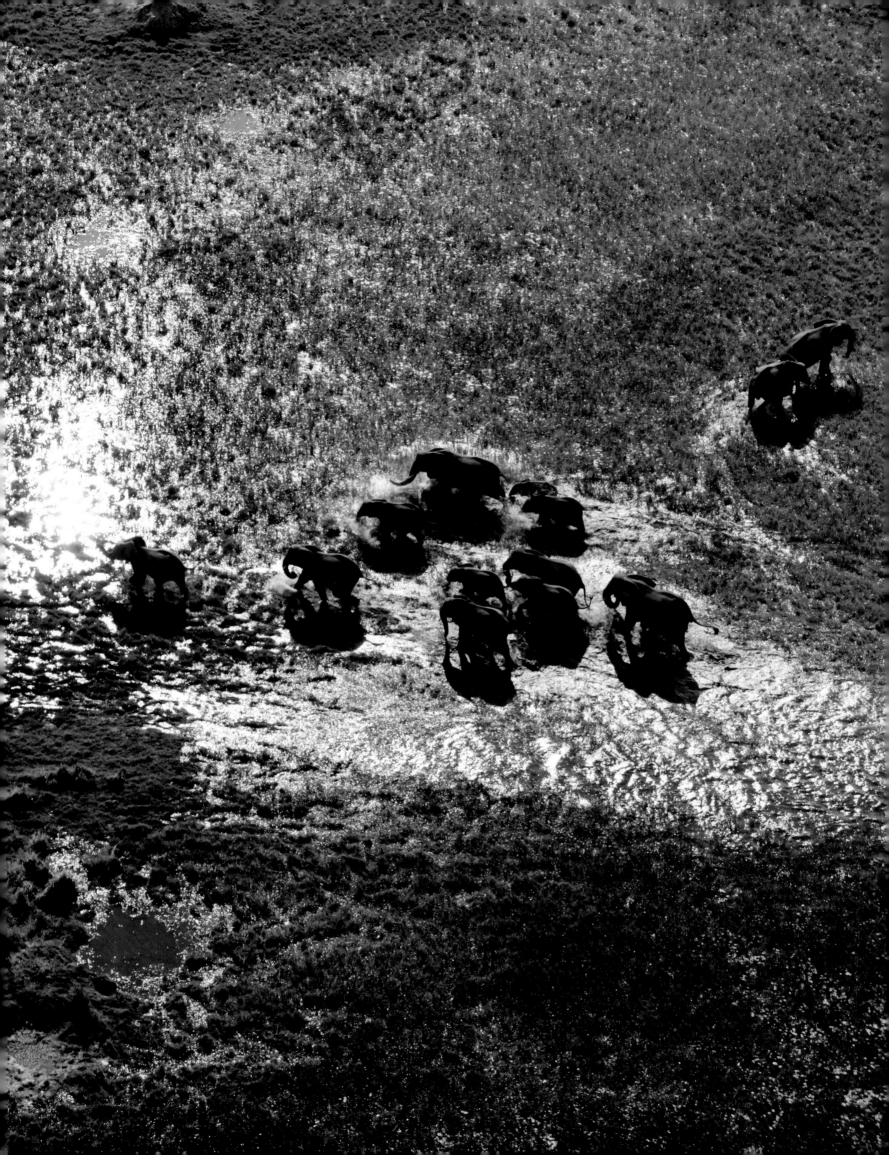

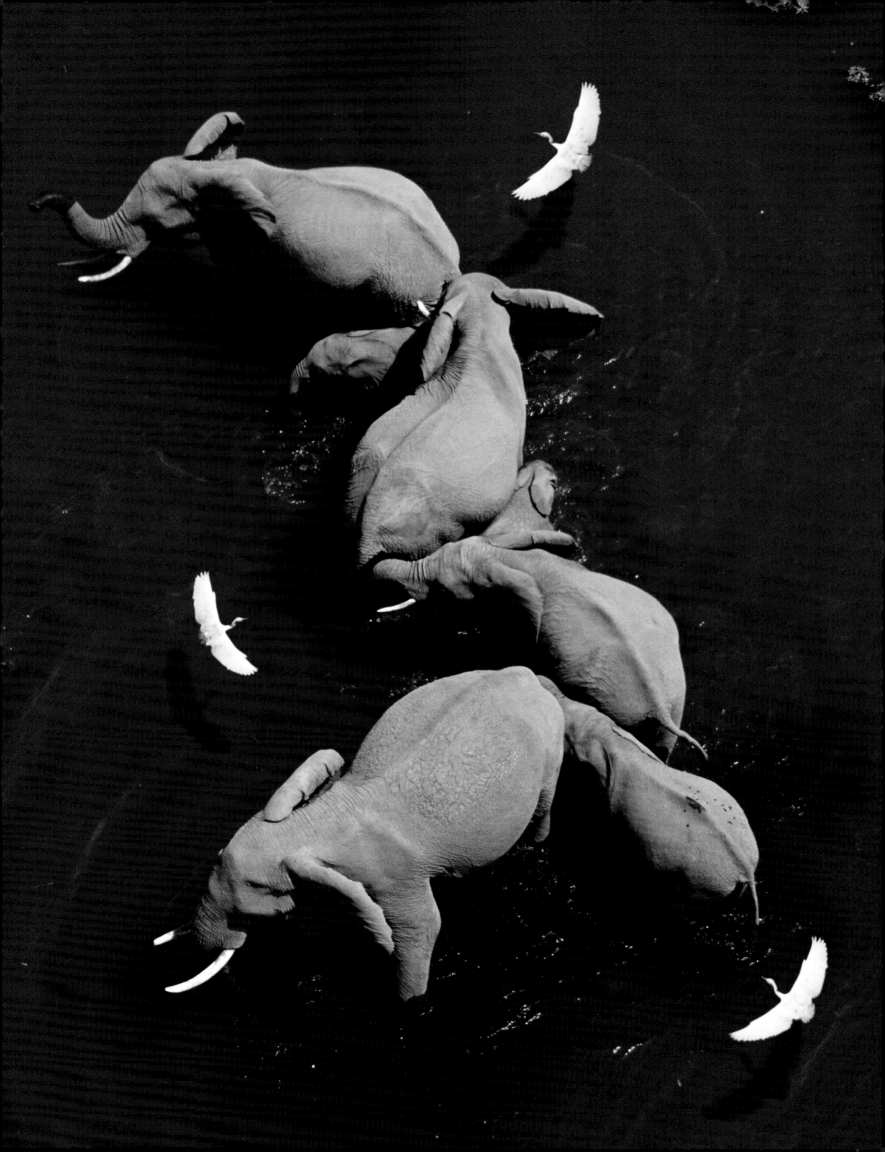

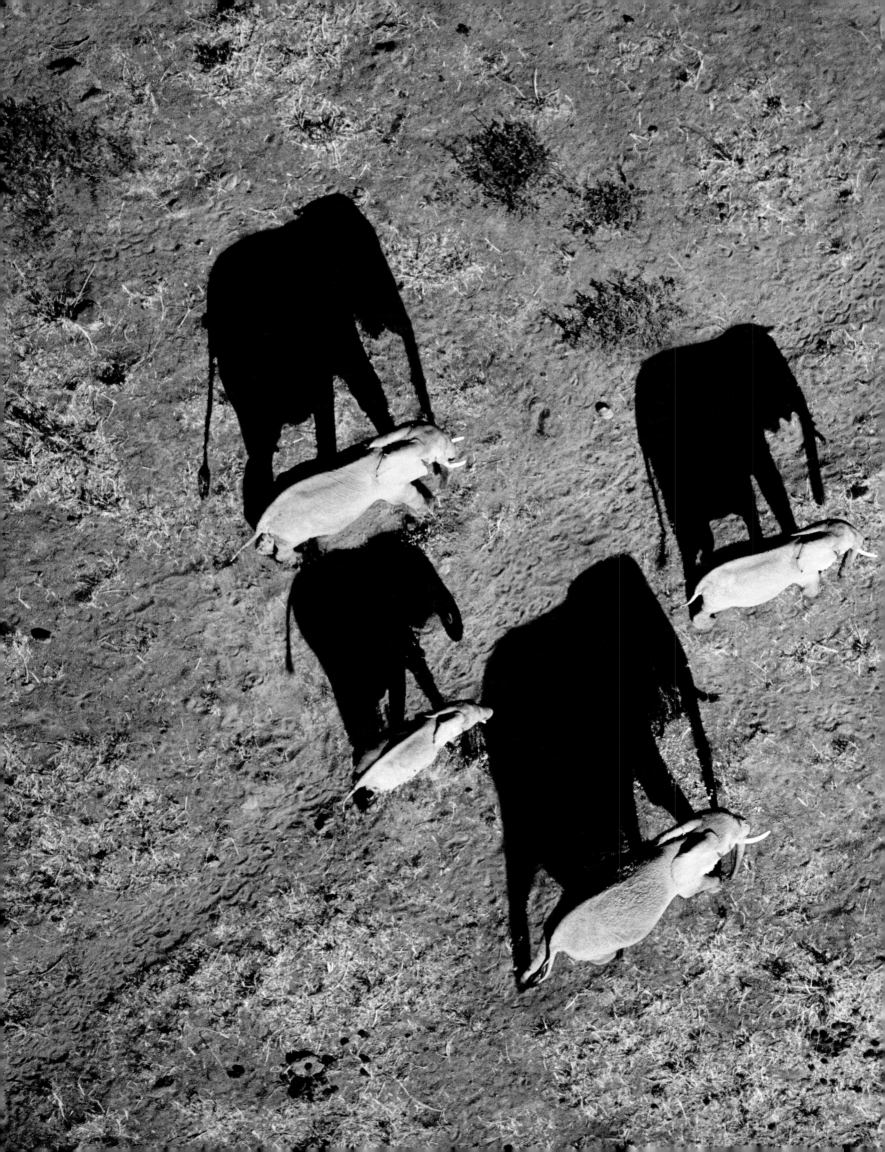

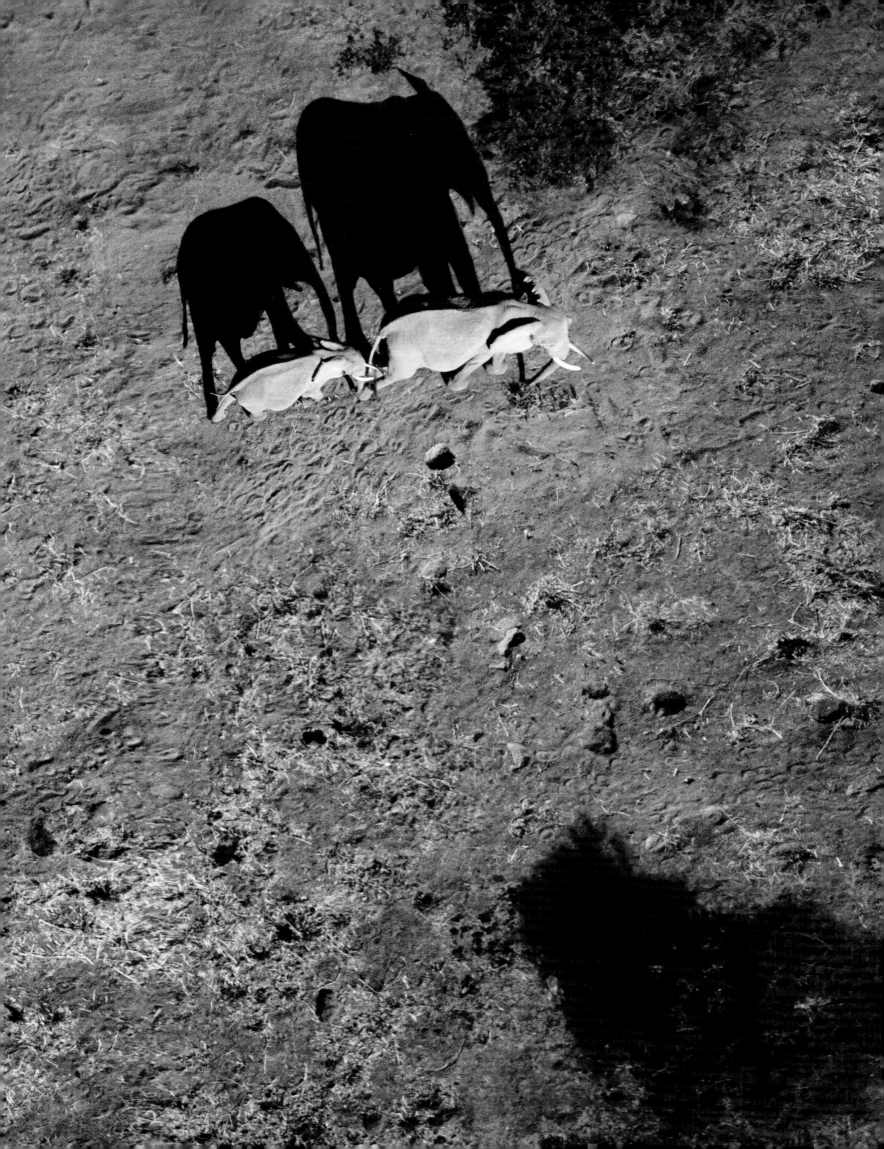

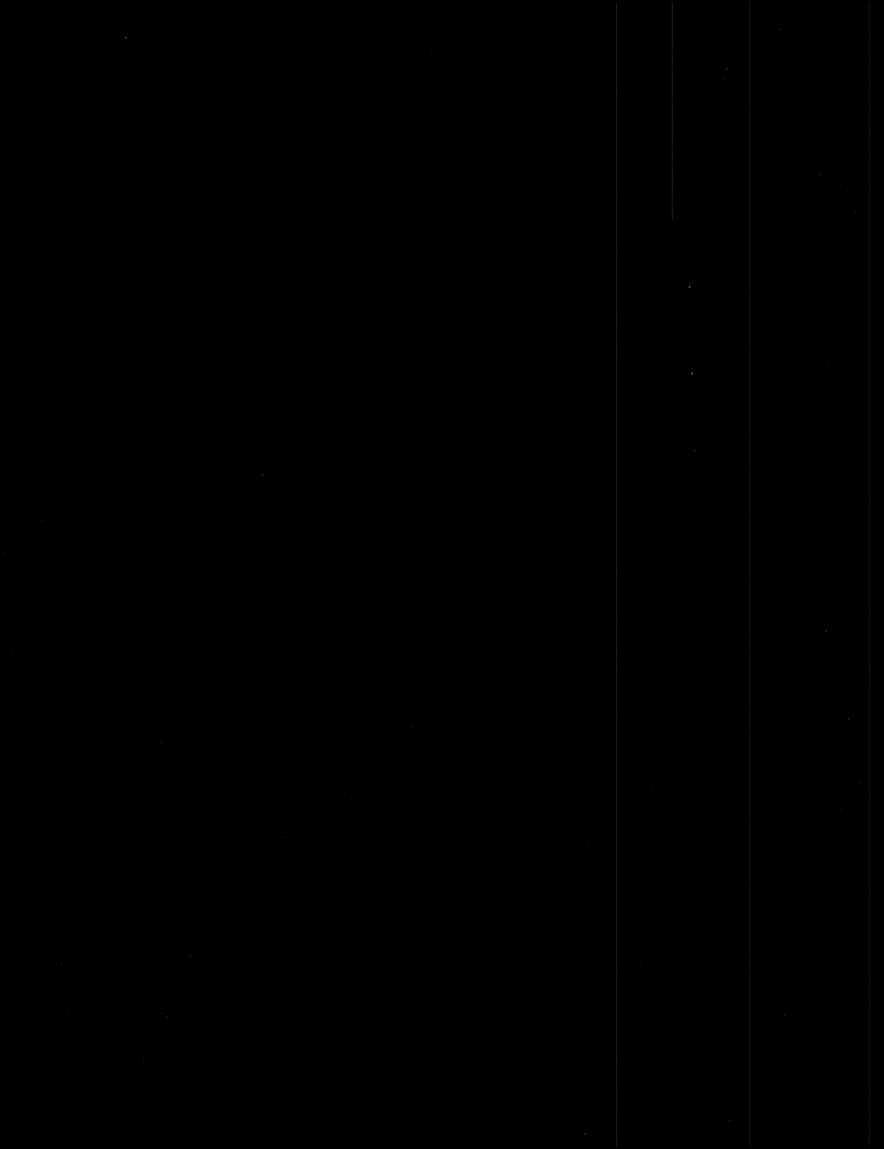

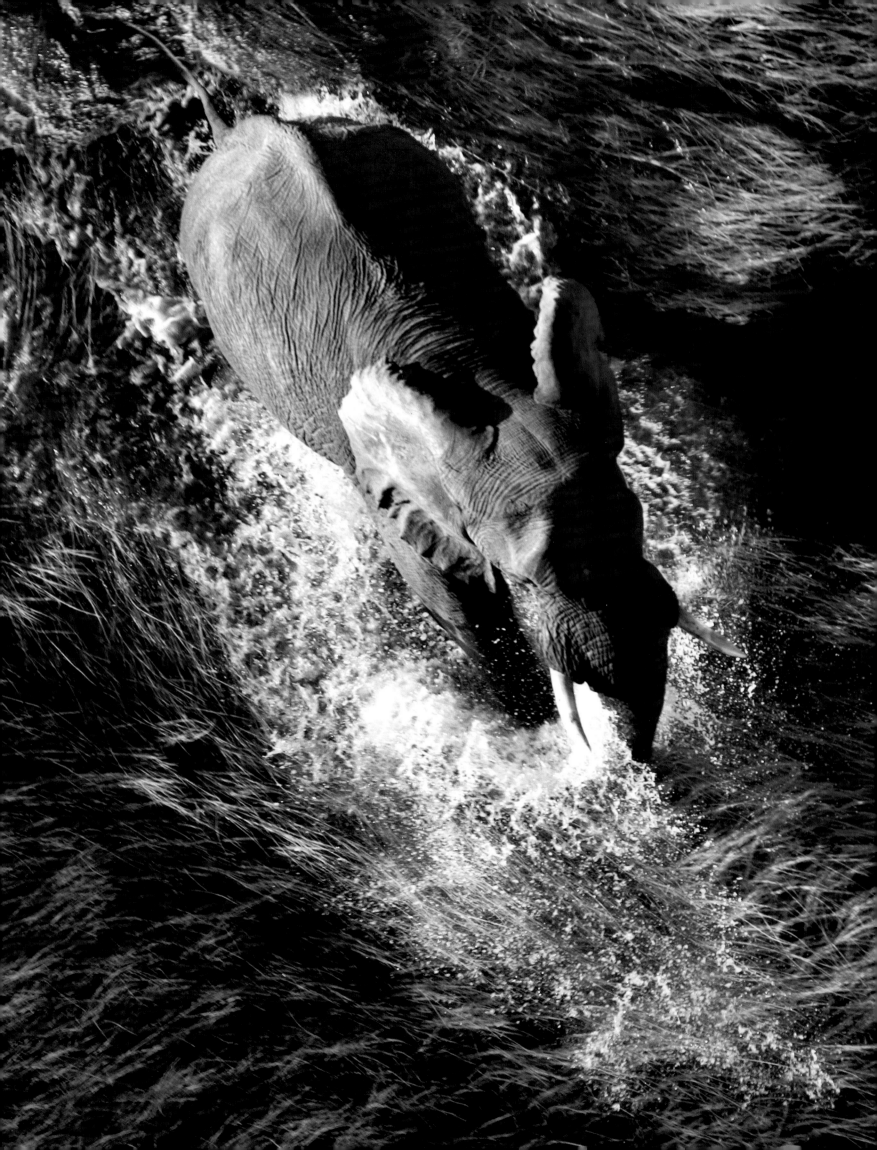

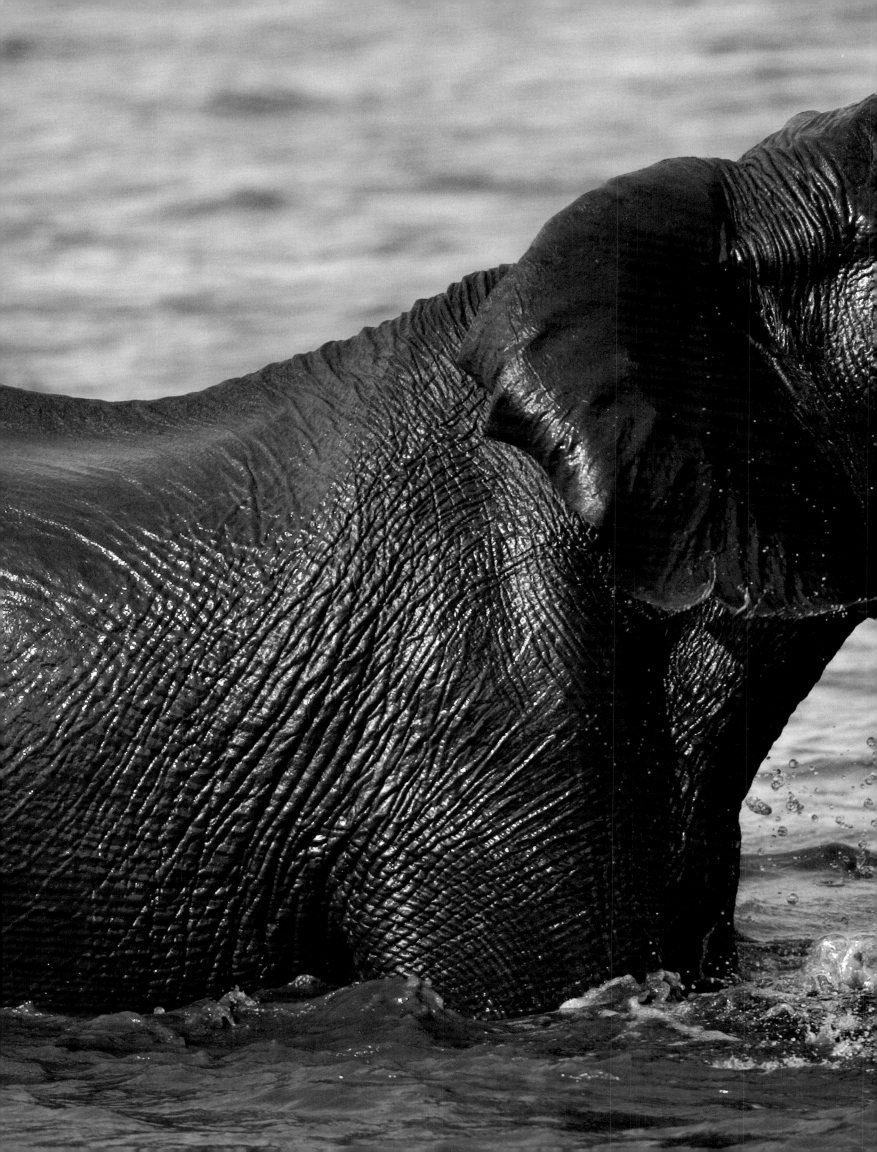

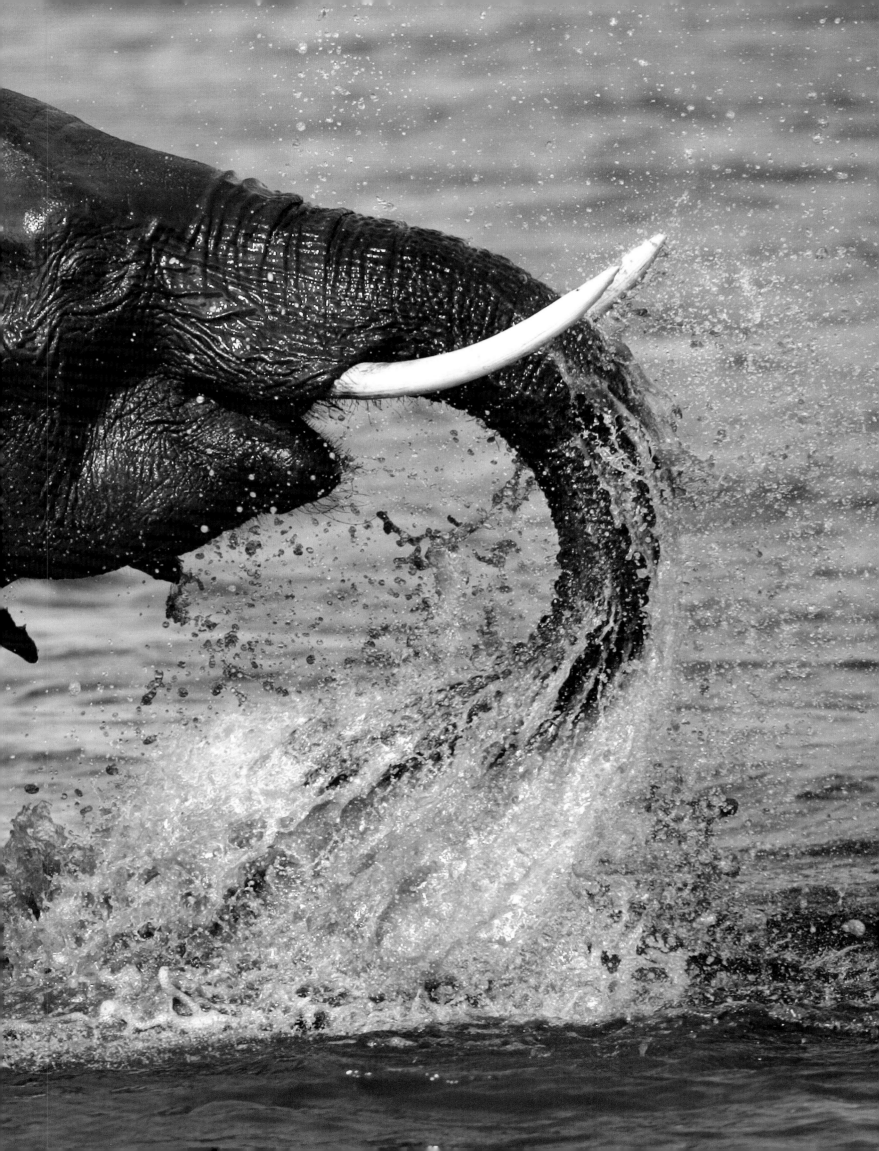

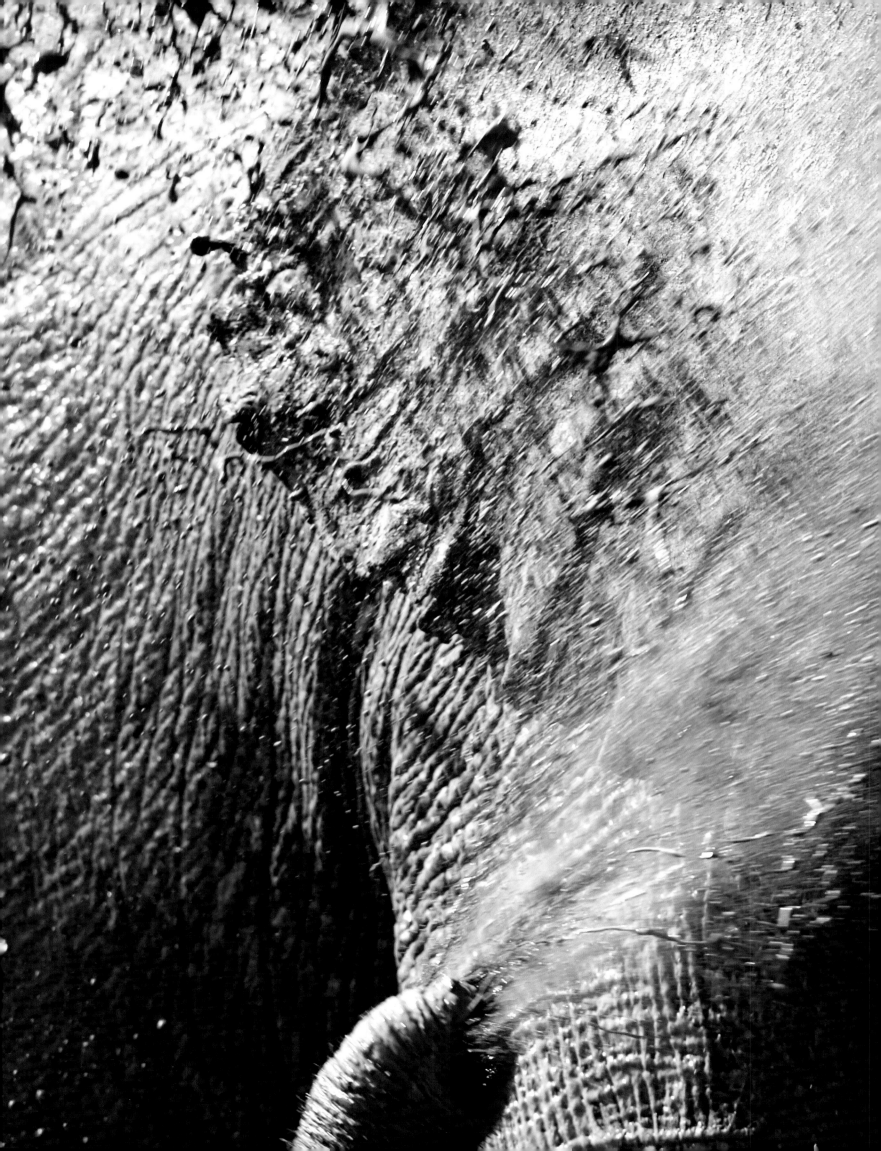

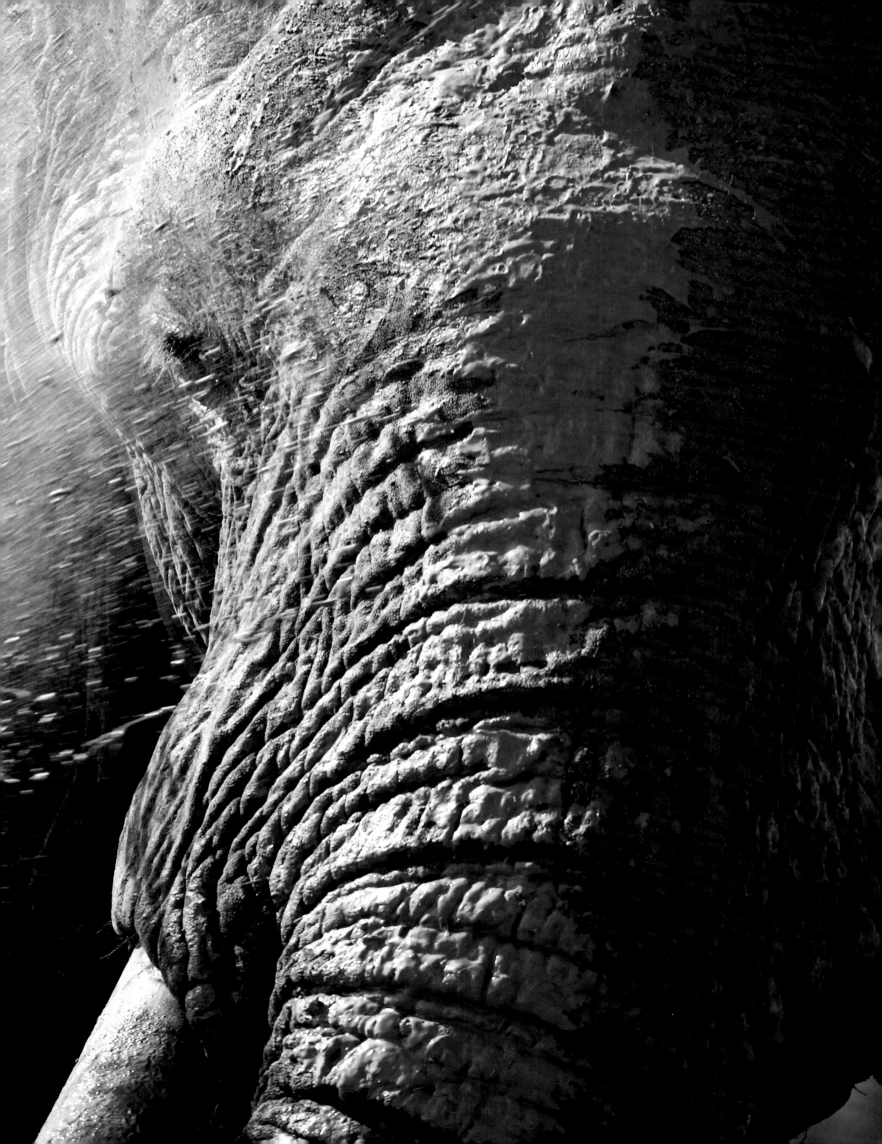

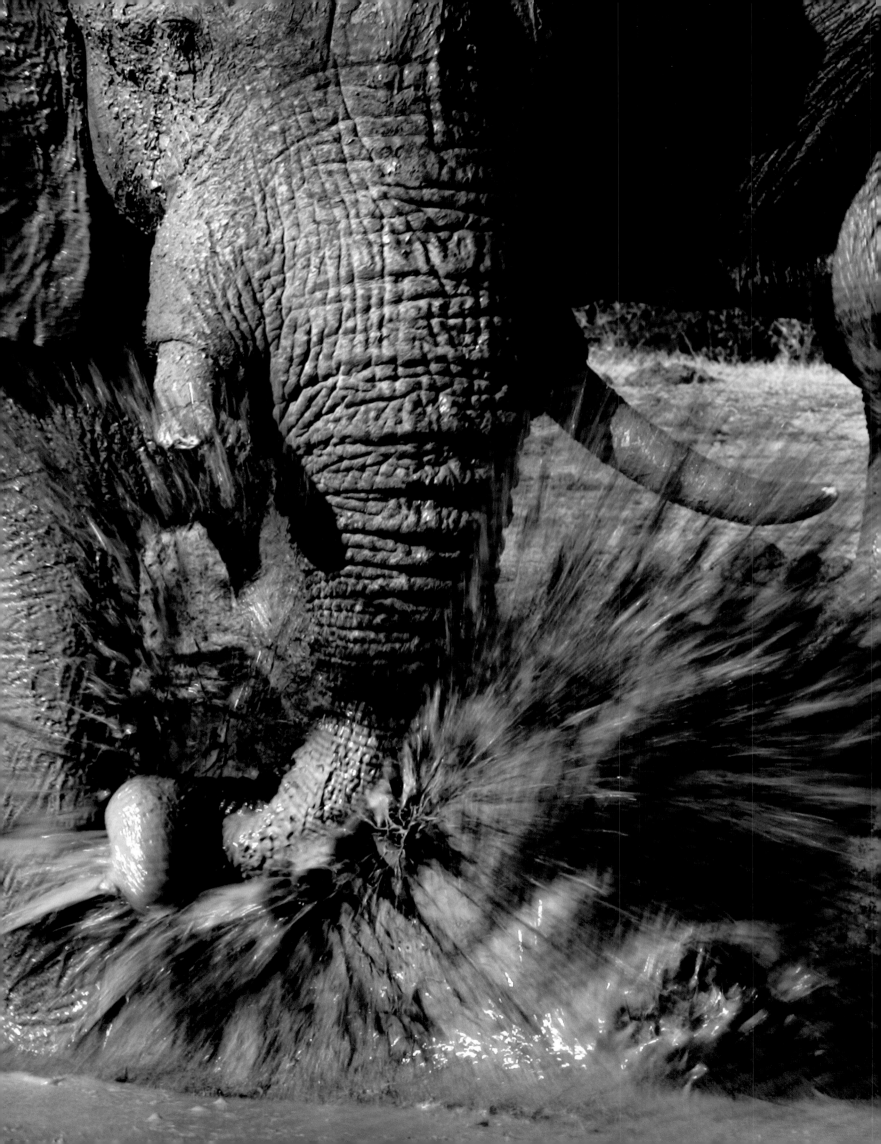

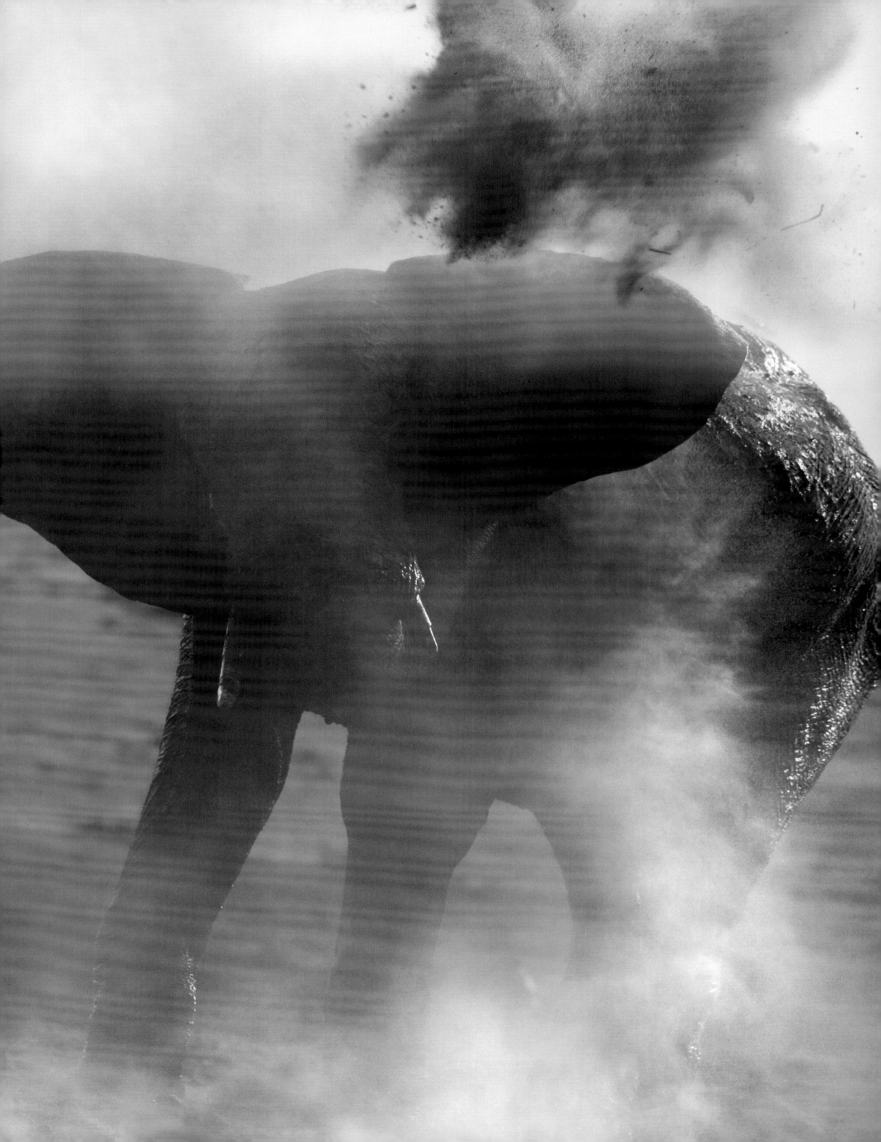

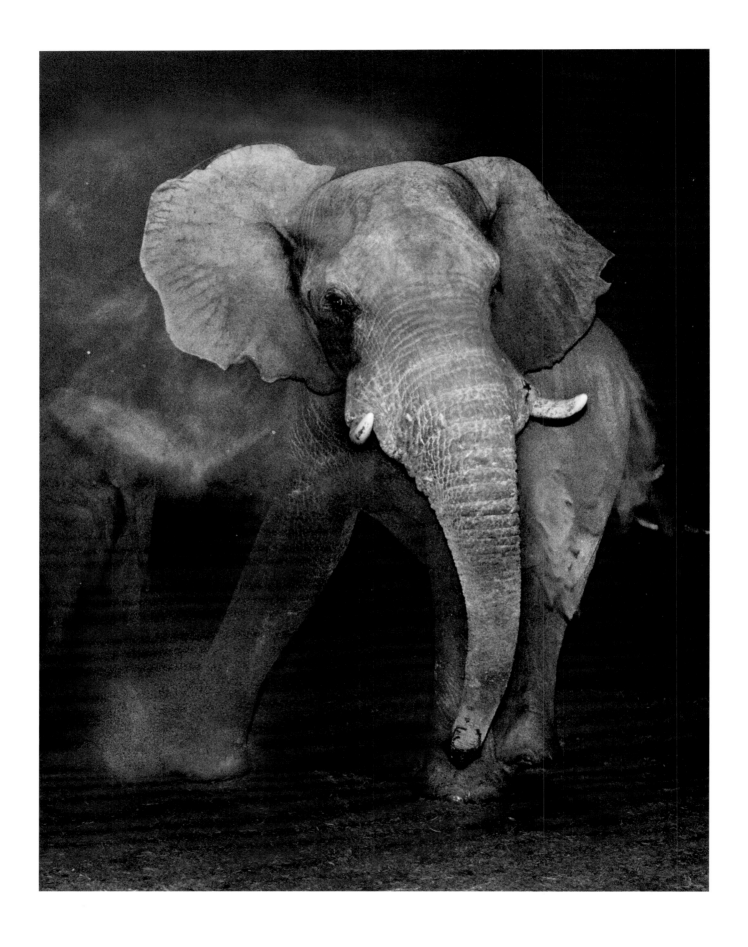

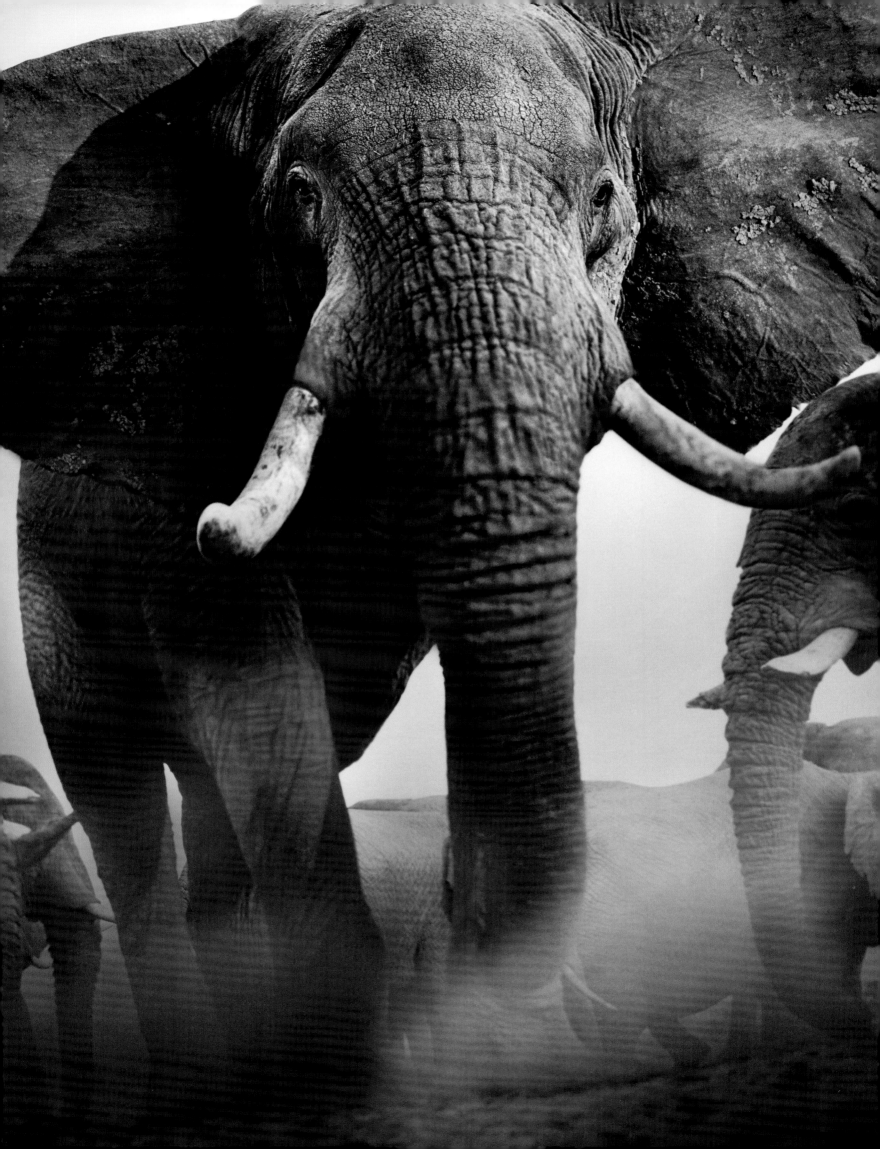

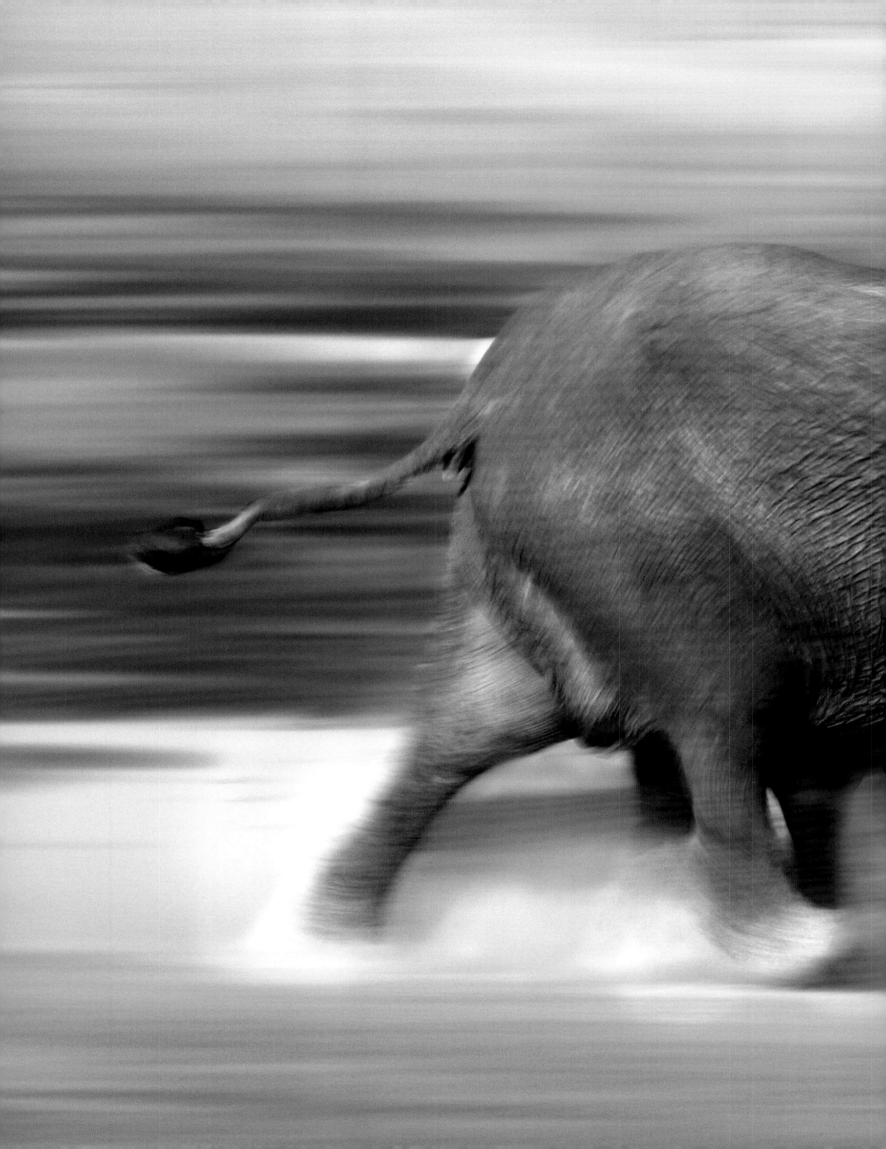

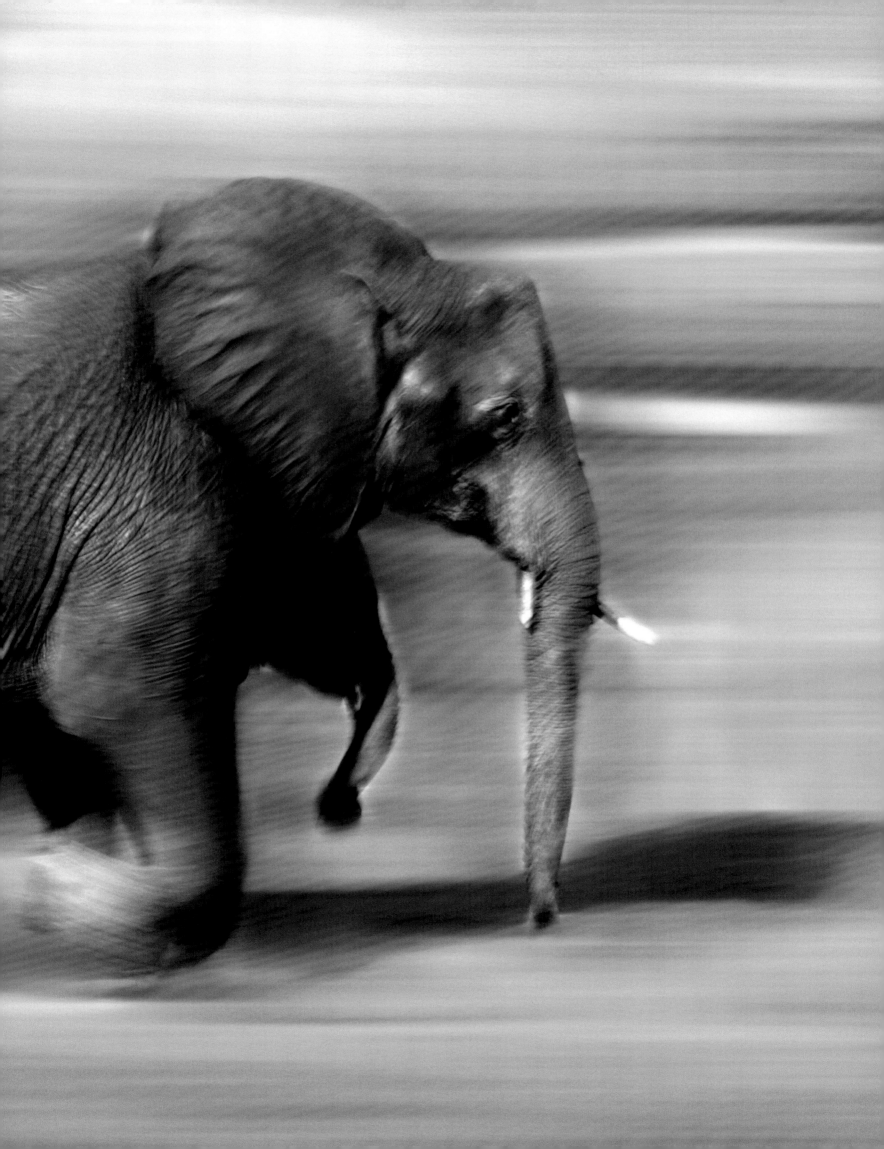

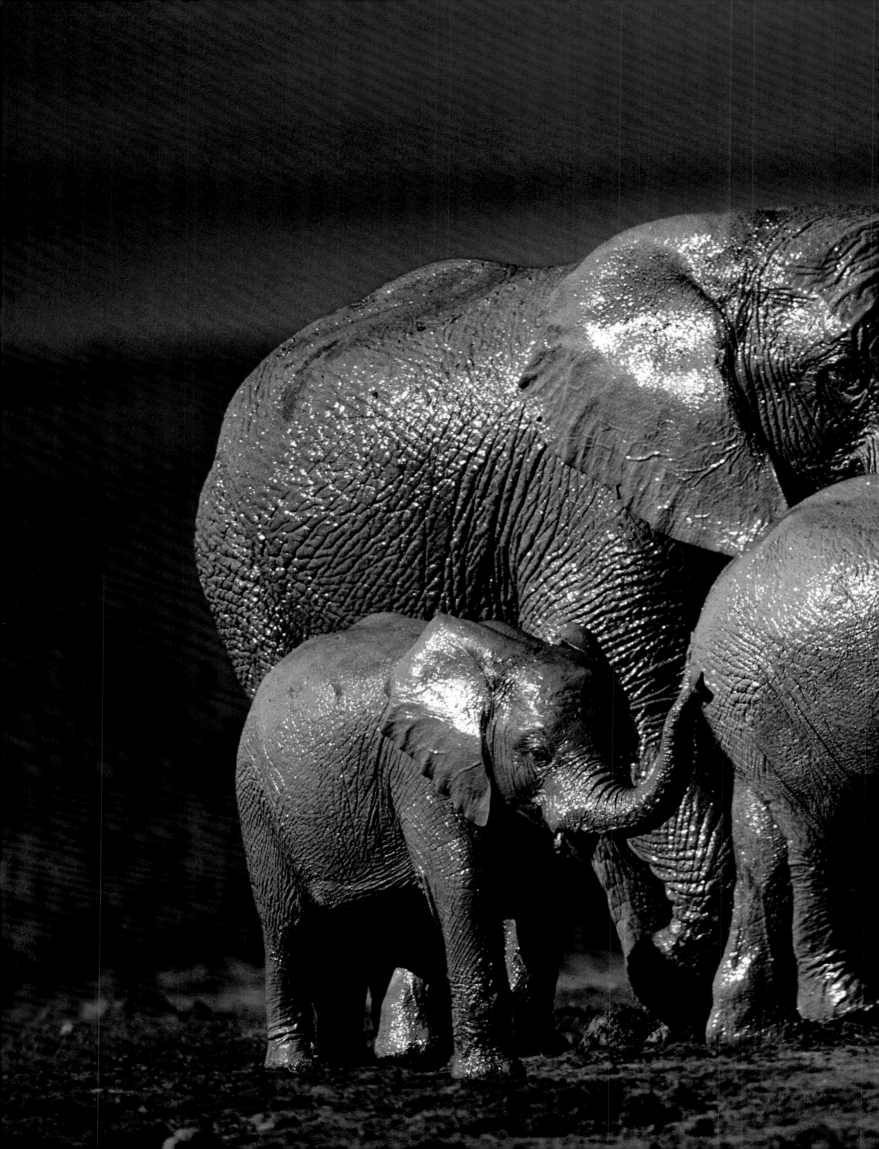

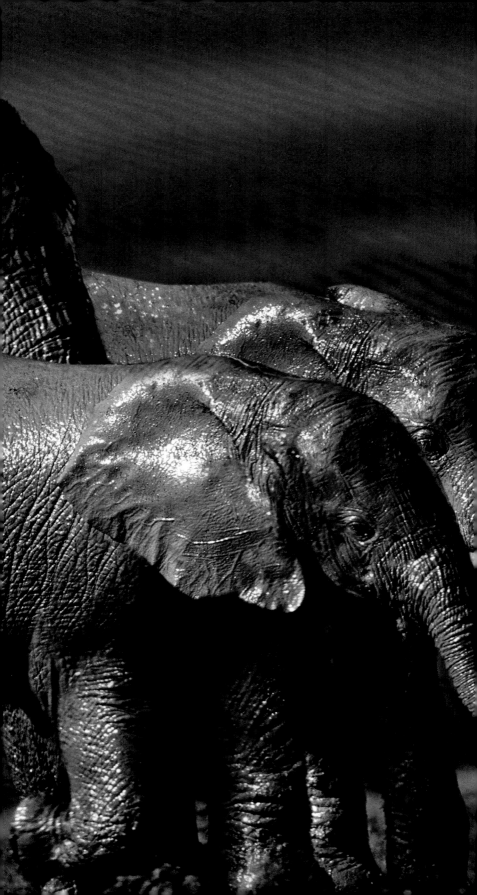

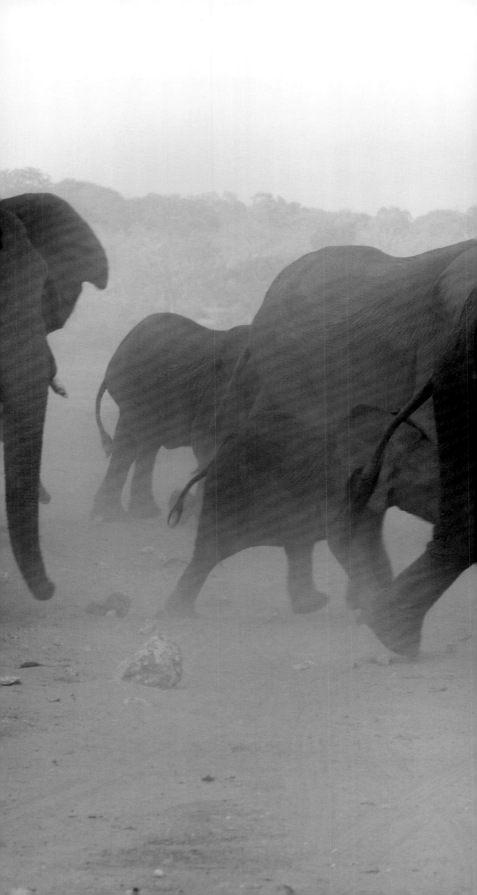

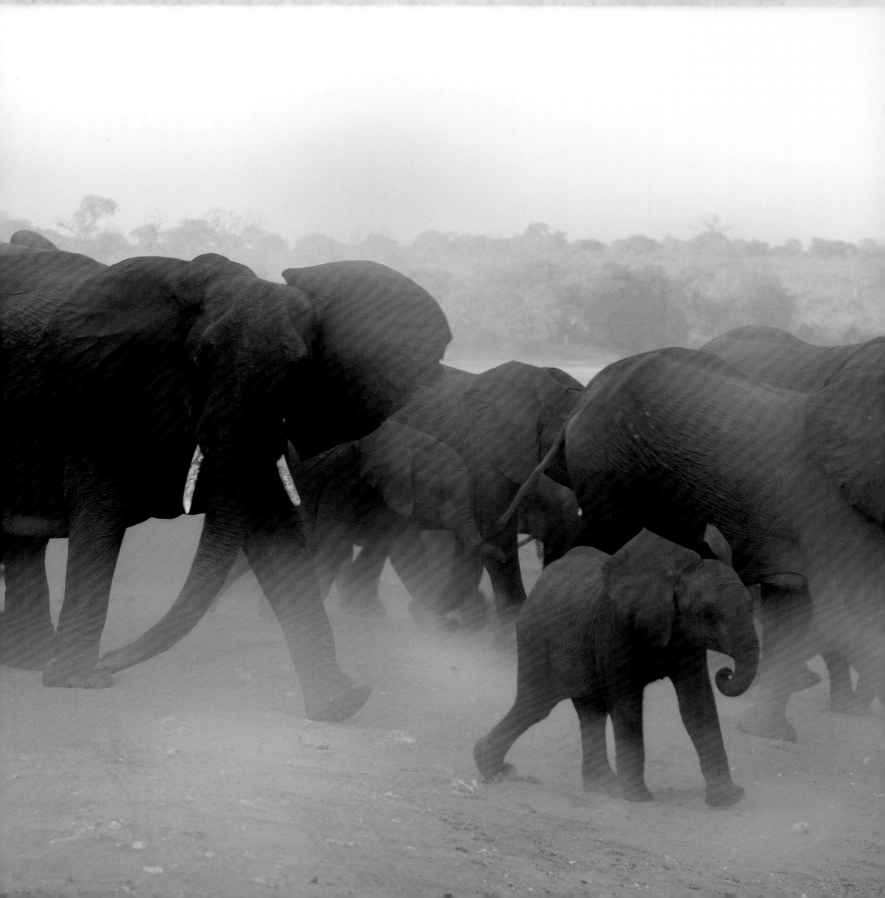

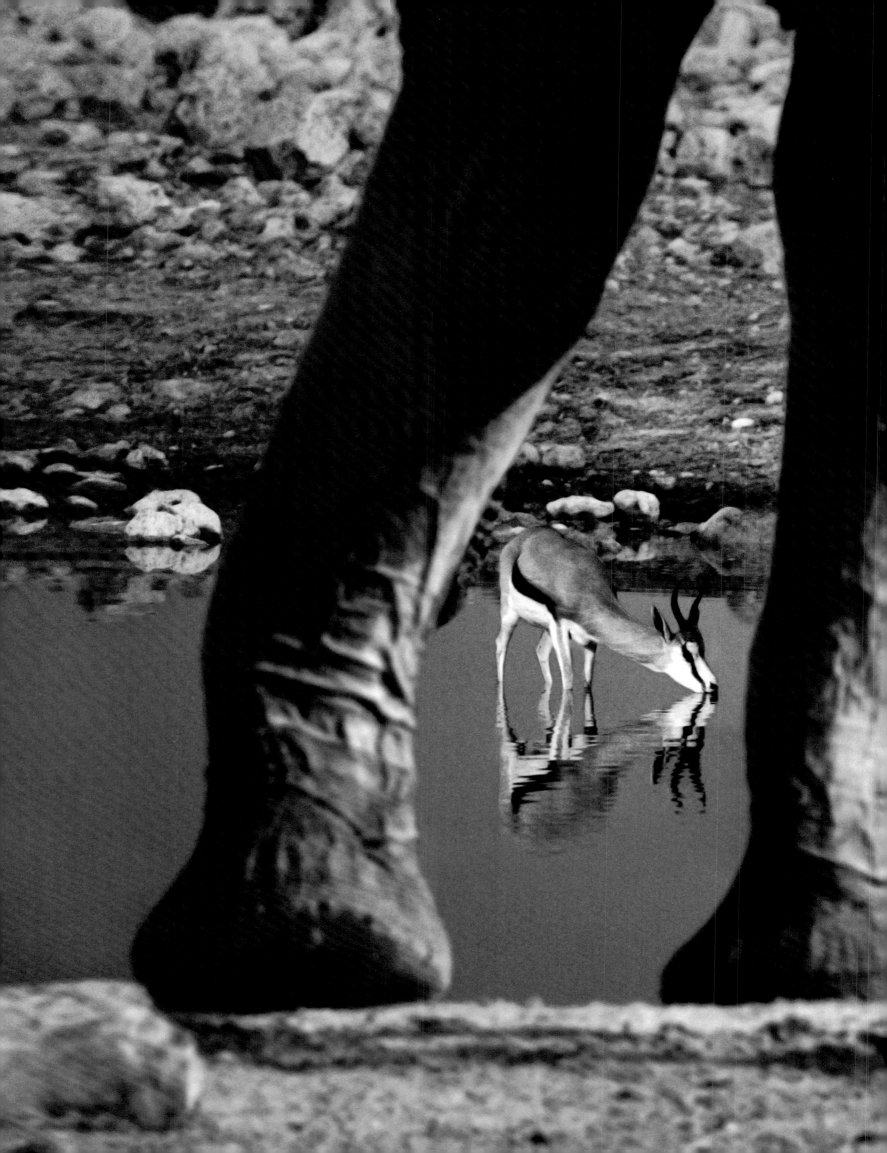

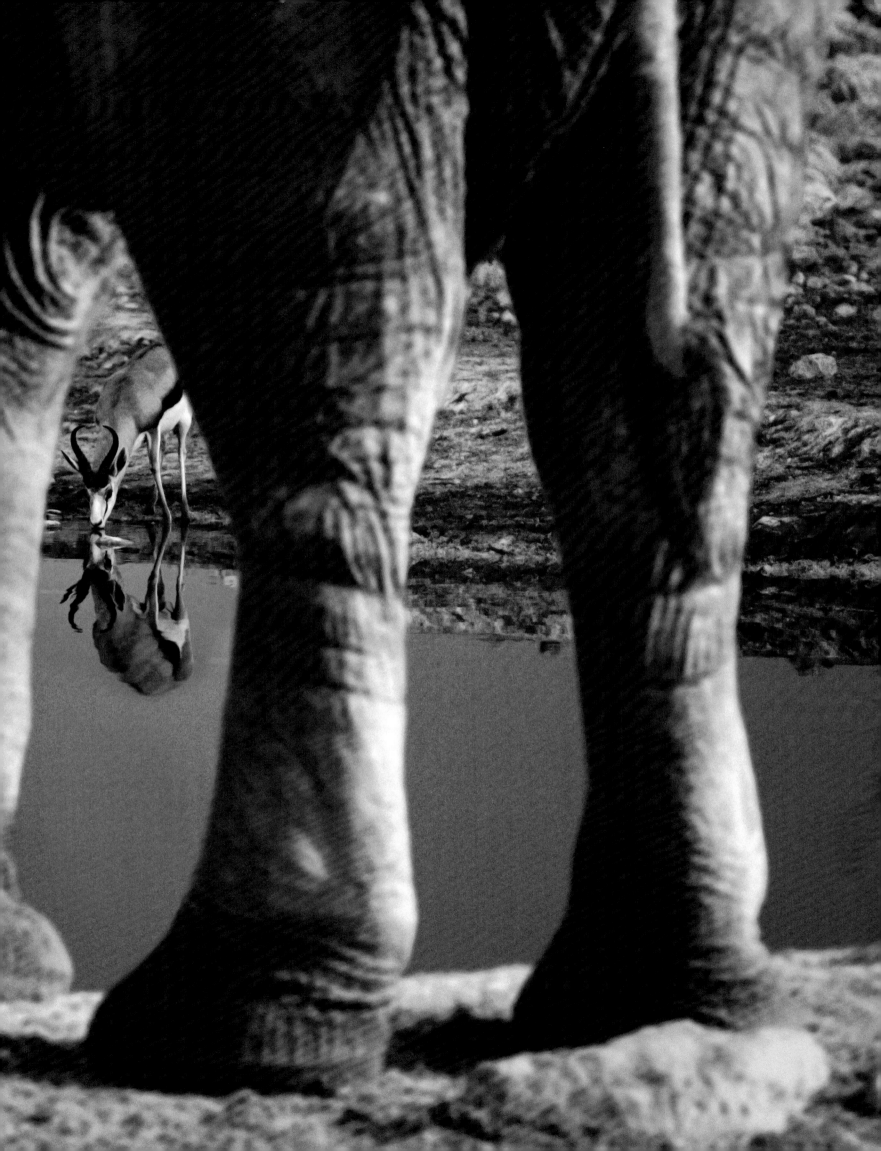

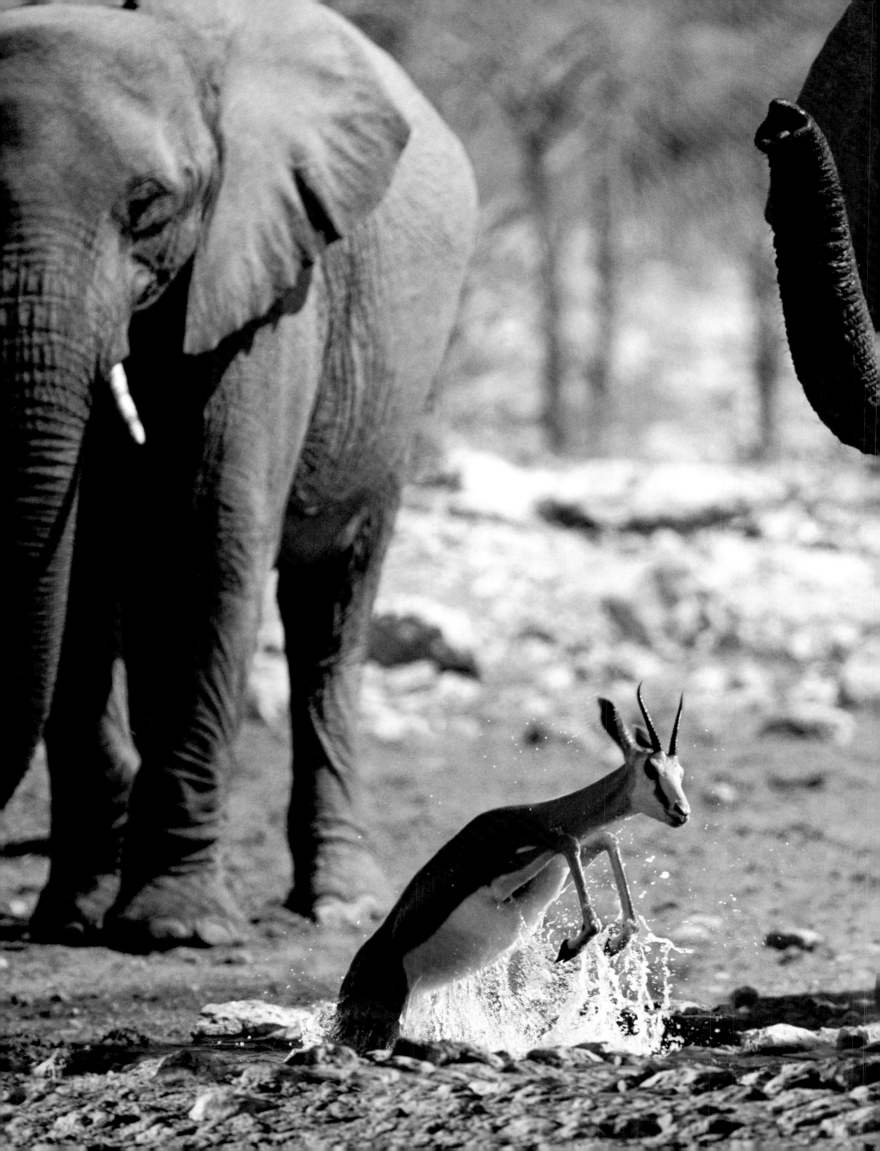

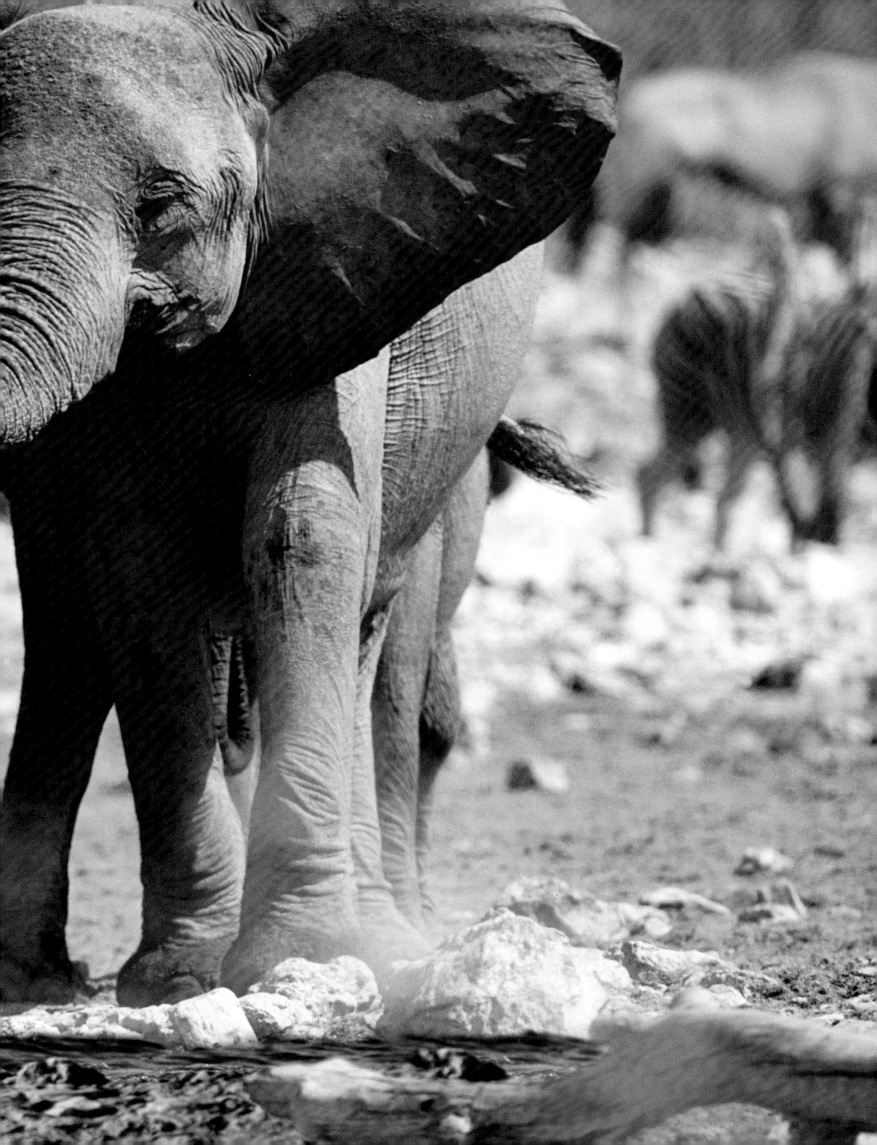

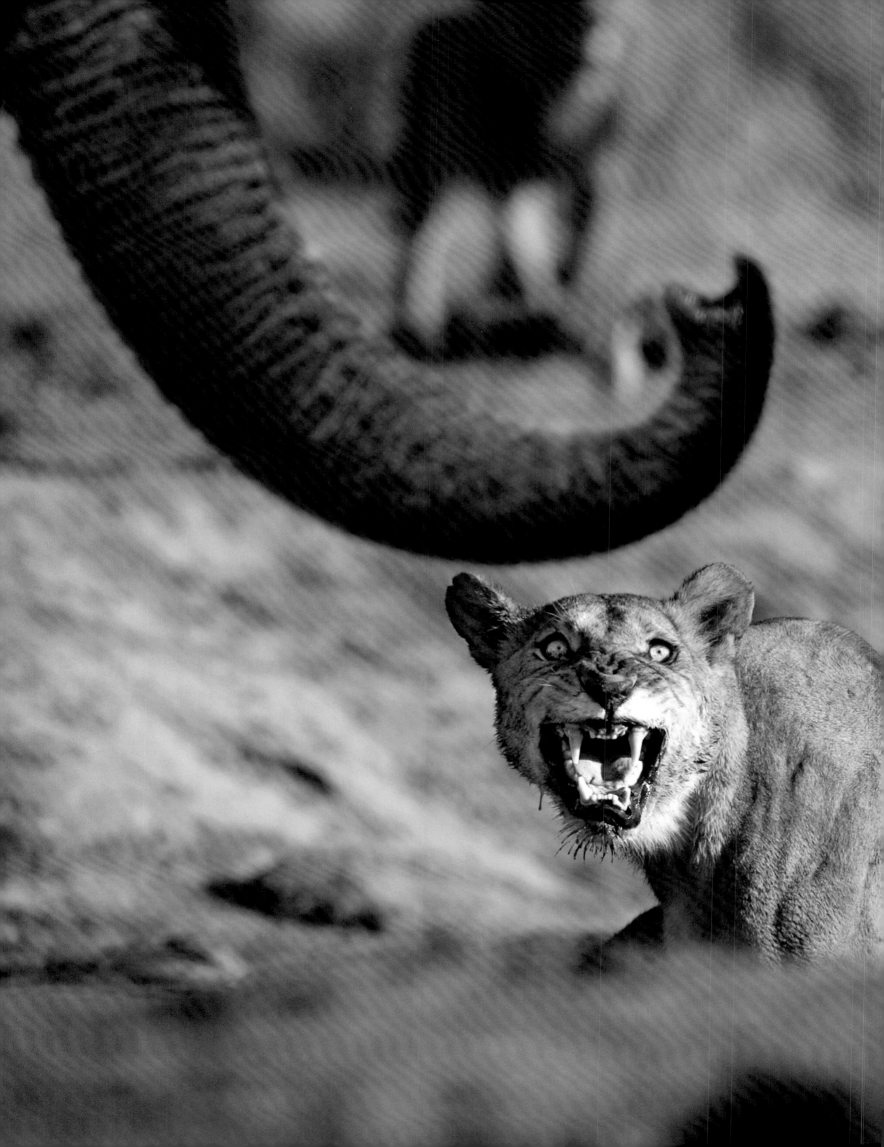

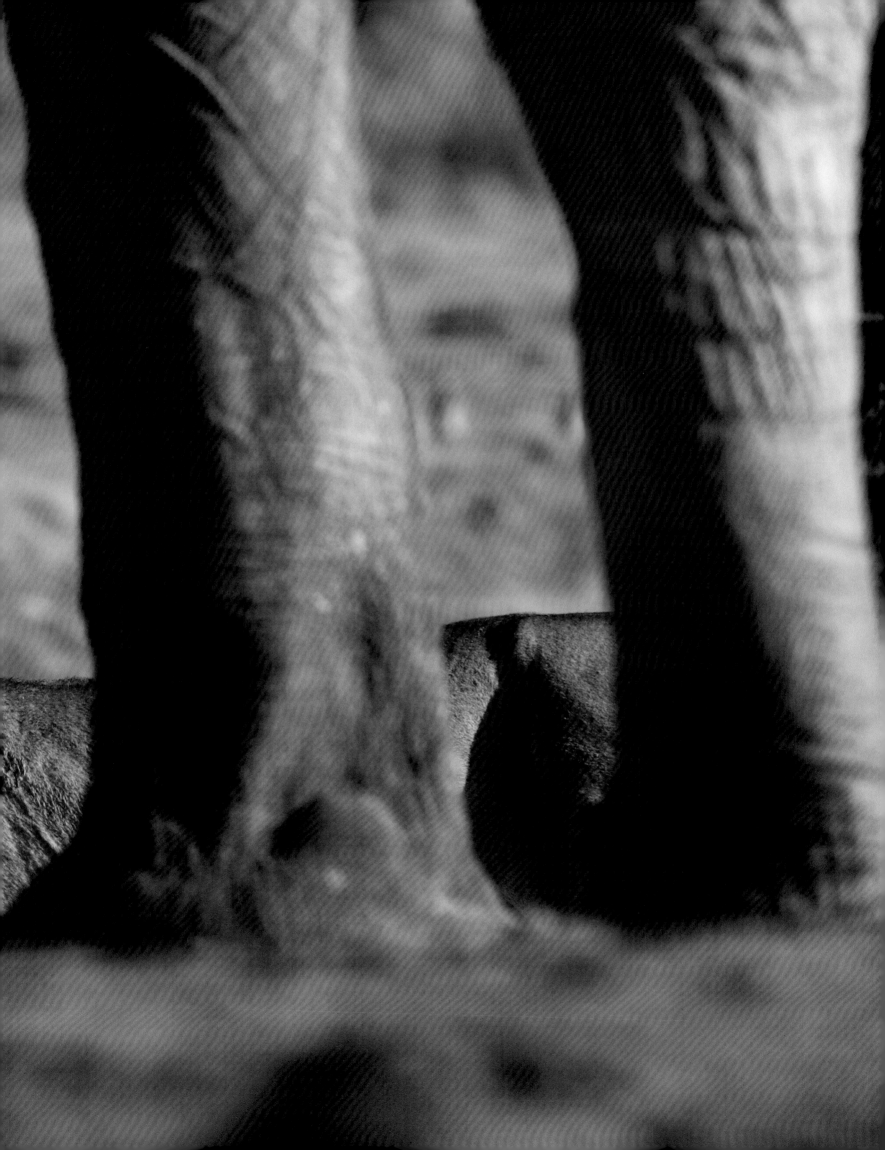

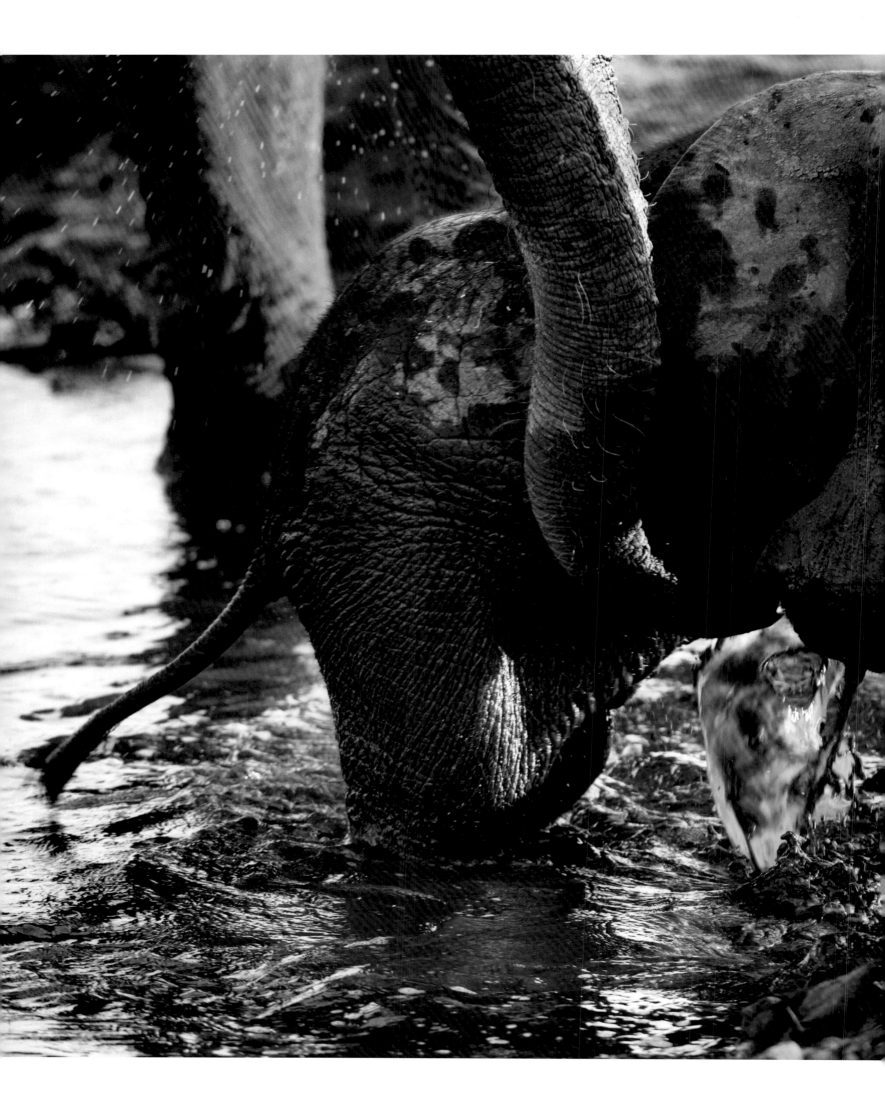

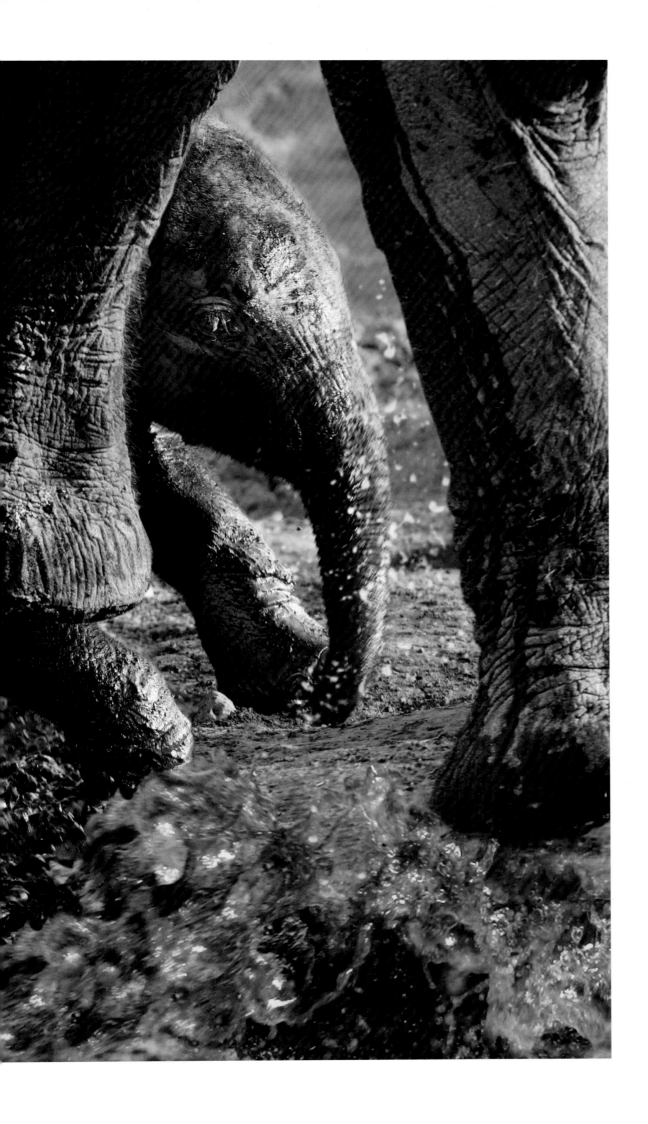

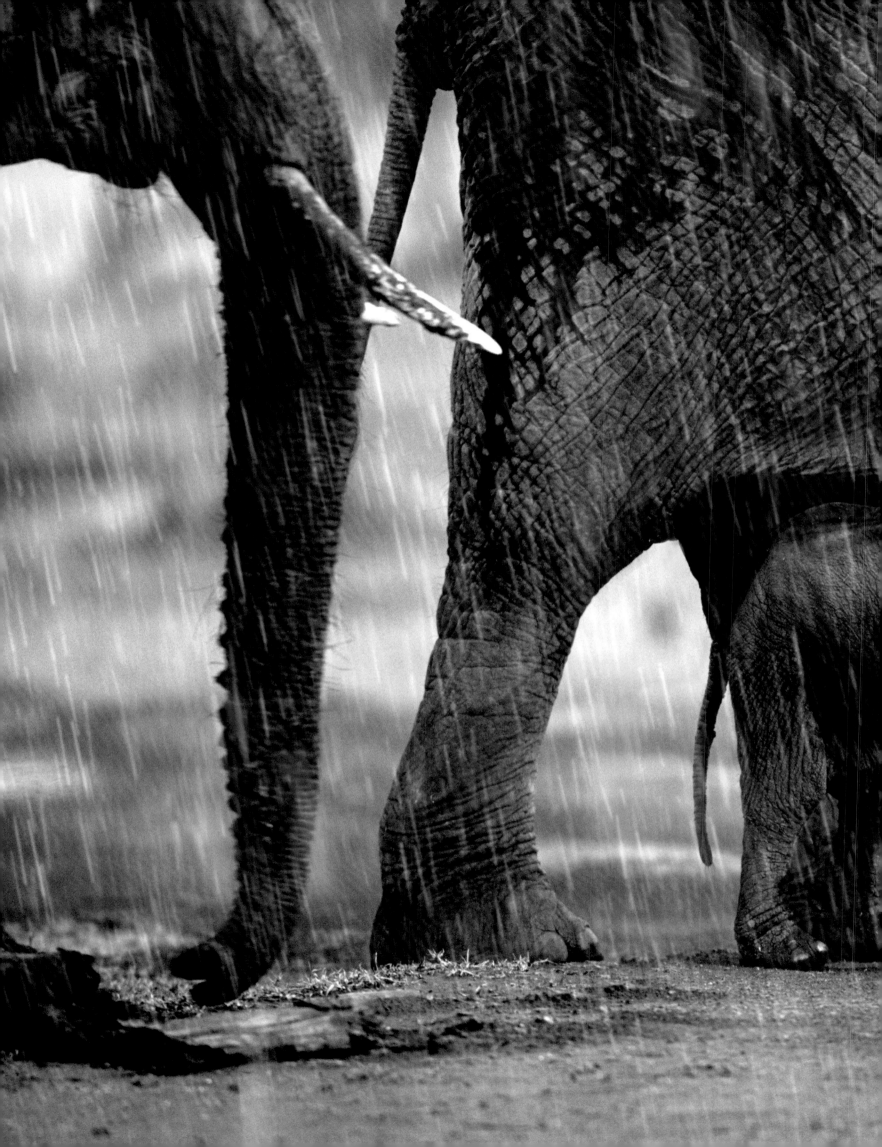

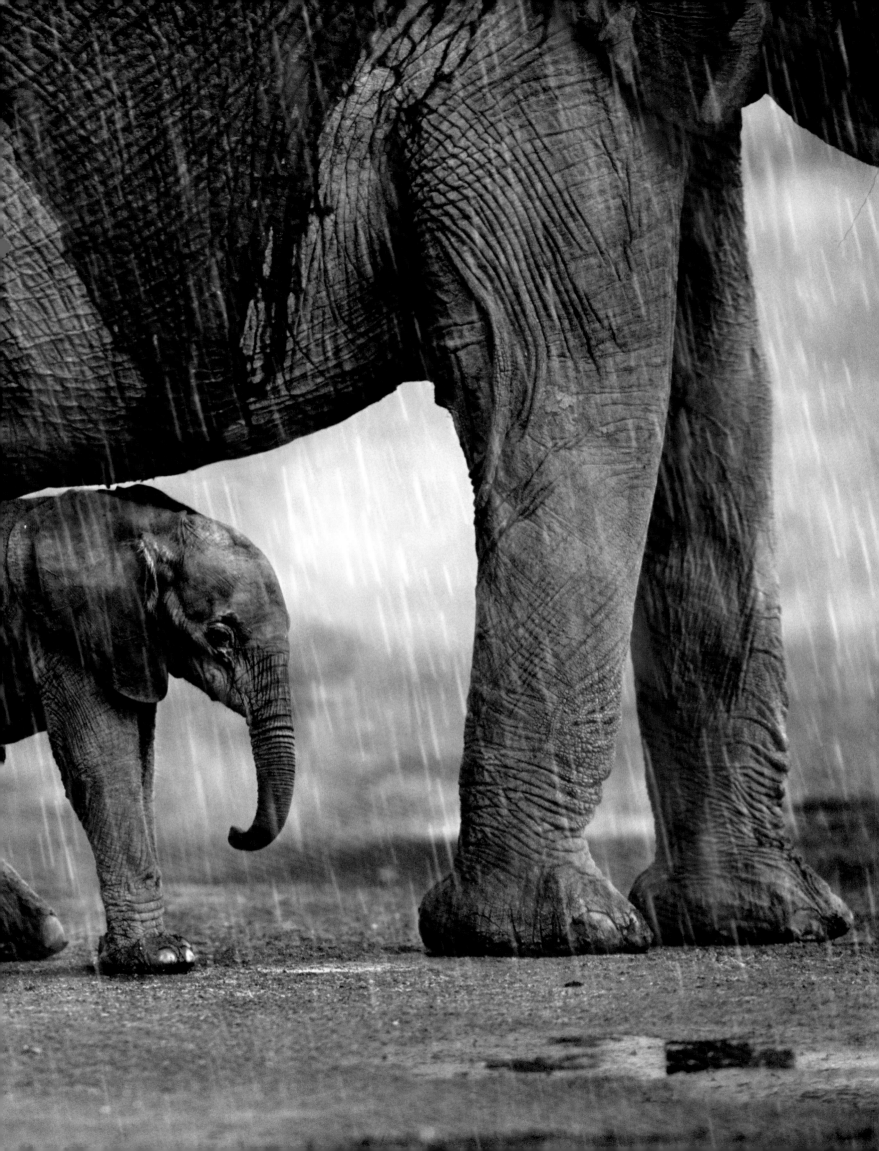

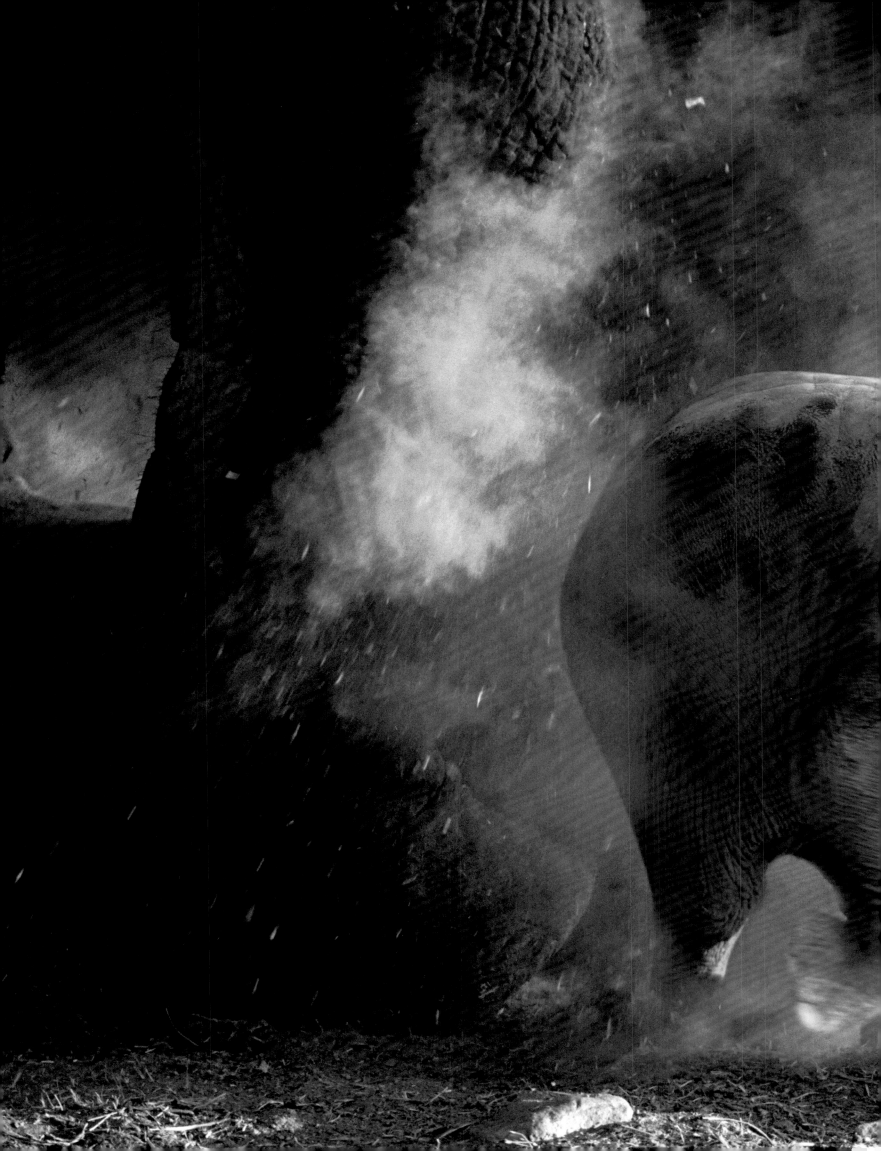

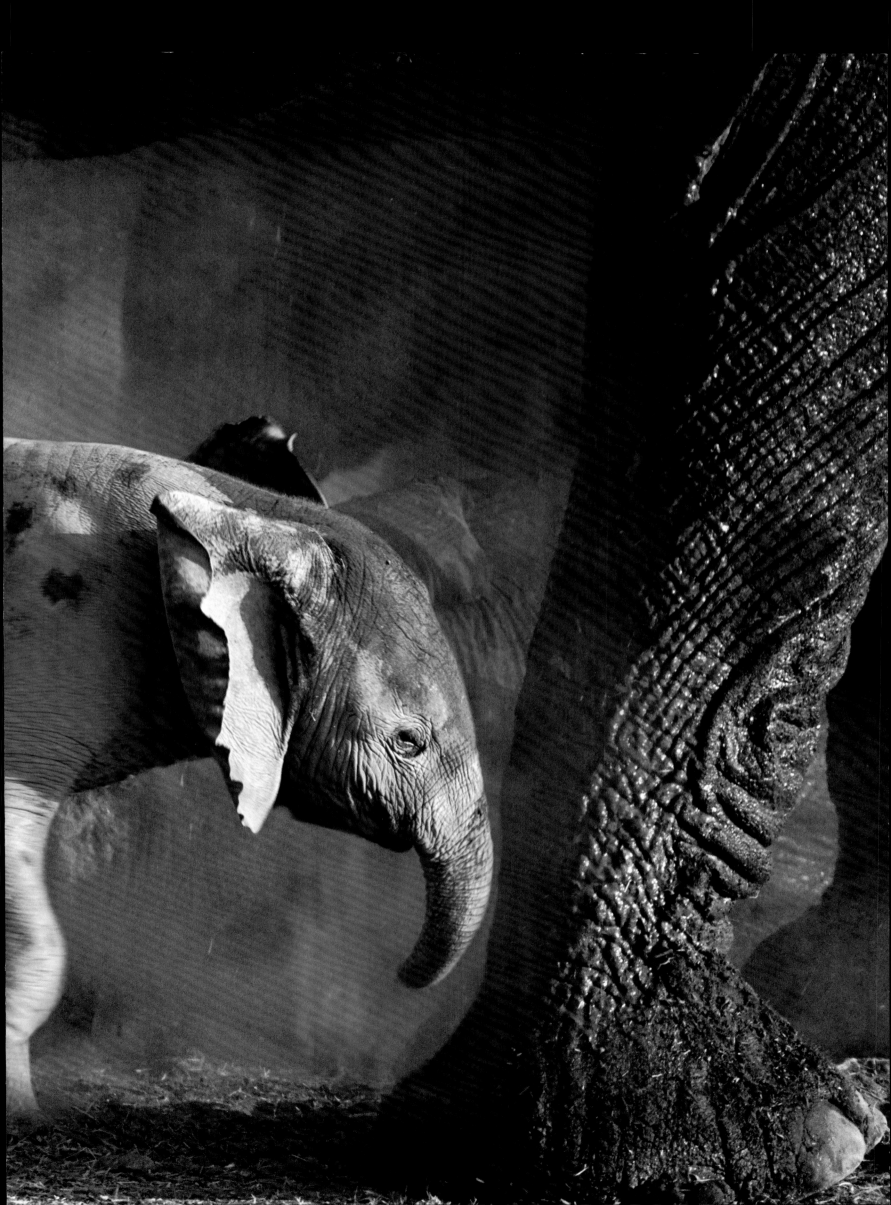

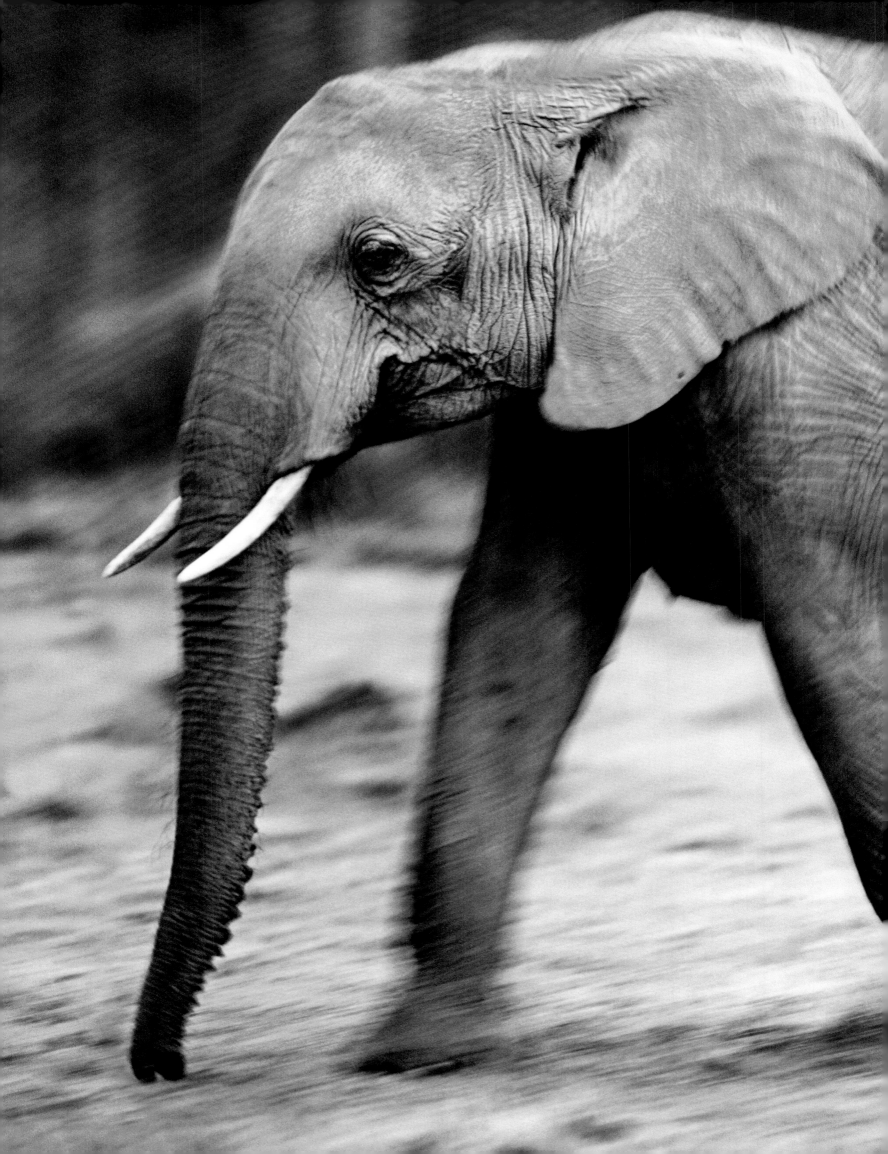

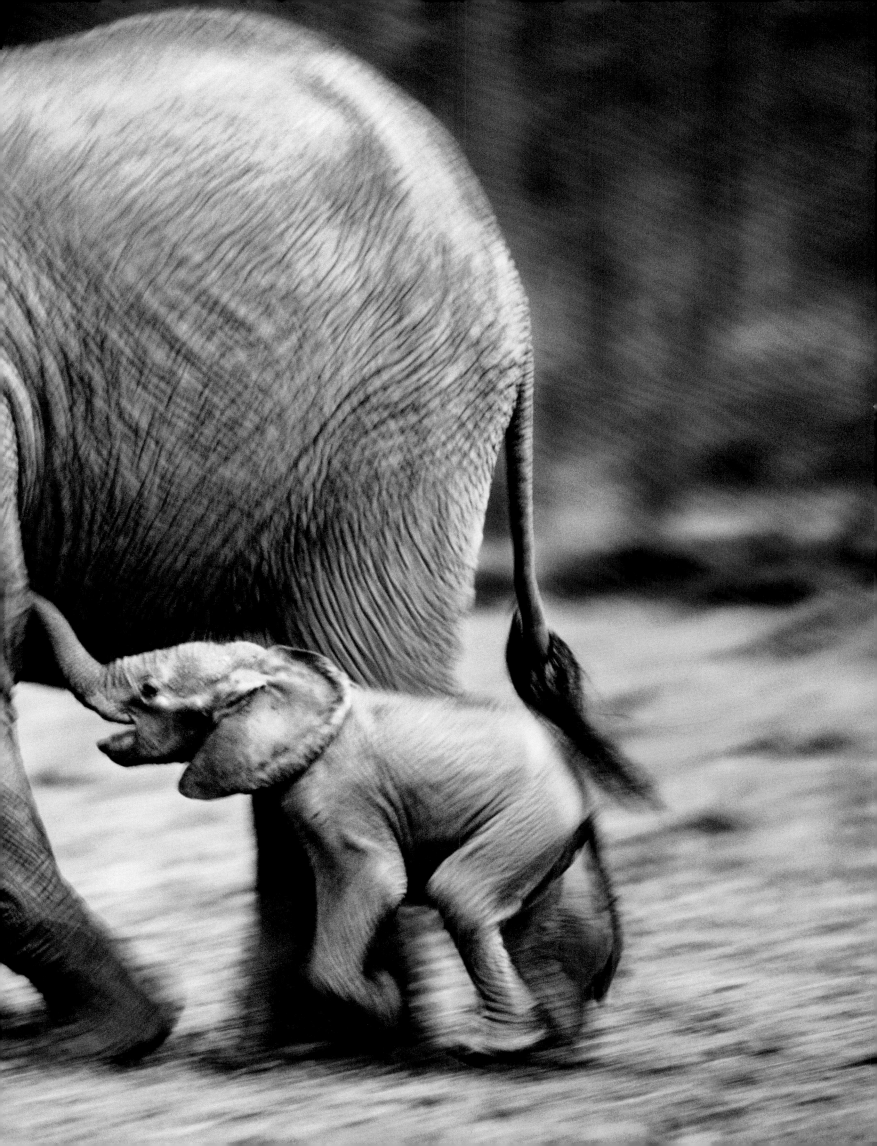

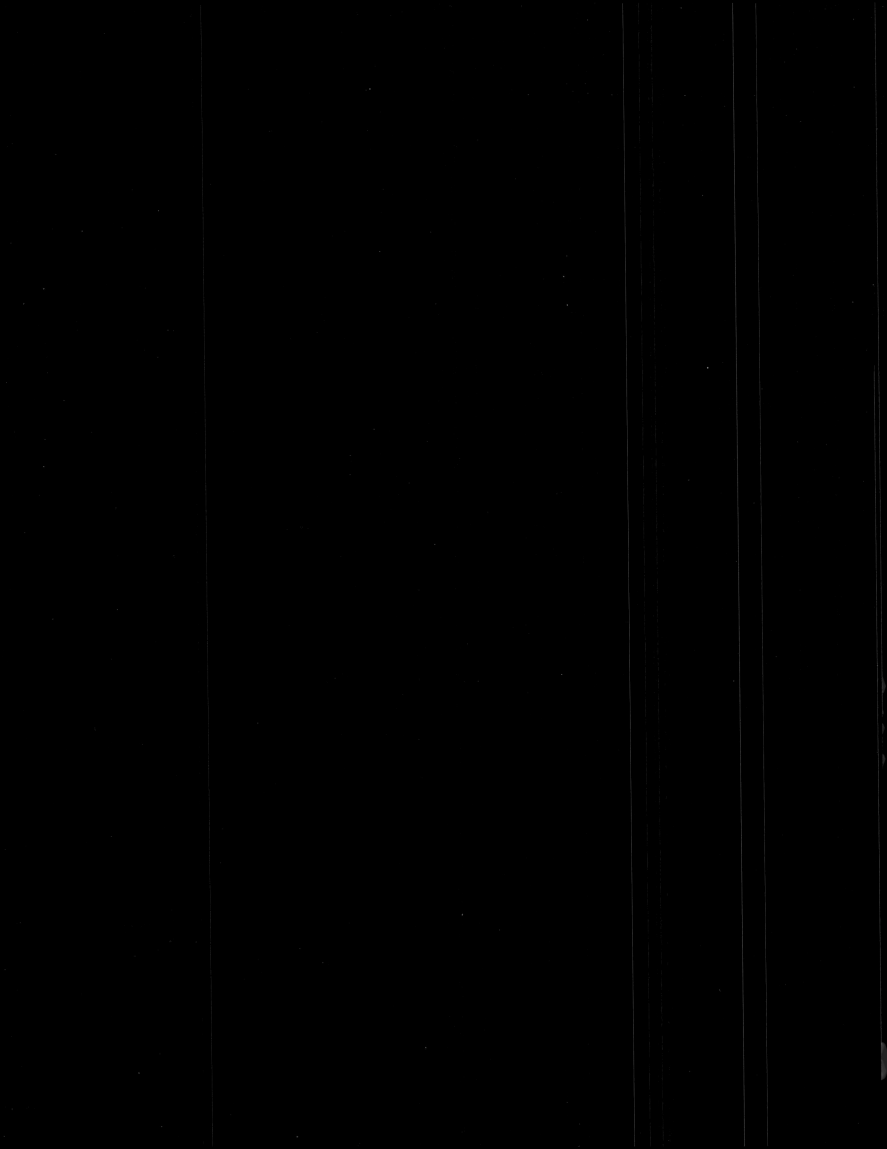

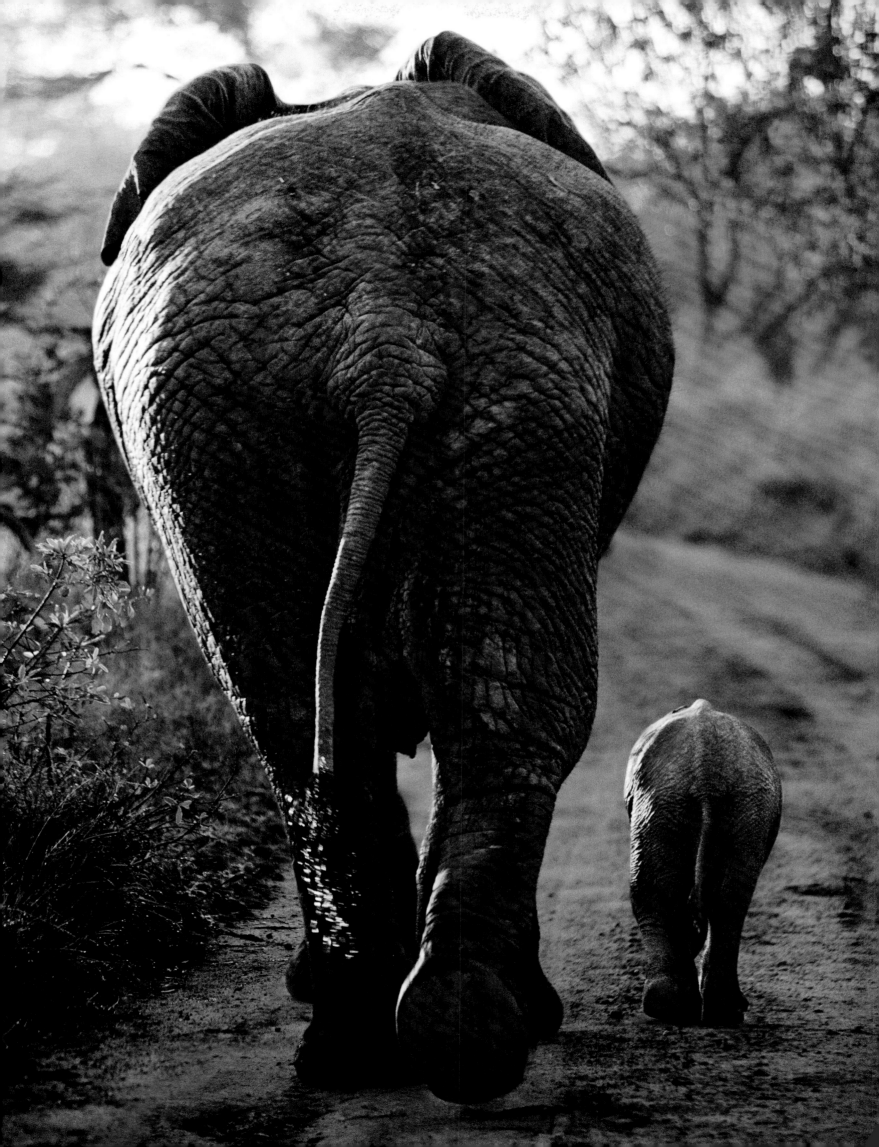

ASIAN ELEPHANT

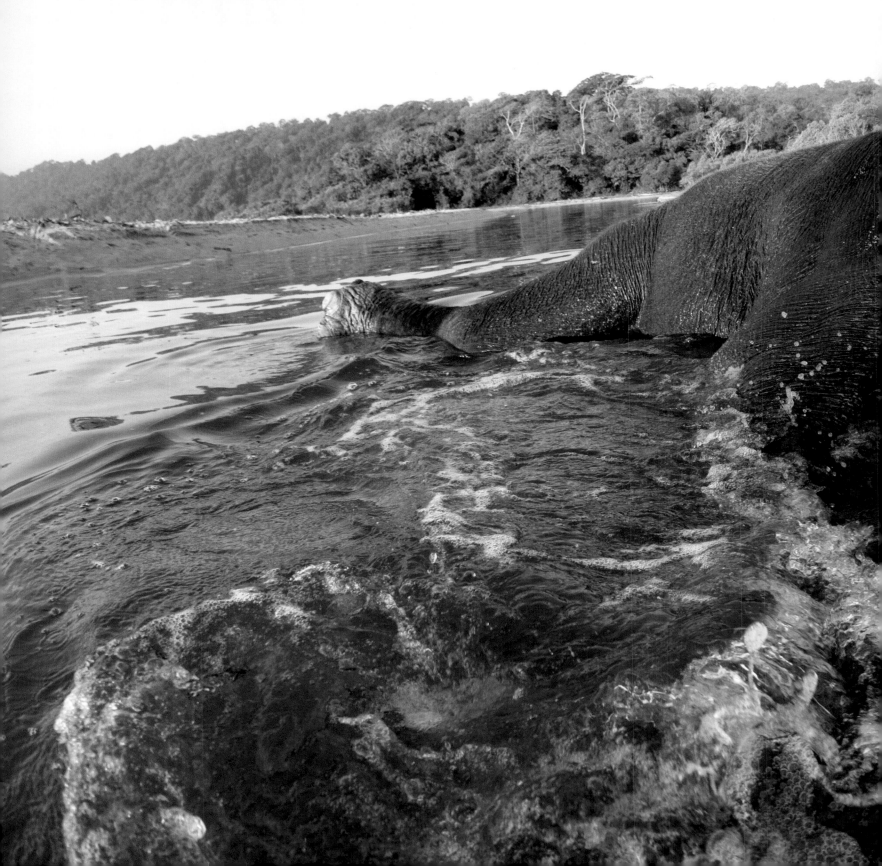

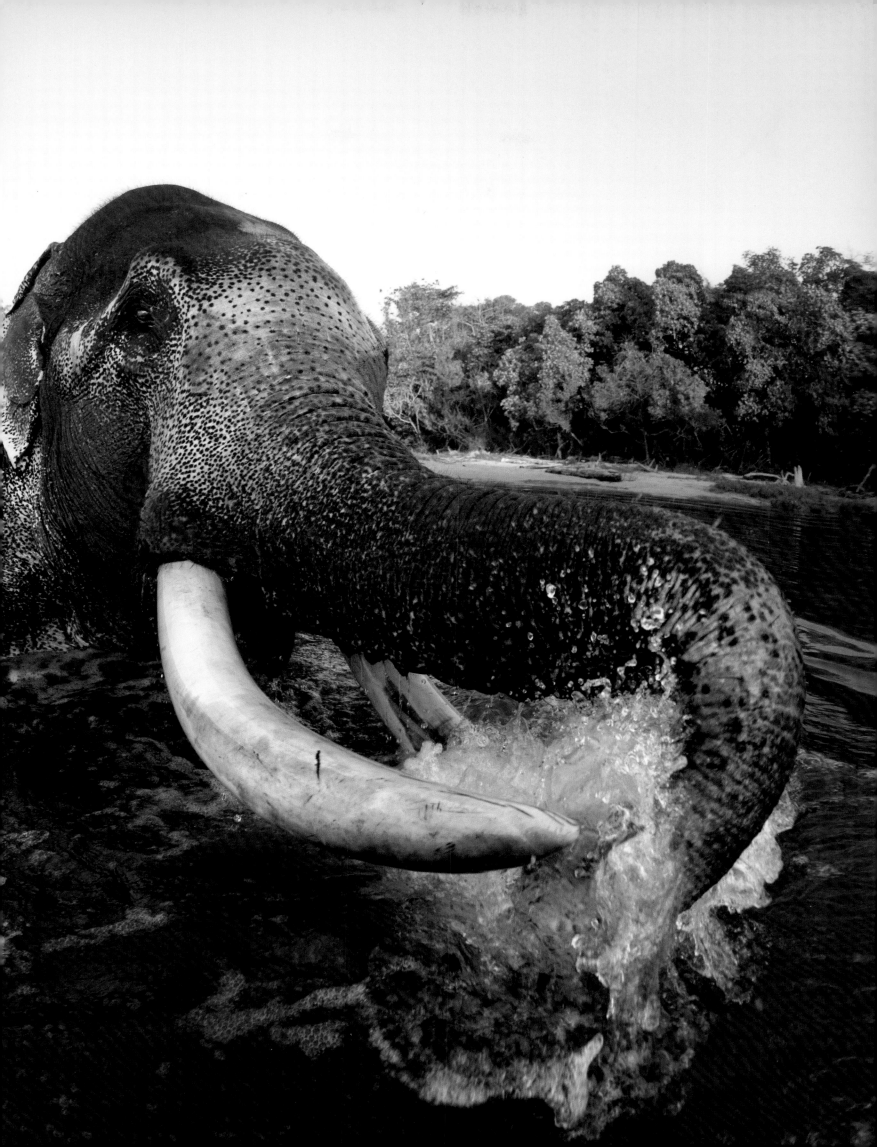

'You're going to do what?' my friends exclaimed, on hearing of my intention to swim underwater with an elephant. My wife, more accustomed to such folly, rolled her eyes in resignation as we began to investigate the possibility of turning my dream into a reality. I had swum with dolphins, heard the haunting song of humpback whales, and seen great white sharks leap from the ocean waves. The prospect of swimming with an elephant in the sea would surely rank alongside such incomparable experiences, and seemed a fitting way to complete the photographic work for this book. I had previously seen some archive pictures and snatches of a documentary film which showed swimming elephants, and these helped to plant a seed. Over time, I became more determined than ever to achieve my goal. We heard that elephants were known to swim occasionally in the sea off Thailand and the Andaman Islands, and we began to search for a suitable location. While formulating our plans, the catastrophic tsunami of 2004 struck the region, putting the project on hold. It was some time before we could resume our research, and it was another full year before I could put my scheme into action. This came about after hearing of a retired logging elephant who spent his days on the beaches of a remote island, and loved swimming in the ocean.

The photo shoot was fraught with potential problems. Water is dense, so visibility is limited. In order to reveal the clarity of something as large as an elephant, I would have to get very close, with extreme wide-angle lenses. Underwater photography is difficult at the best of times, and I was a novice in this field. When I discovered that the elephant swam at considerable speed, like an over-exuberant dog releasing all its pent-up energy in the waves, I realized that just keeping up with him would require considerable skill and dexterity. The challenge was becoming ever more daunting.

I arrived on the island with little diving experience, and immediately undertook a brief course in scuba diving. For safety reasons I decided to have two skilled divers accompany me at all times. One was essentially my engine, and would steer me where I wanted to go, directing me from behind, so freeing me to concentrate on the photography. Most of the time I would be composing in the viewfinder, with little peripheral vision to warn me of impending danger. The second diver would provide backup, and shoot some video. We developed an intricate system of hand signals, and had lengthy briefings over sweet Indian tea, discussing light and physical positioning in relation to the elephant.

On arrival I was introduced to the mahout, Nasru, who took me to meet the elephant, Rajan. They had been together for thirty years, and both lived a quiet life of retirement on the island. Rajan was a large bull, with magnificent tusks, and he towered high above my head. Having previously worked in the logging industry, he had lived on the island for two years. He seemed content, surrounded by an abundance of trees and an unlimited supply of bananas, a favourite treat, which he would swallow in bunches of twenty at a time. Slightly older than me, it went through my mind that we had lived parallel lives through the same passage of time. No doubt he, too, had his own separate memories; however, for a brief period we would swim together in the ocean.

As we came to know each other, I was offered an opportunity to ride on Rajan's bare back. From this vantage point high on top of a mature bull elephant, vertigo gives a true perspective of the enormity of the earth's largest land mammal. The prospect of swimming anywhere near Rajan's feet filled me with unease, and I needed positive focusing to come to terms with what I was about to do. Little by little, the allure of swimming with an elephant began to over-ride my fears, and adrenalin then took over.

On the first morning of the photo shoot, we took our equipment to the edge of the beach and prepared for the job in hand. As the air tank, lead weights, regulator and other paraphernalia associated with diving were attached to me, I became more convinced than ever that my rightful place on Earth is firmly on dry ground. I had left the sea millions of years ago, and, with good reason, did not feel quite ready to return.

I entered the water slowly, and as I submerged, holding my large domed underwater camera and its shiny fisheye port, I must have looked like an astronaut. We lay low, under the water, some distance from the beach, and waited. After a while, in the murky green–grey sea, I saw an indistinct shape

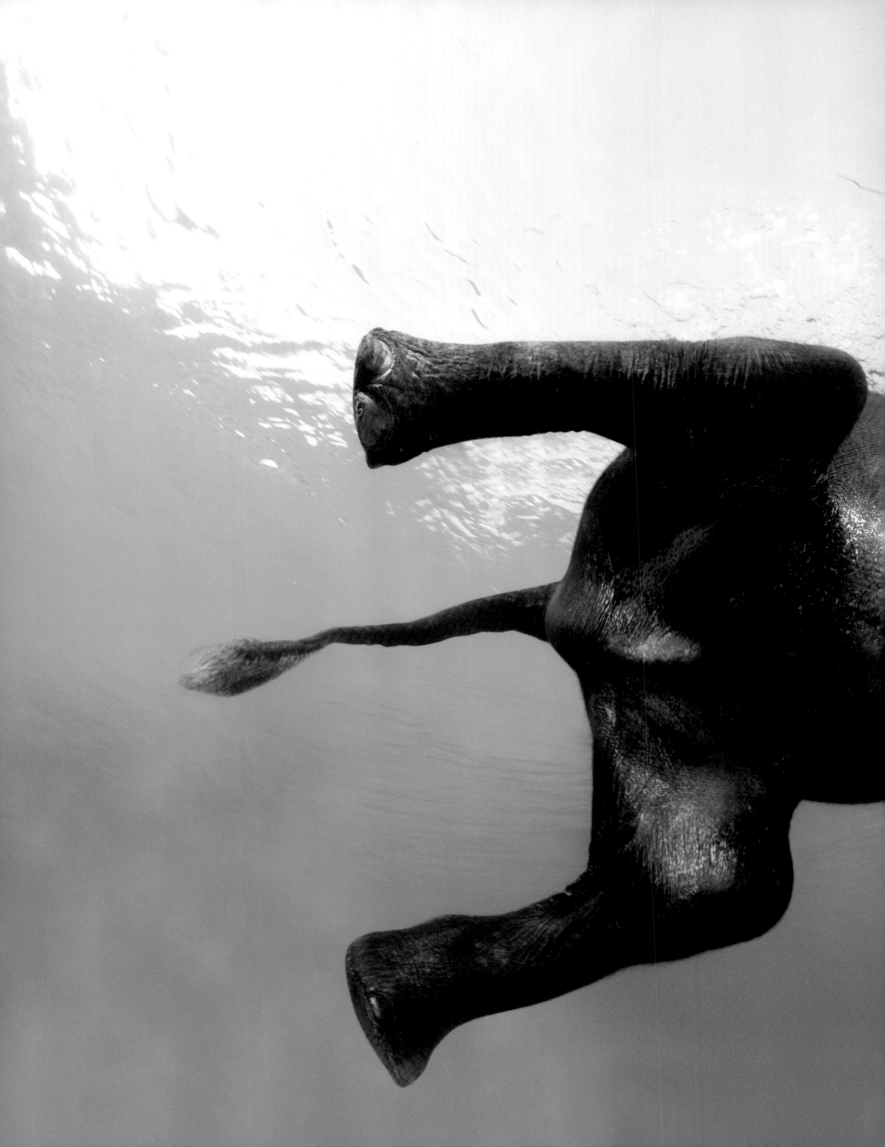

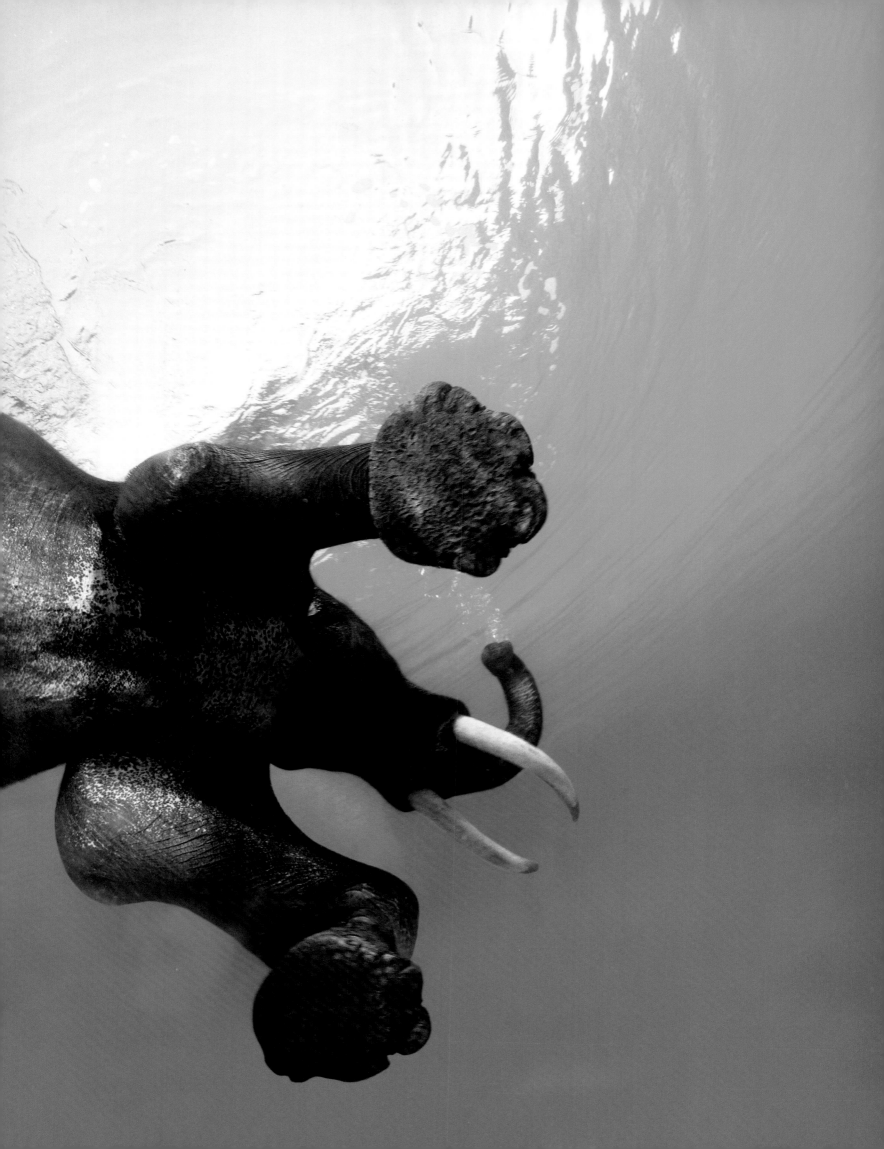

approaching from the distance, and as it grew larger, I was finally able to make out the pale highlight of a tusk. Suddenly, as if he had burst through a translucent shield, Rajan appeared in vivid detail, legs kicking wildly, trunk waving madly, all in a swirl of giant bubbles. Yes, elephants do fly, and Rajan was coming straight for me! He seemed to erupt with joy as he bounded up from the ocean bed, which dropped away from his feet amid exploding clouds of fine sand. For a while I was transported into an exquisite, dreamlike world, where elephants are weightless and dance a kind of surreal ballet. Rajan, liberated from his enormous bulk, explored his own free spirit.

I cannot imagine what he must have thought of our scuba team; bizarre creatures of the deep with strange feet, wetsuits and goggles, blowing frequent bursts of bubbles. At times I swam extremely close to him and could see the warm glint in his eye. With one swift turn of his head, he could have struck me with his giant tusk and killed me. For most of the time my eye was firmly focused on the viewfinder which reduces the image, giving the illusion that the elephant is much further away than he really is. When I momentarily moved my eye from the viewfinder, I was immediately struck by a sense of shock and amazement. How magnificent he was, and how uncomfortably close!

I am, however, convinced that he recognized me, and took great care to ensure I was not harmed, often turning away to avoid a collision. During the many sessions we spent together, we learned to swim in tandem, performing the dance of the diving elephant and the encumbered photographer. The pictures were borne out of our mutual harmony; the meeting of two species in an alien world.

Later, while cleaning the equipment, my thoughts drifted far away to my first experience of meeting mountain gorillas in the wild. A few years previously, I had travelled to central Africa, and struggled with great difficulty through thick jungle in search of gorillas. After a long trek, the forest gave way to a clearing and suddenly I found myself surrounded by a large family of gorillas peacefully relaxing in the undergrowth. Such rare experiences sometimes have the effect of briefly shifting the traveller onto another level of experience, so giving a deep sense of being at one with the world and all its inhabitants.

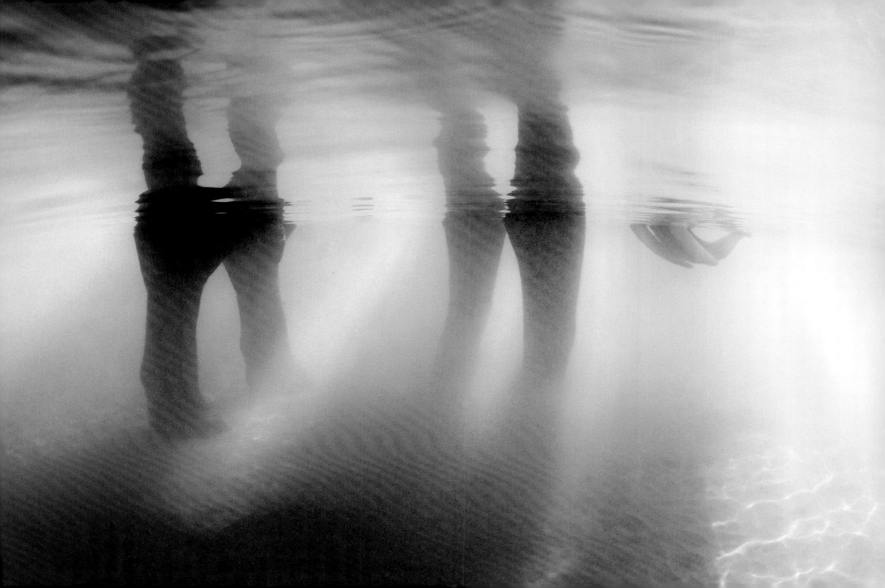

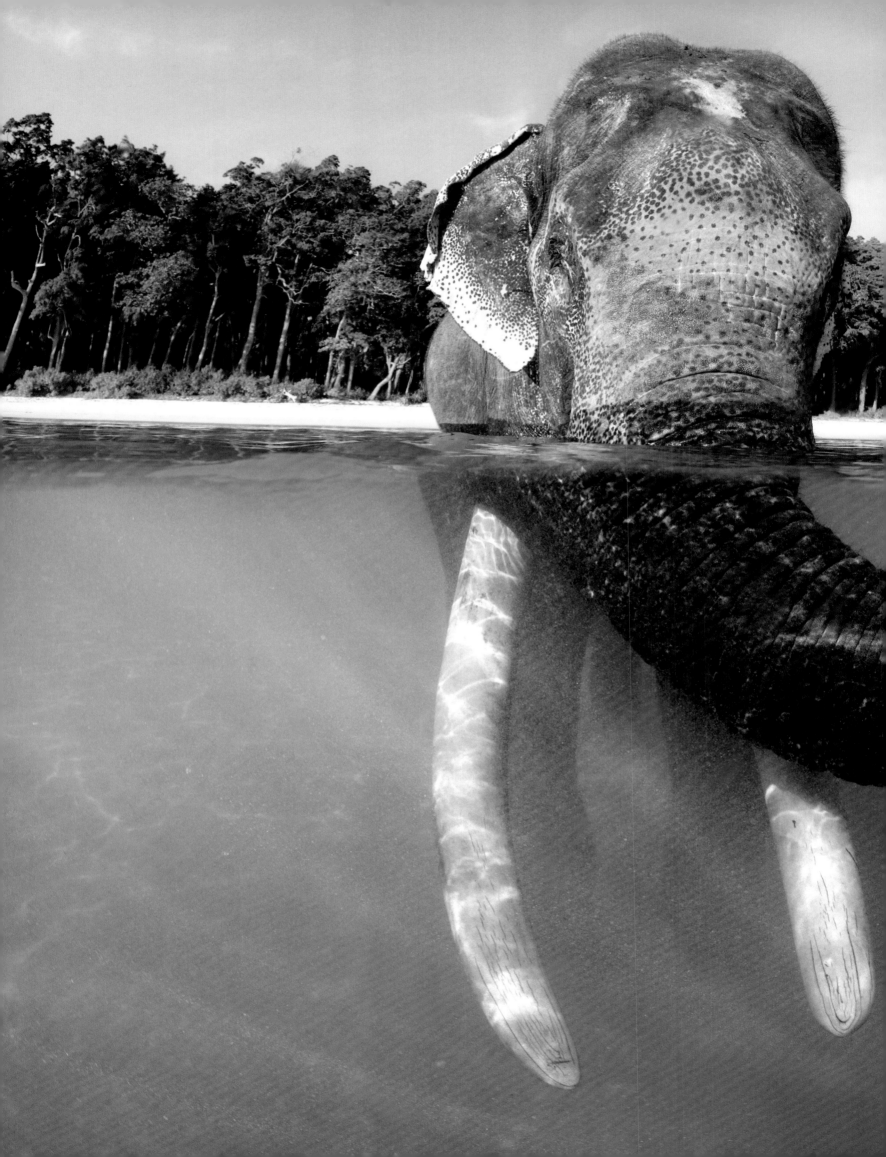

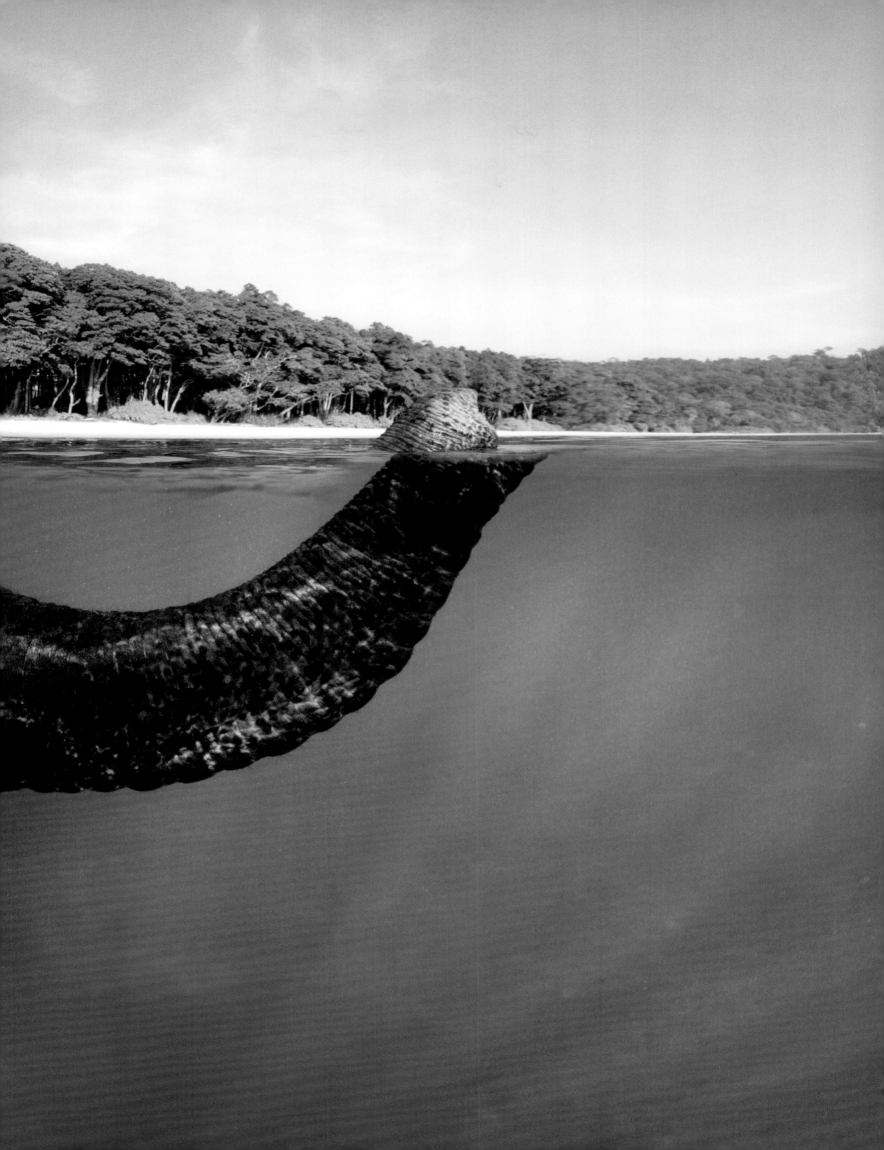

Seeing Rajan swim under water had a similar profound effect on my diving partners, who were deeply moved by the experience. I am a persistent photographer, and will often drive myself to exhaustion over long periods in pursuit of aesthetic harmony. Sometimes dogged perseverance pays off, proving that time spent pursuing an image is seldom wasted.

On my final day on the island, I took a walk along the deserted beach in the warm light of the late afternoon. I was pleased with the pictures, and contented in my solitude. A thick forested cliff rose high above the long white beach, and as I walked, listening to the waves, I noticed a small shape in the far distance, silhouetted against the intense green of the forest. It was some time before I could clearly make out the distinctive form of an elephant and a man moving towards me. When we finally met, we stopped for a short time and I said my goodbyes to Rajan and Nasru. Rajan blew gently over me, rocked his head, snorted and then ambled off in the opposite direction. I walked on alone, and took great pleasure in making giant strides, firmly planting my feet in the large round footprints in the sand.

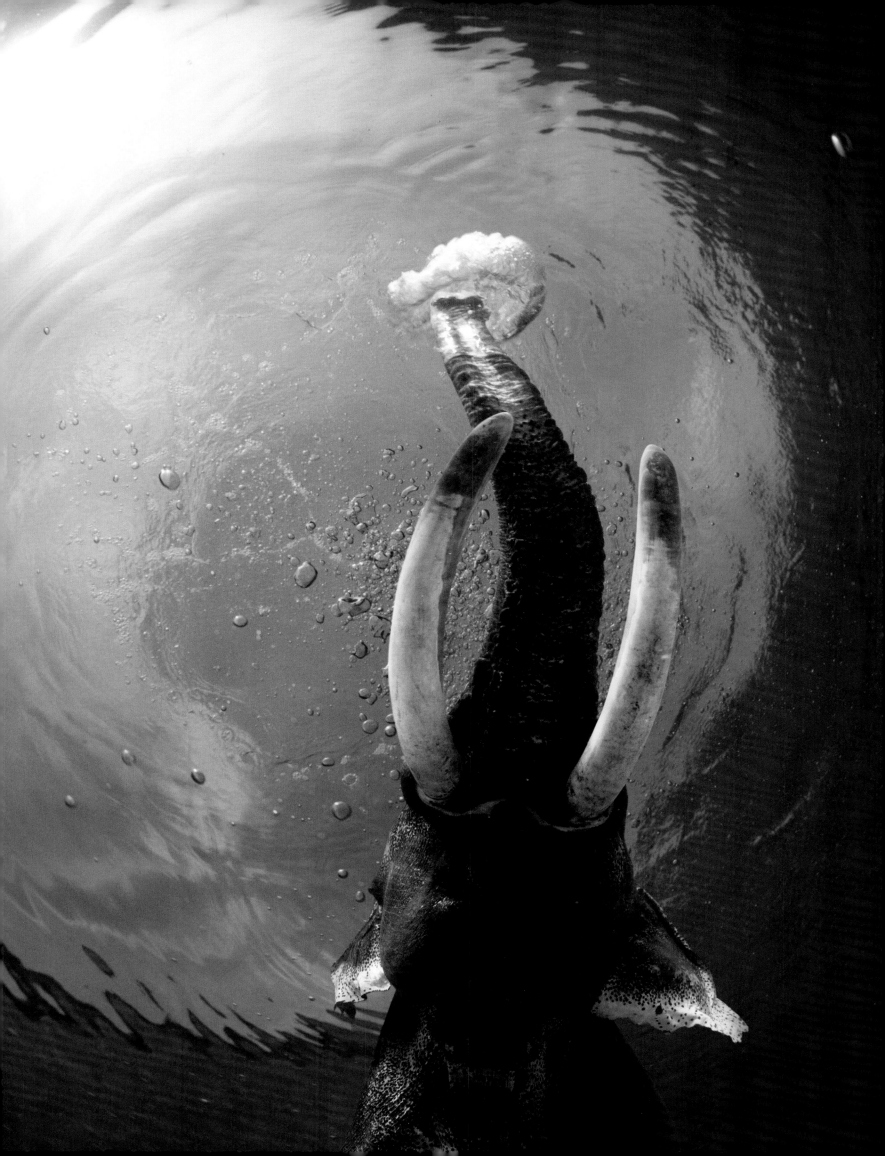

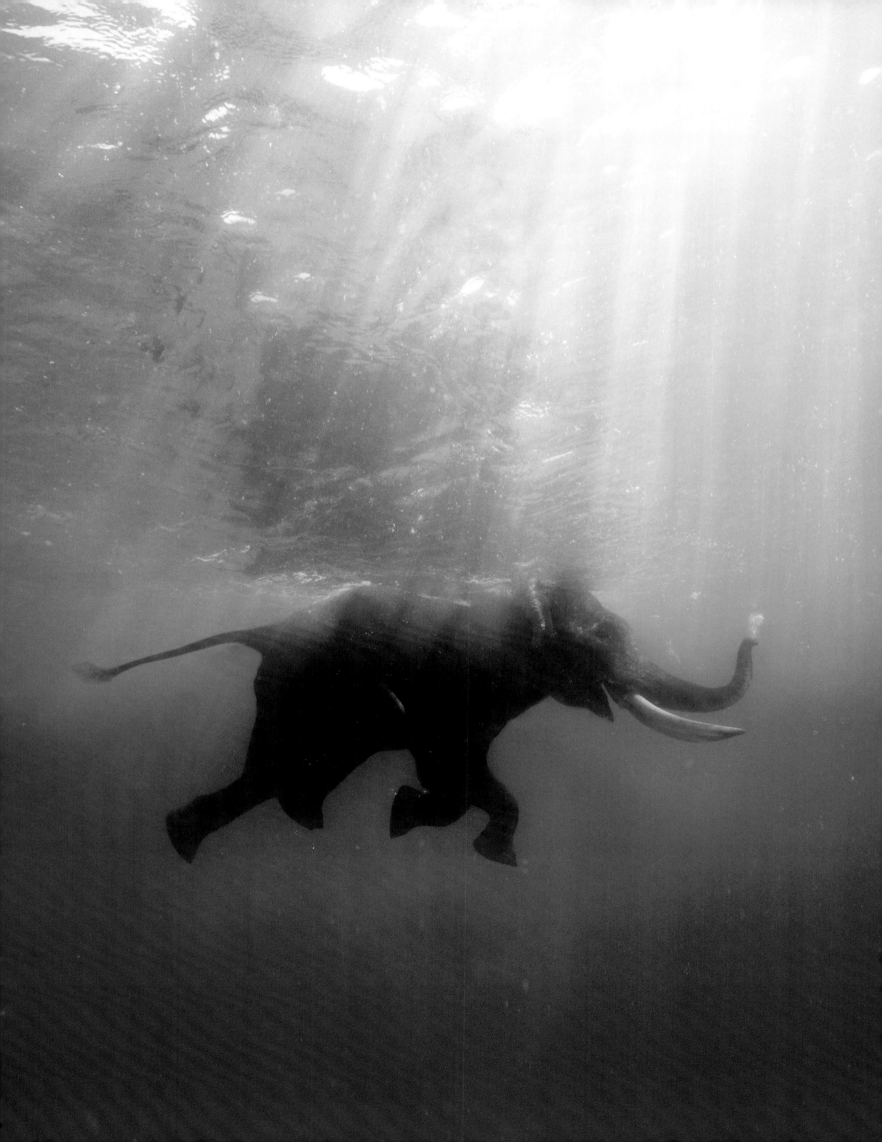

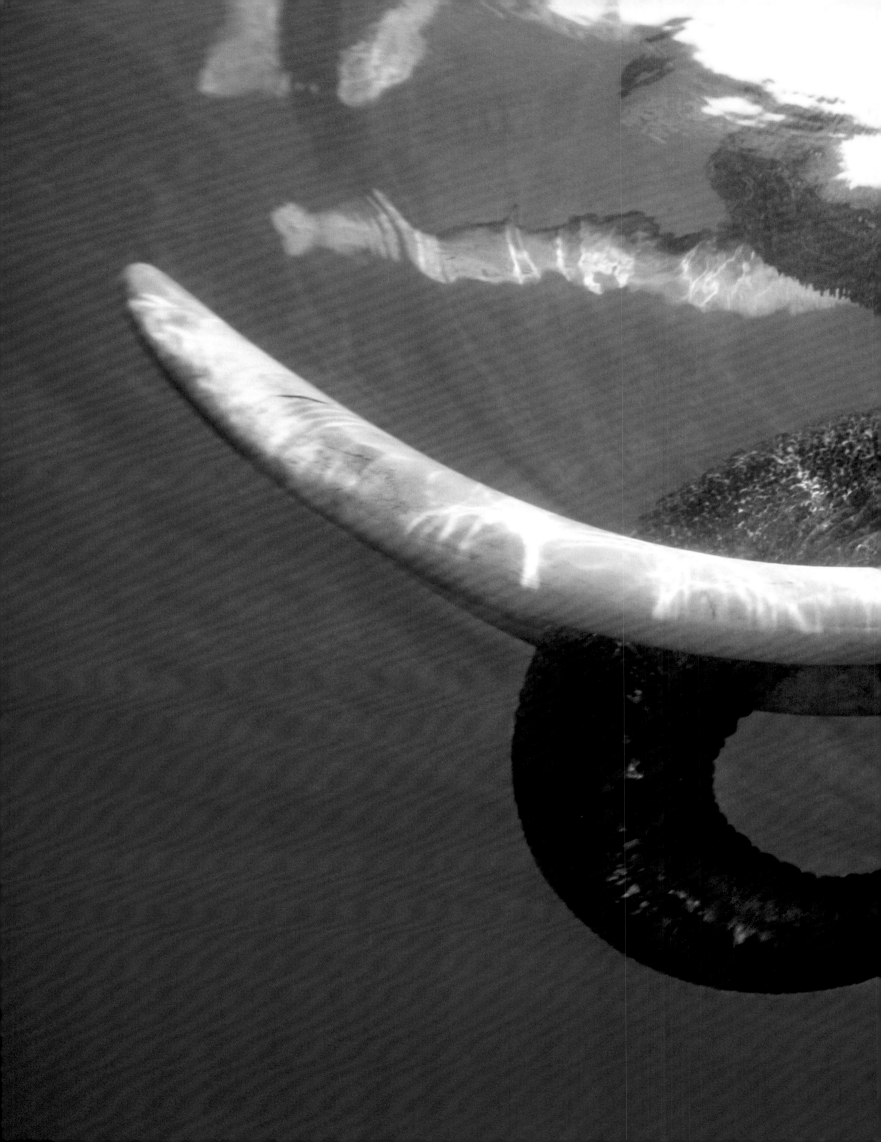

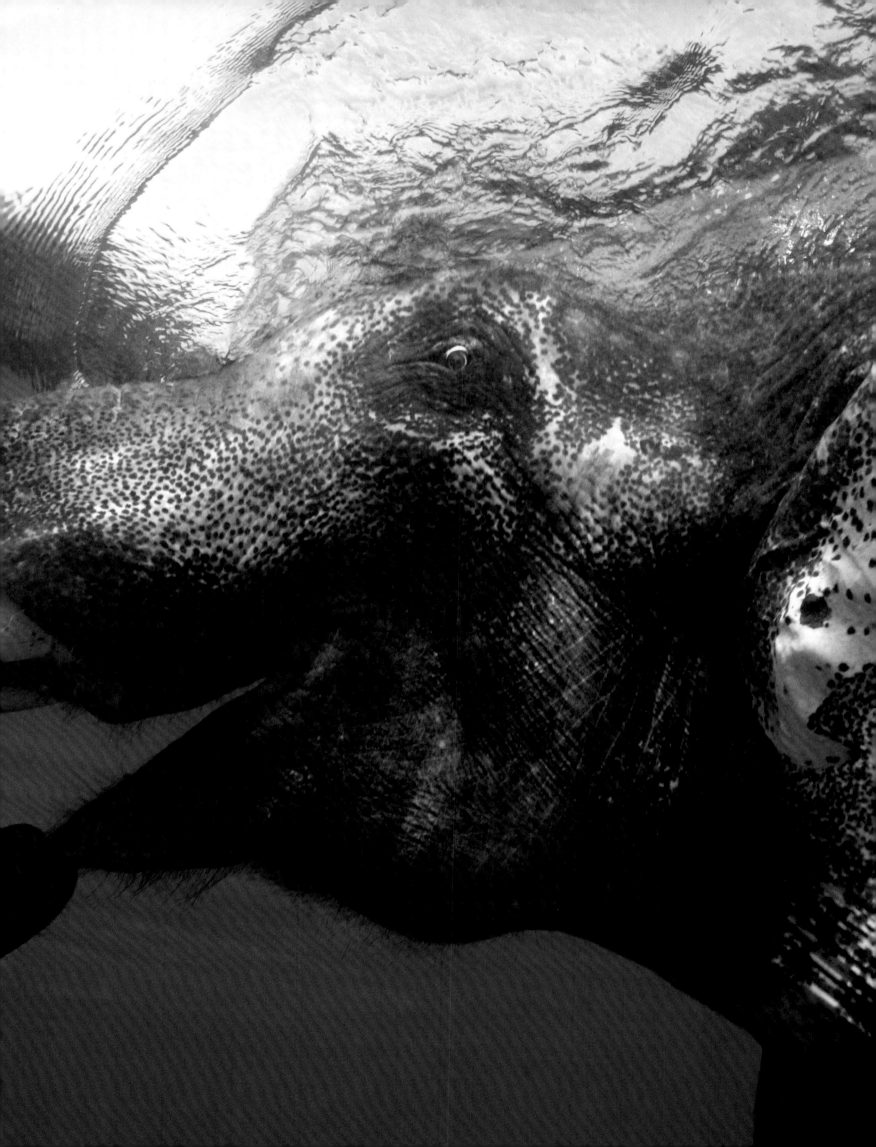

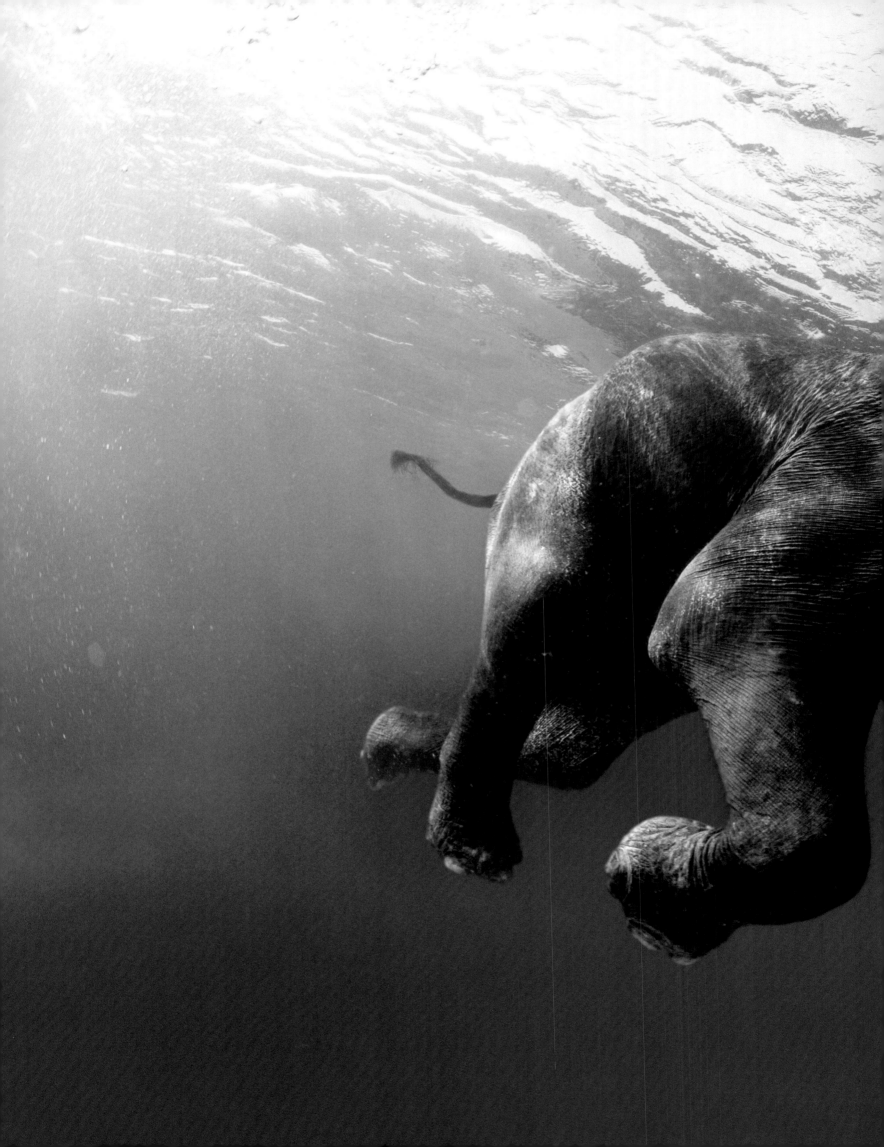

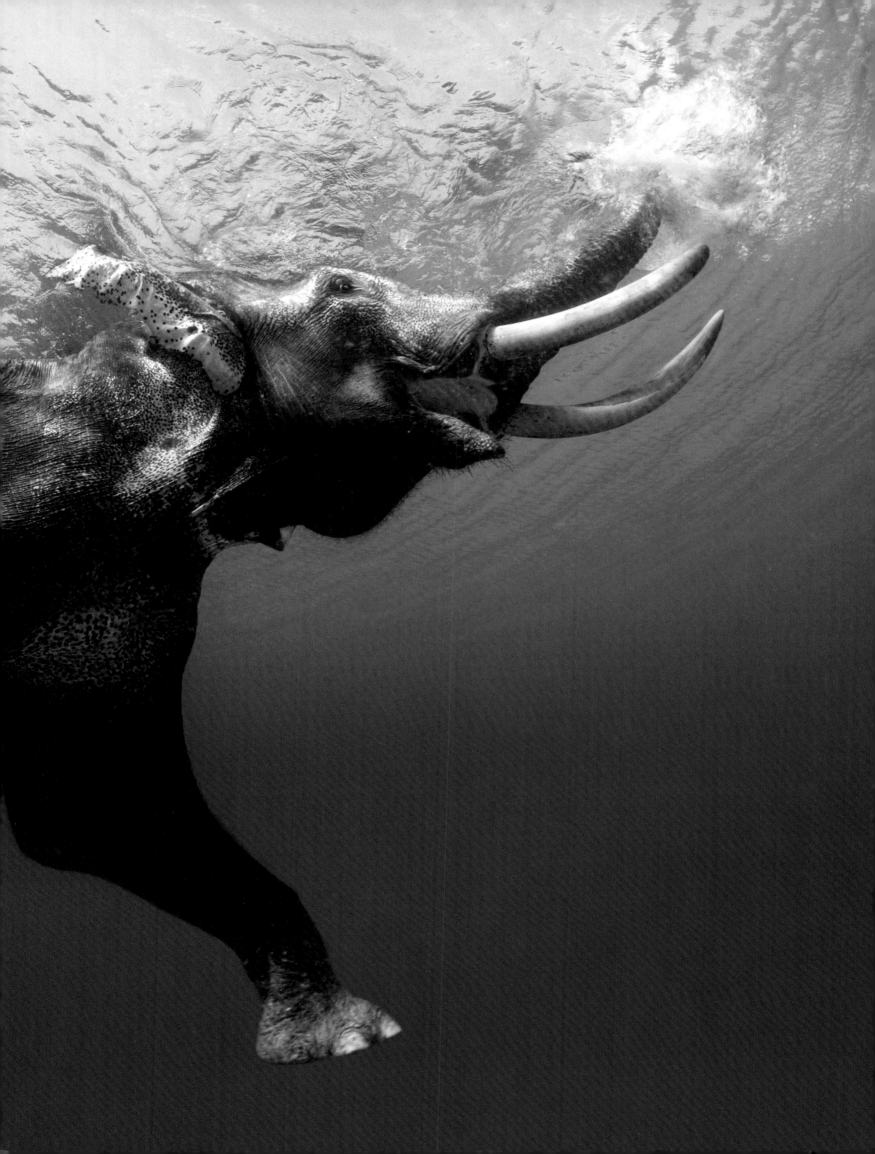

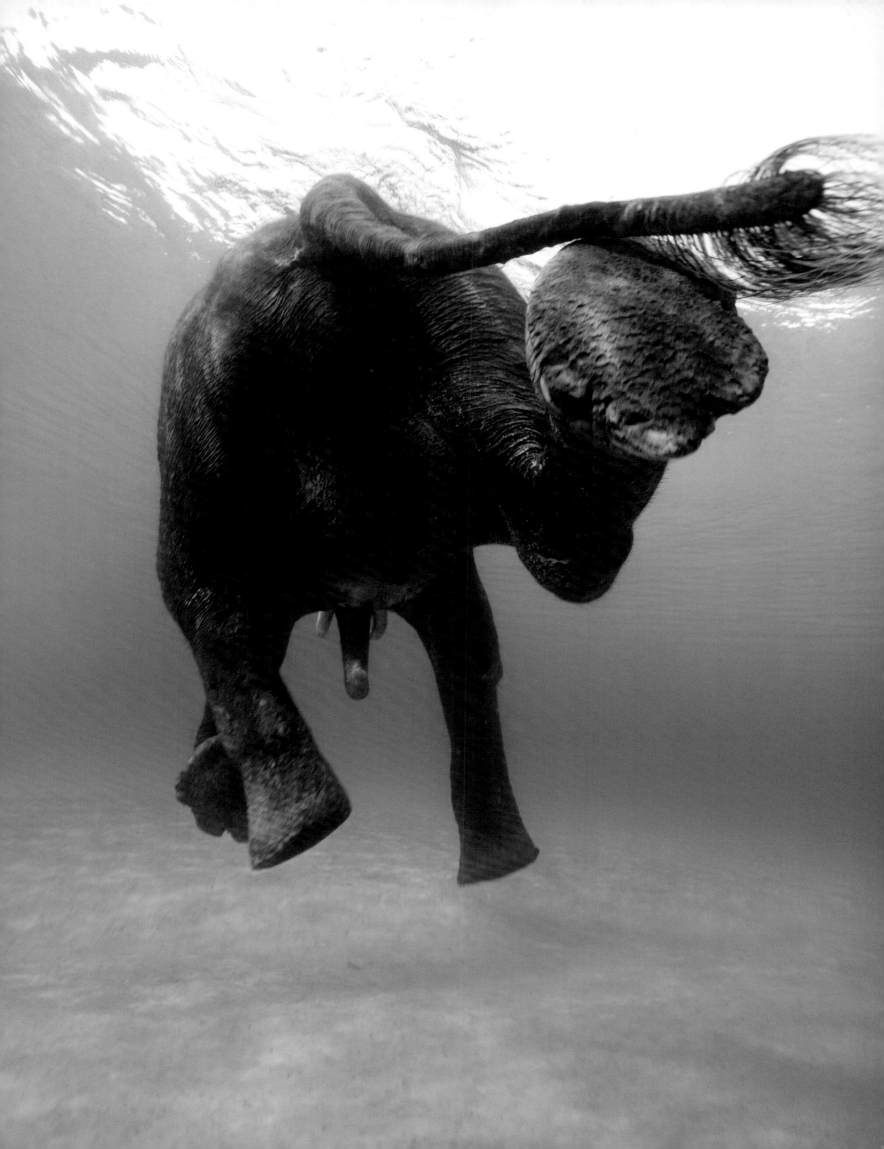

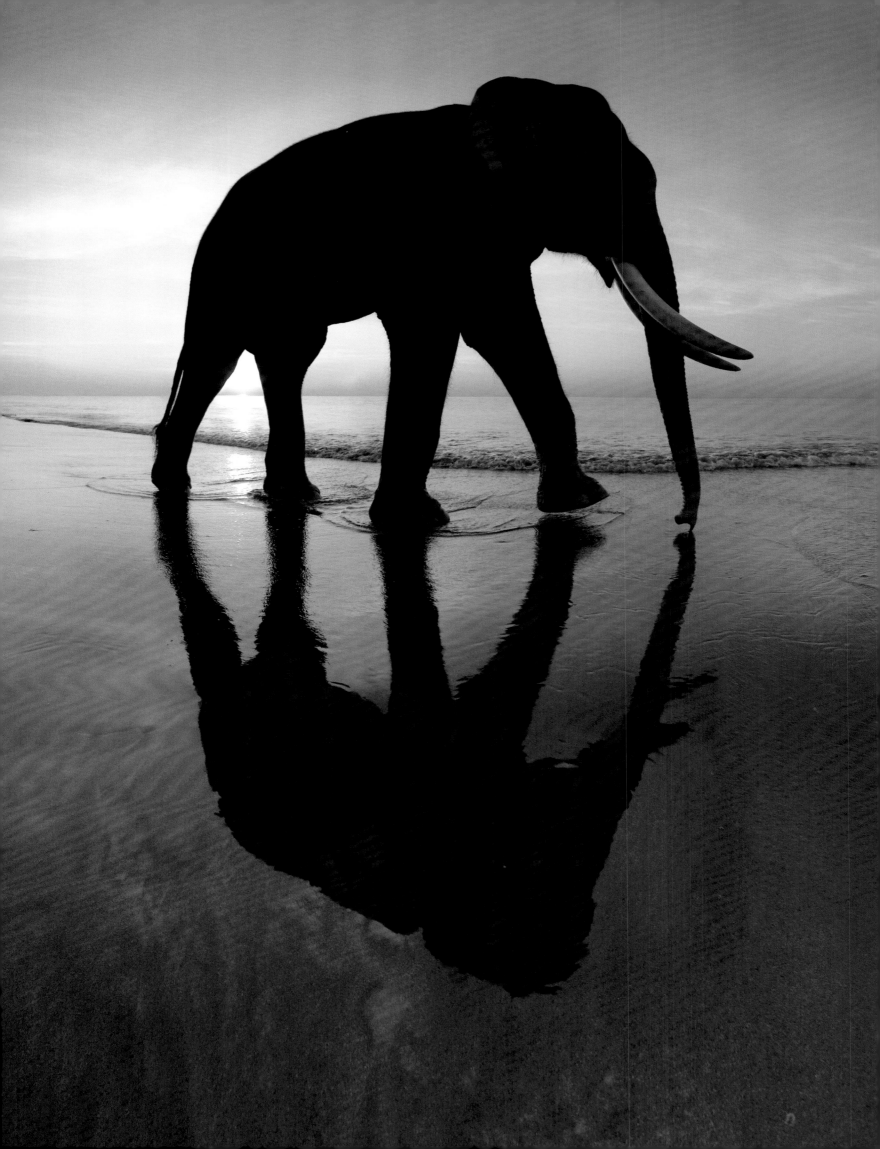

The elephant is venerated in India. The most compassionate and humane of the Hindu gods is Ganesh, who has the head of an elephant; a head that symbolizes Atman, or the universal essence of ultimate supreme reality. His broken tusk represents sacrifice. Bearing in mind the ivory trade, it would be hard to find a more fitting symbol of sacrifice than an elephant's tusk. The Buddha is said to have once been a magnificent white elephant, appearing to his future mother in a dream in which he bowed and presented her with a lotus flower, entered her womb and emerged nine months later in human form. A general respect for living things is visible throughout the Indian subcontinent. It is seen in small details such as pigs roaming freely down the road, gnawing on scraps. Cows bizarrely choose the middle of the busiest thoroughfares to stand motionless, while the bustle of the city is a chaotic, rushing blur around them. By comparison, European domestic animals are fenced in or caged, their movements always under strict human control.

In Hindu culture, elephants are held in high esteem. A small boy running behind an elephant was badly scratched by the coarse hairs of the elephant's tail as it flicked at the flies. Blood dripping, he ran crying to his parents. Rather than lose their tempers, they considered it a great honour that their son had been blessed by Ganesh. On a separate occasion, a resident of northeast India was driving home at midnight when an angry elephant attacked his car. The man jumped out and rolled down a bank, narrowly escaping with his life. When he returned, even though his car had been demolished, he gave thanks to Ganesh for saving his life. When people are killed by elephants in India, it is often considered to be the fault of the victims. Such is the reverence in Indian culture for Ganesh and his physical counterpart, the elephant.

When I stand beside an Indian elephant, I feel dwarfed by her bulk; slightly wary knowing that, if she chose, she could break my back and pulverize my body, with a speed that would leave me no time to even comprehend my fate. I feel reassured as I run my hand along the folds of her coarse trunk, pleasant to the touch and prickly with her thick hairs. I sense the mutual pleasure of the caress, as she rumbles and purrs like a giant kitten. She gently explores with her trunk, then nuzzles up against me, blowing warm damp air as she reaches out with the delicacy and finesse of a human hand tenderly touching another hand. Our special relationship with elephants is reinforced by these aspects of close contact which would be impossible with an animal such as a hippo.

There is a legend about a tiger and elephant who witnessed the arrival by boat of the first humans in Asia. The tiger ran away, convinced that any animal who could harness the wind and travel the ocean had to be feared. The elephant stayed behind, confident that he was much larger and stronger and could easily destroy the humans if they tried to exert control. However, he was captured, and for the last five thousand years elephants have been domesticated. The notion of humans dominating elephants is something that has always made me feel uncomfortable, but after visiting the home of an elephant owner, and seeing how mahouts behave, I felt encouraged by the warmth and total care they showed.

The relationship between the mahout and the Asian elephant is intensely personal and they win trust by lavishing the elephant with close contact and constant attention. Sometimes they grow up together, forging lifelong bonds. Because elephants can become easily confused and unsettled, the mahout should be able to use his skills to pacify. This can best be achieved when a great amount of mutual understanding and loyalty is present. The physical contact between mahout and elephant is profound. The bathing ritual may last for hours, and much bonding takes place during these sessions which the elephants obviously enjoy with great enthusiasm. Mahouts throw water over the elephants, climb on to them when they lie down, and scrub them energetically, showing great attention to detail, with neither a fold nor crevasse untouched. Elephants can master up to sixty commands, and respond using their own repertoire of sounds. In the wild, elephants live in a hierarchal society, with individual families usually ruled by a matriarch. In captivity, where they live in close proximity with people, the mahouts must take control. However, elephants can never be fully domesticated, and will at heart always remain untamed. Captive elephants are either descended from wild elephants, or caught in the wild; and it is not possible to completely breed out their natural feral instincts.

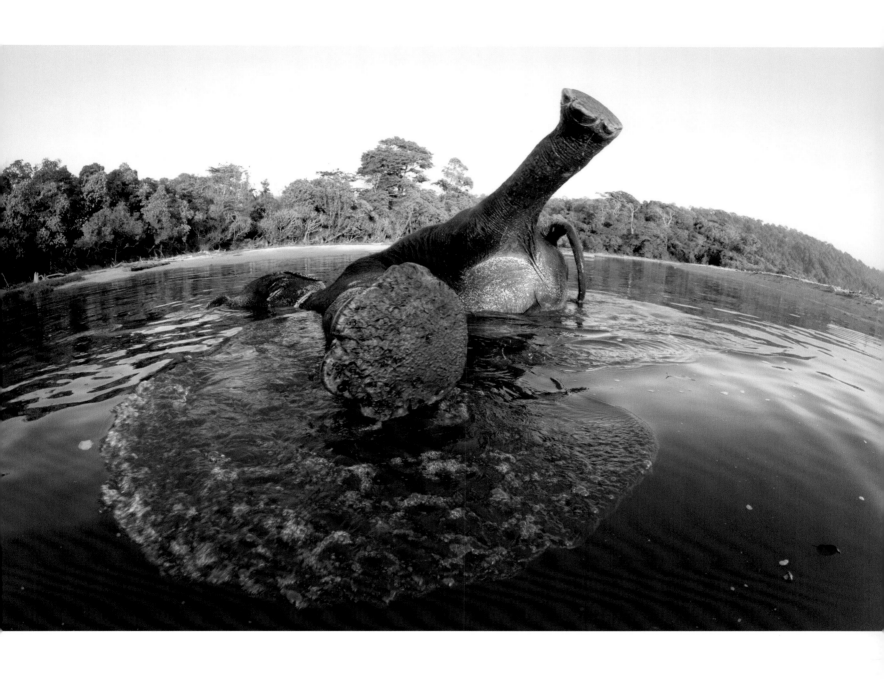

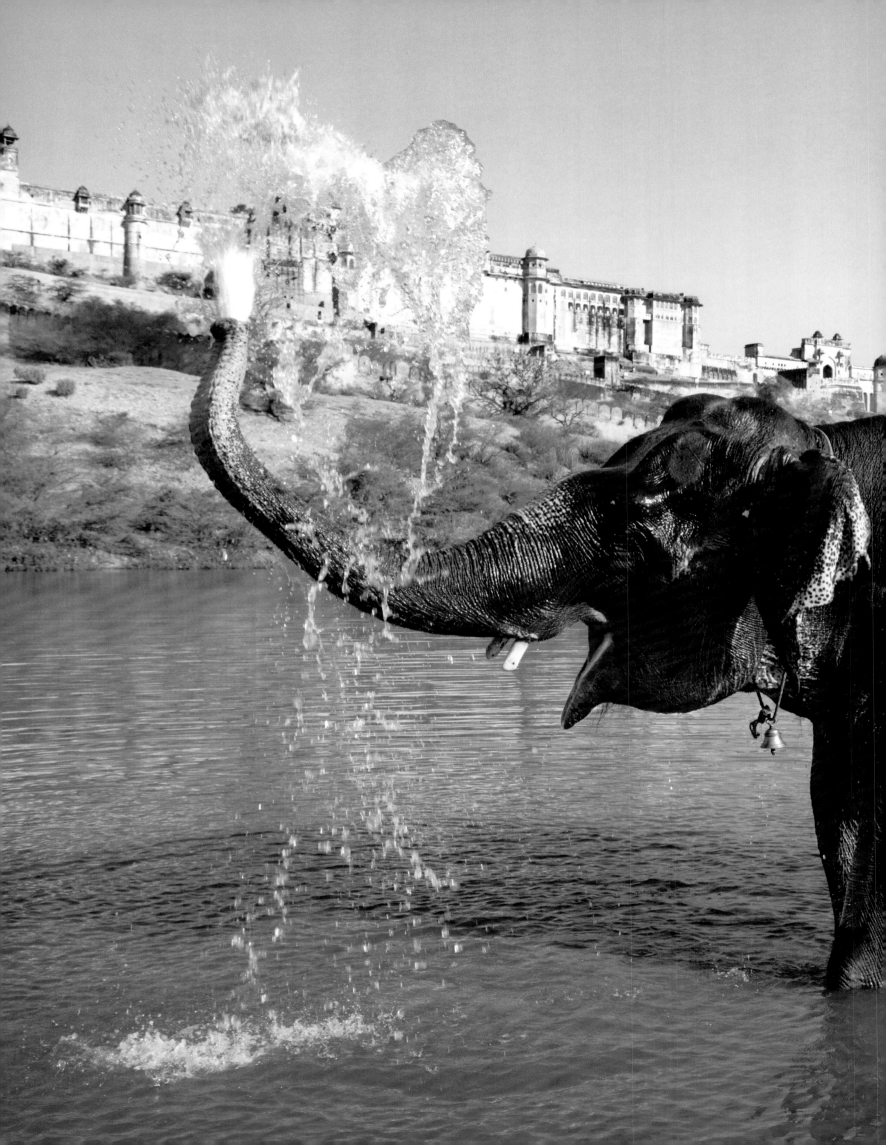

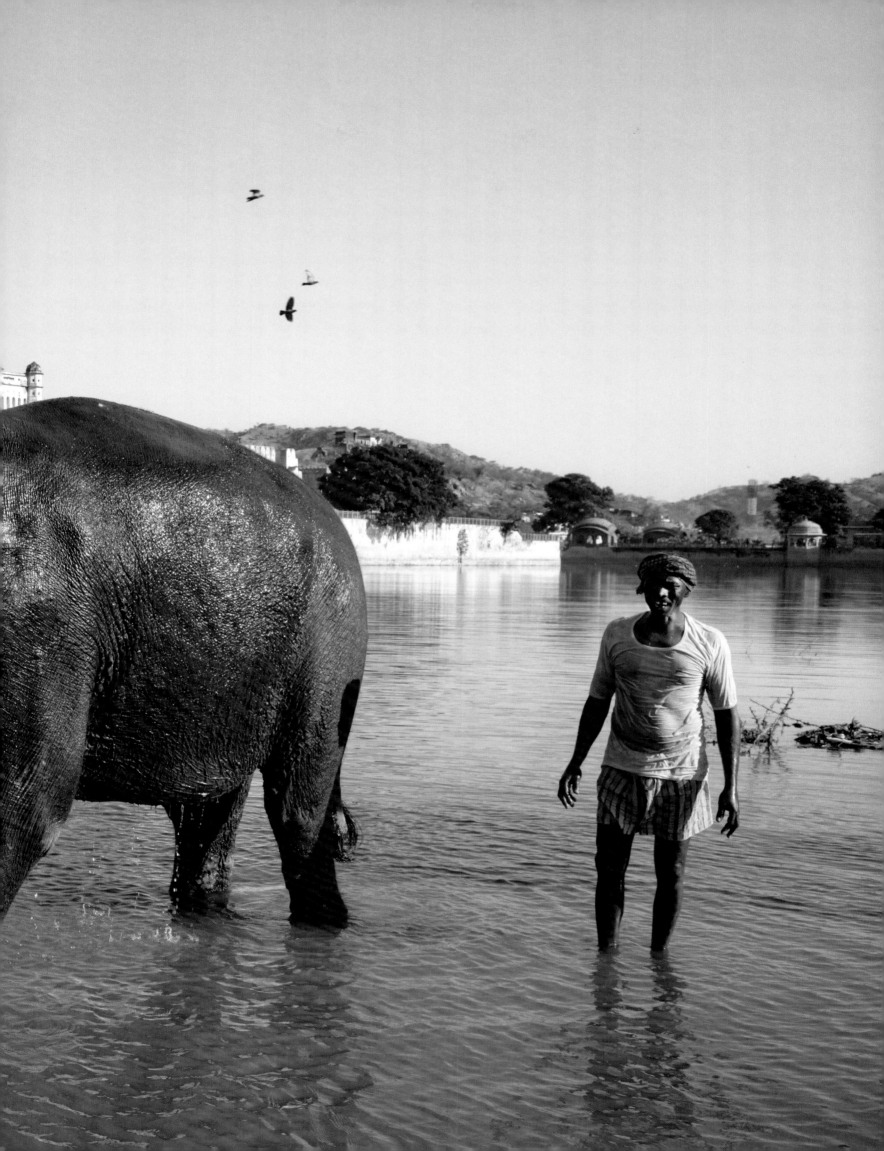

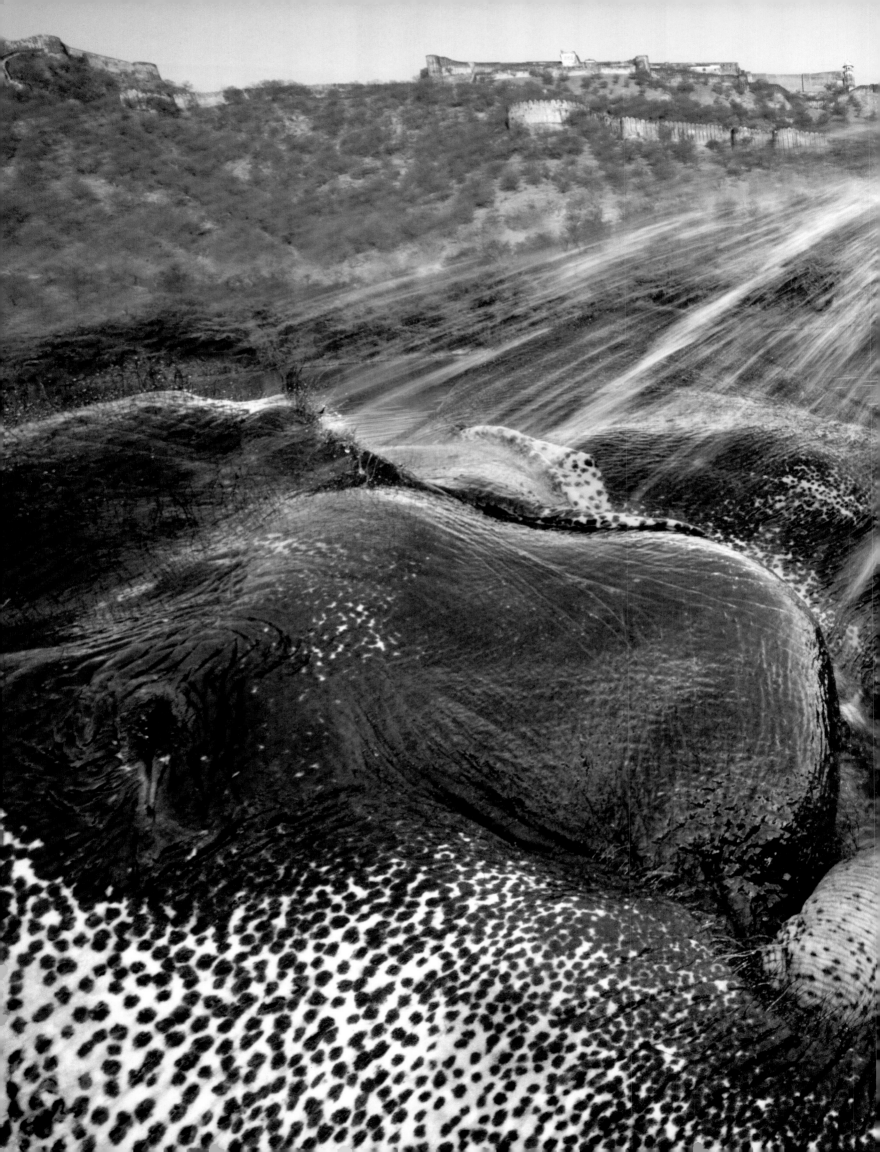

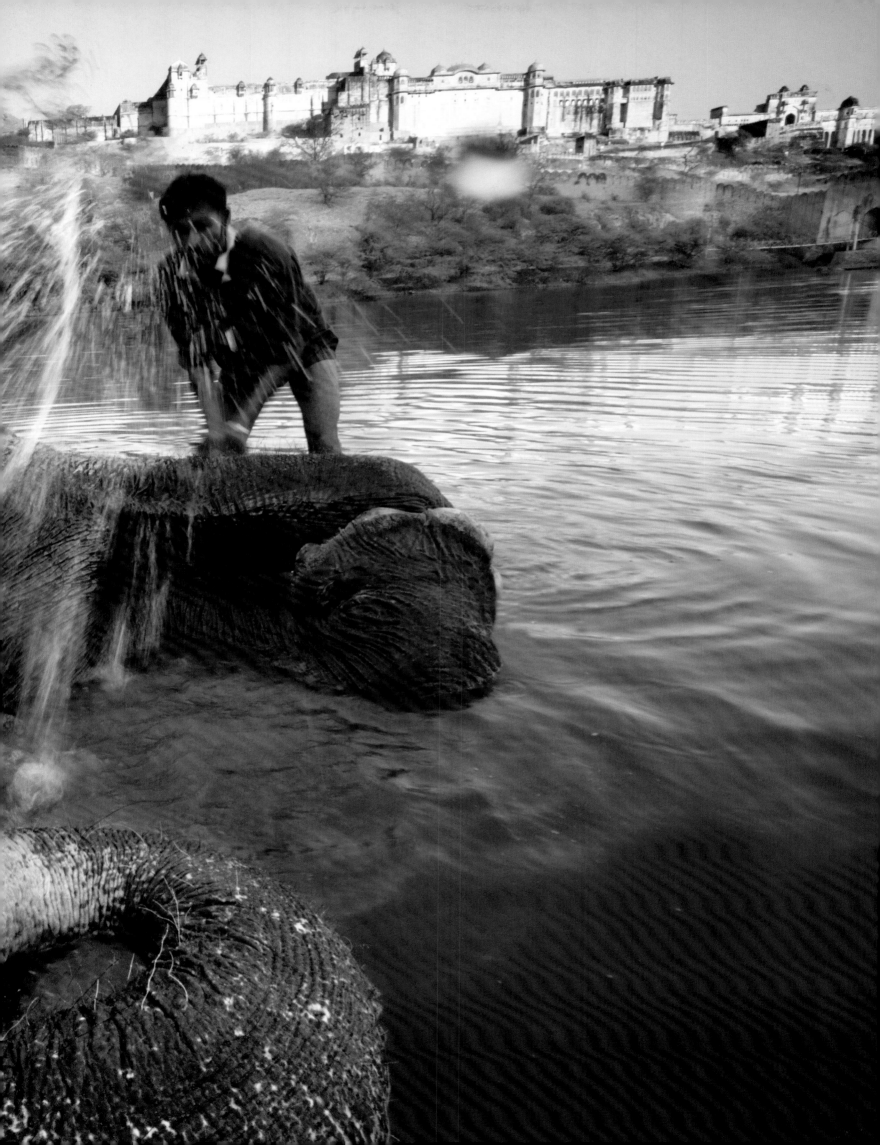

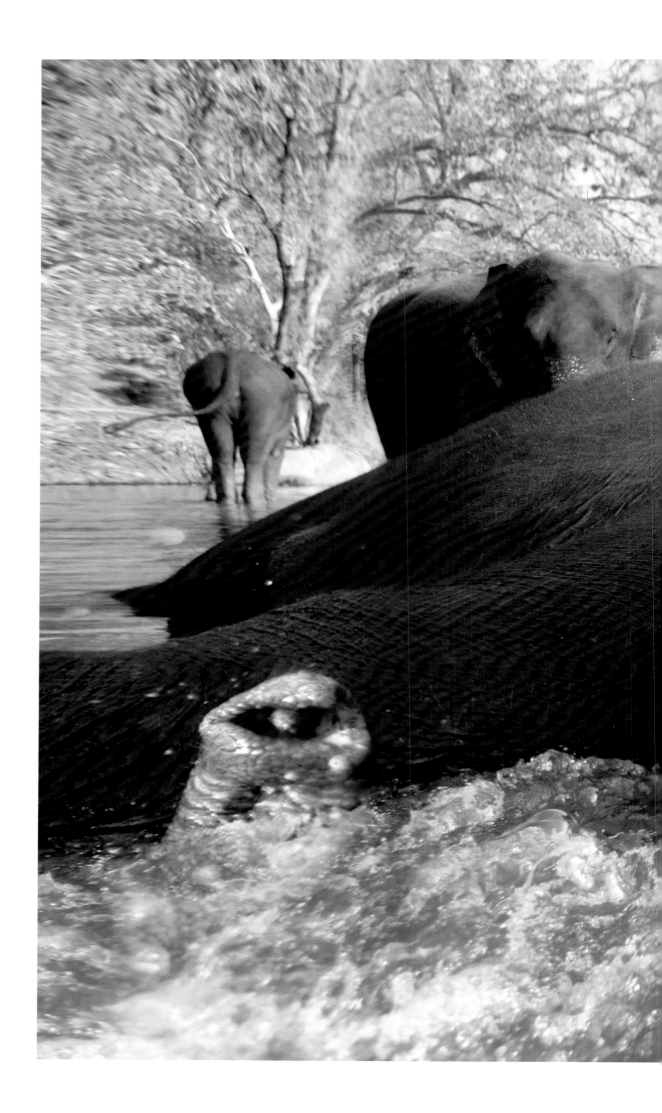

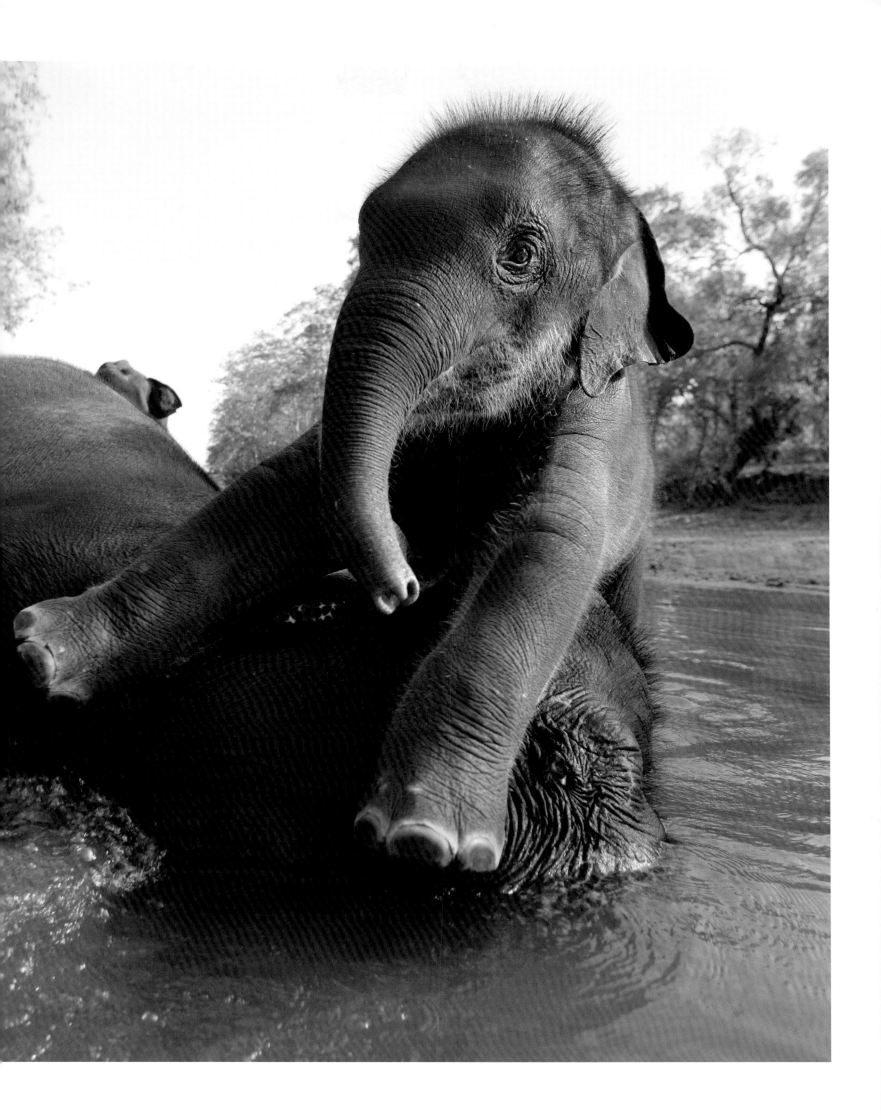

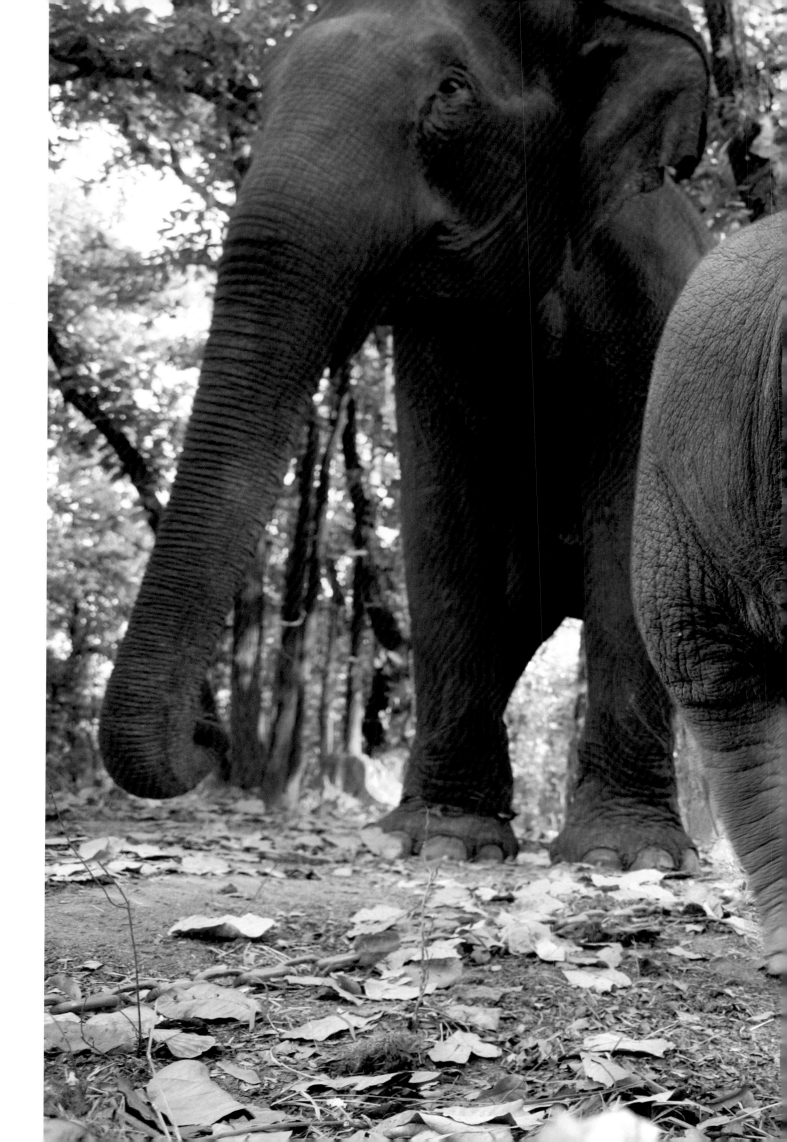

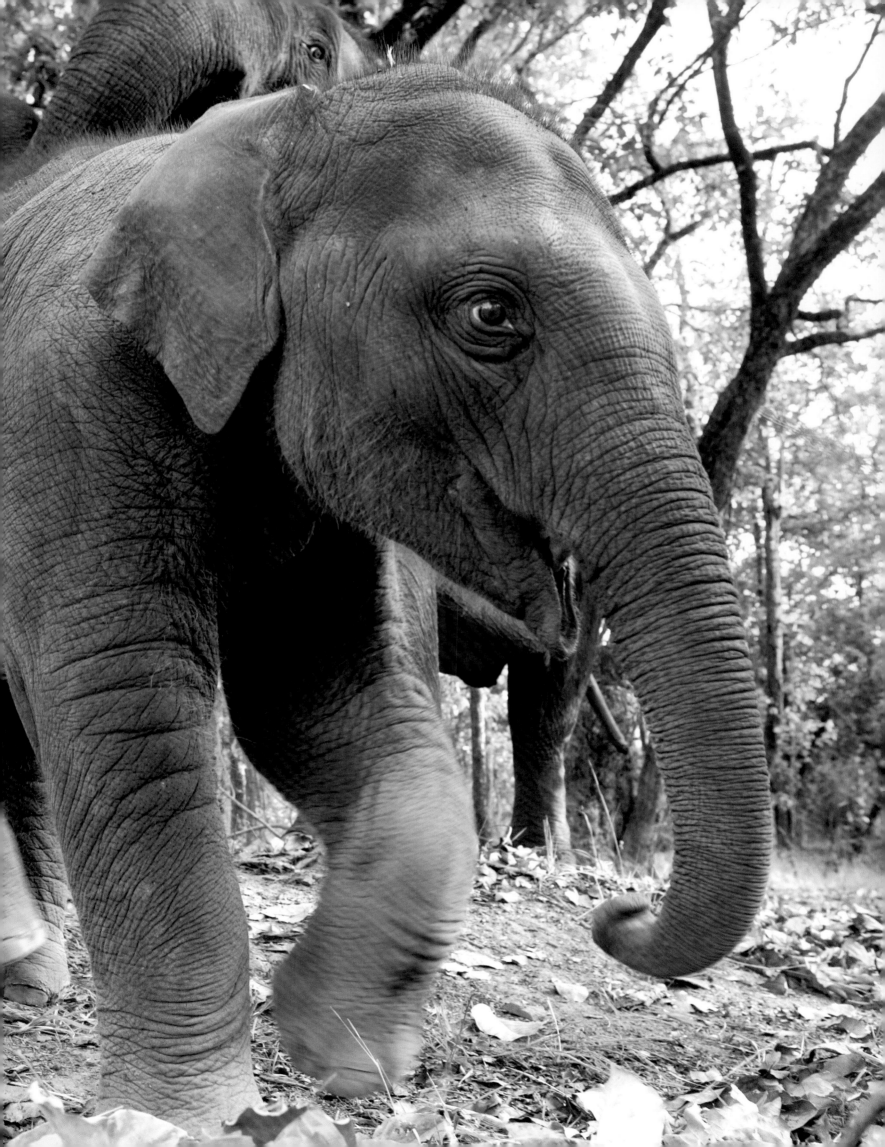

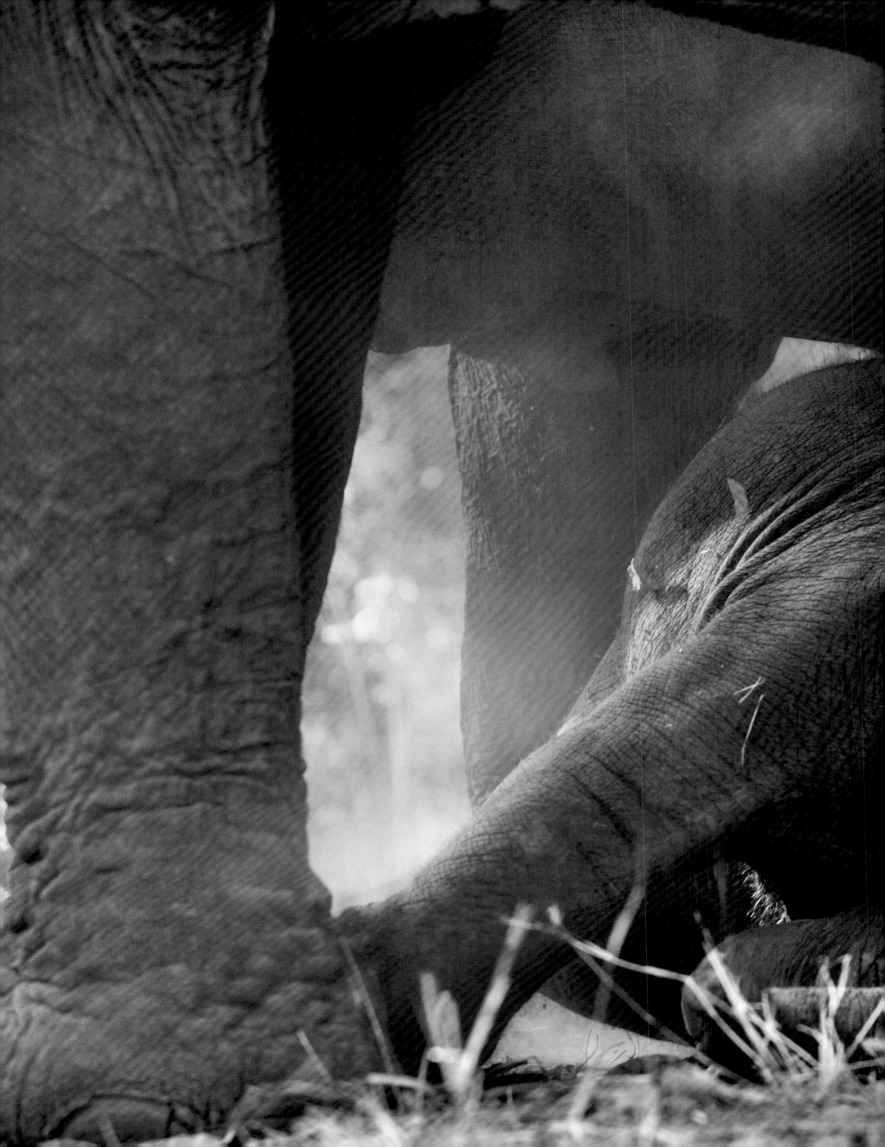

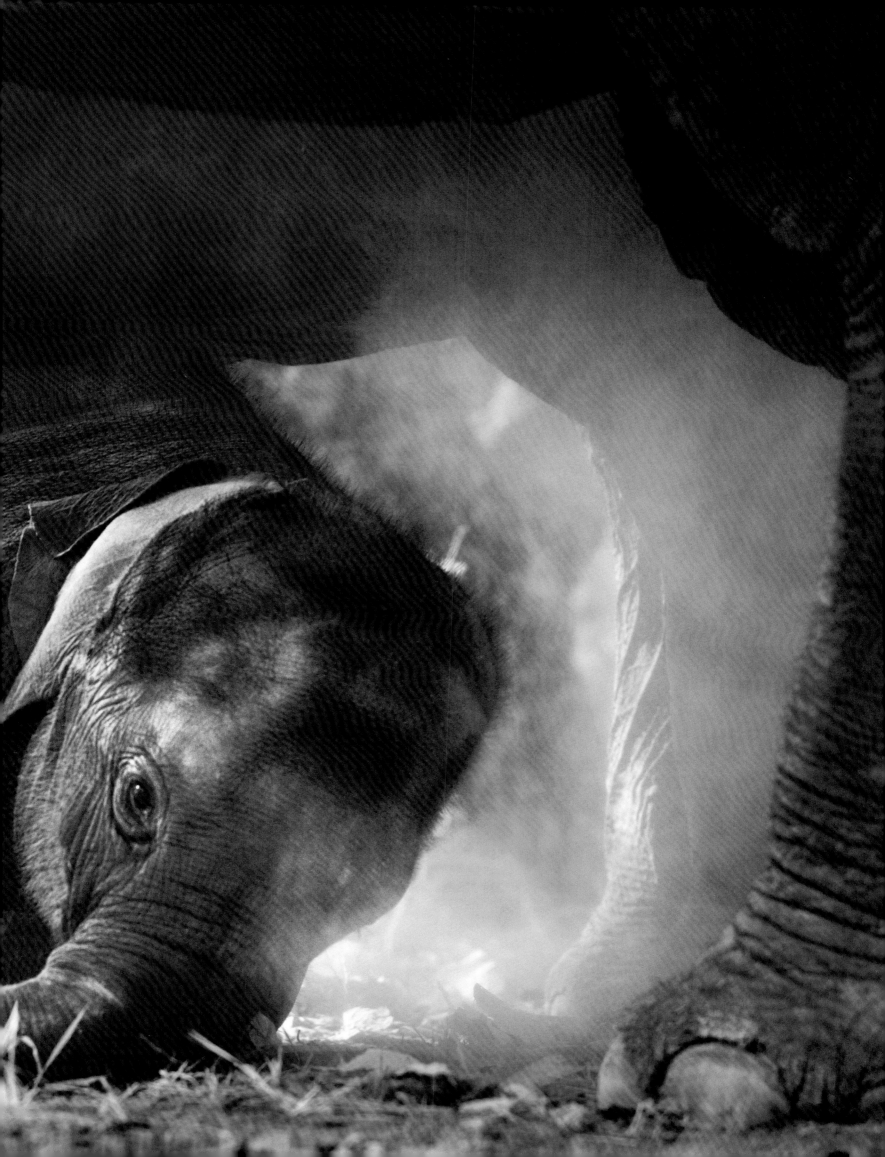

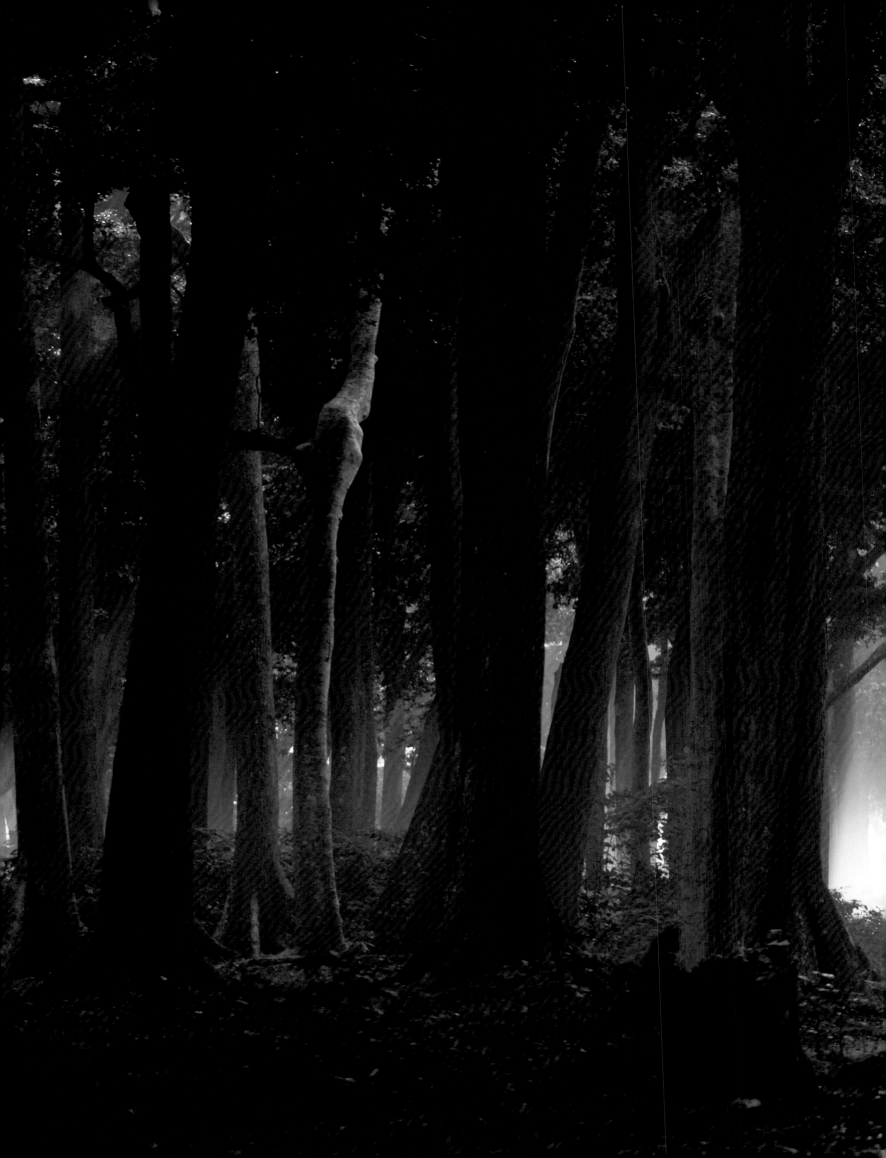

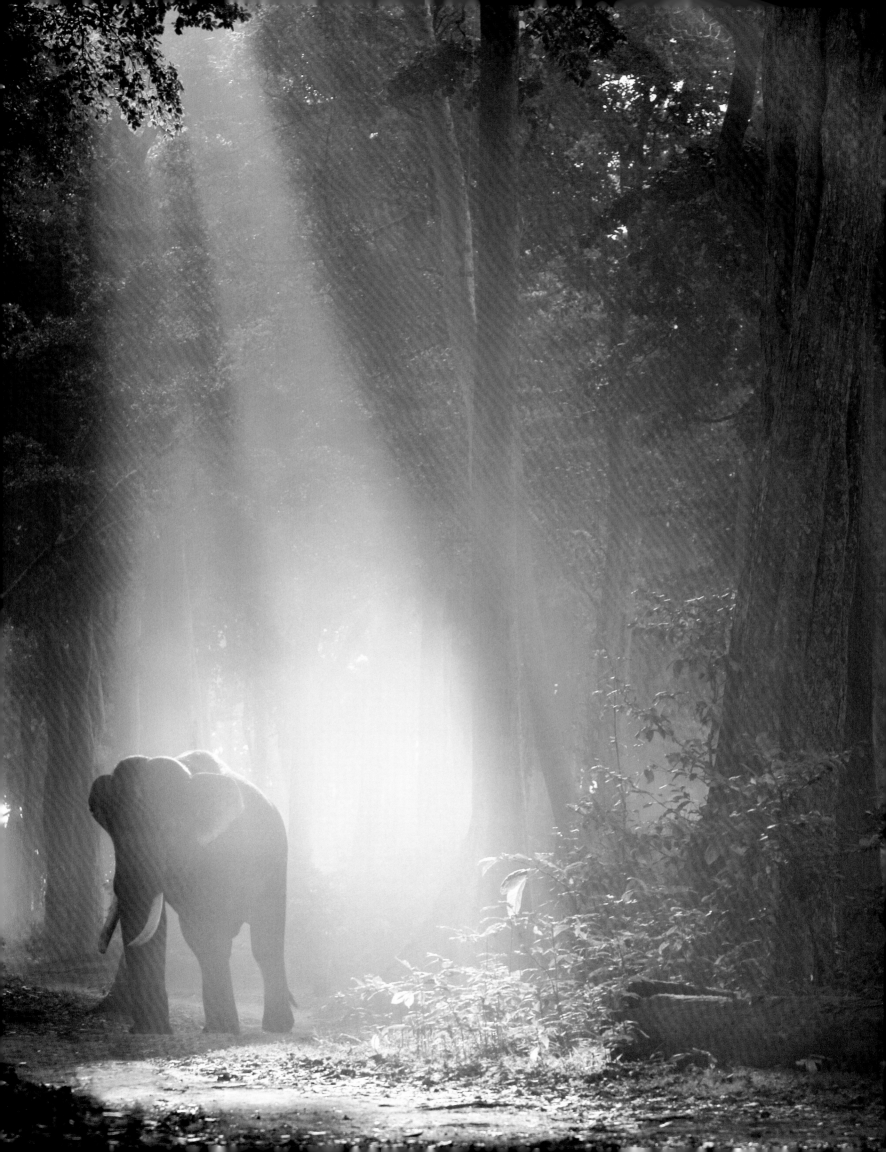

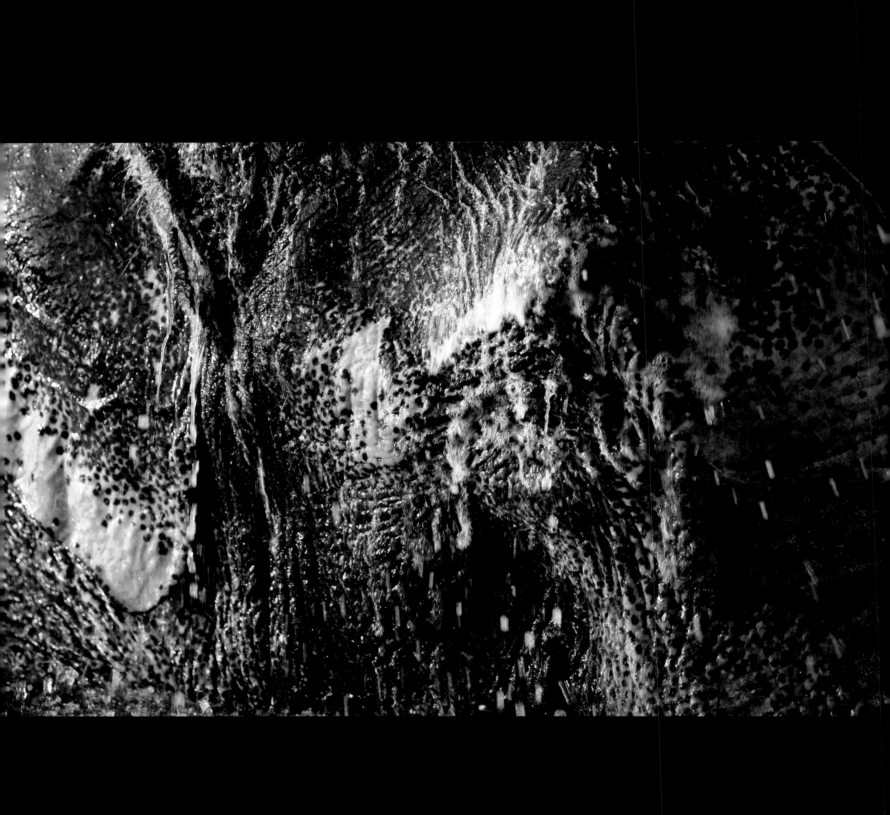

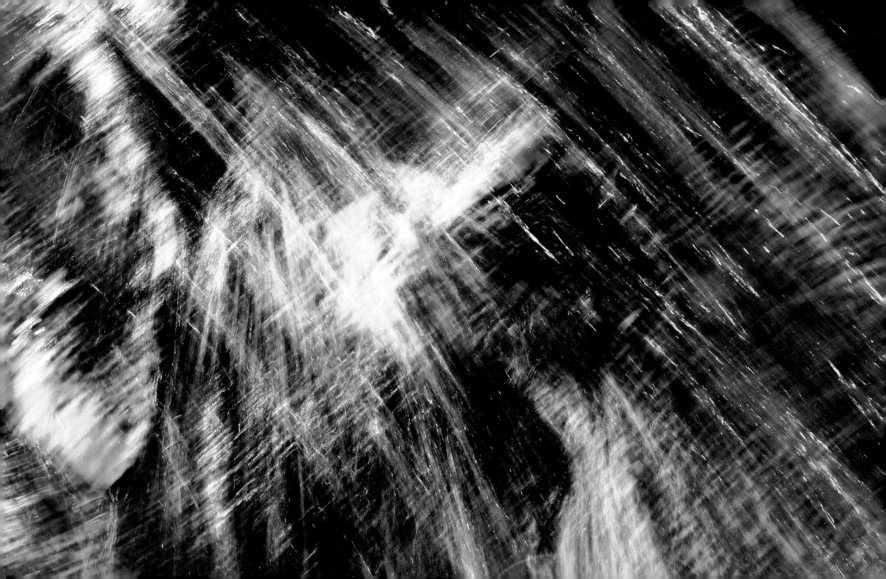

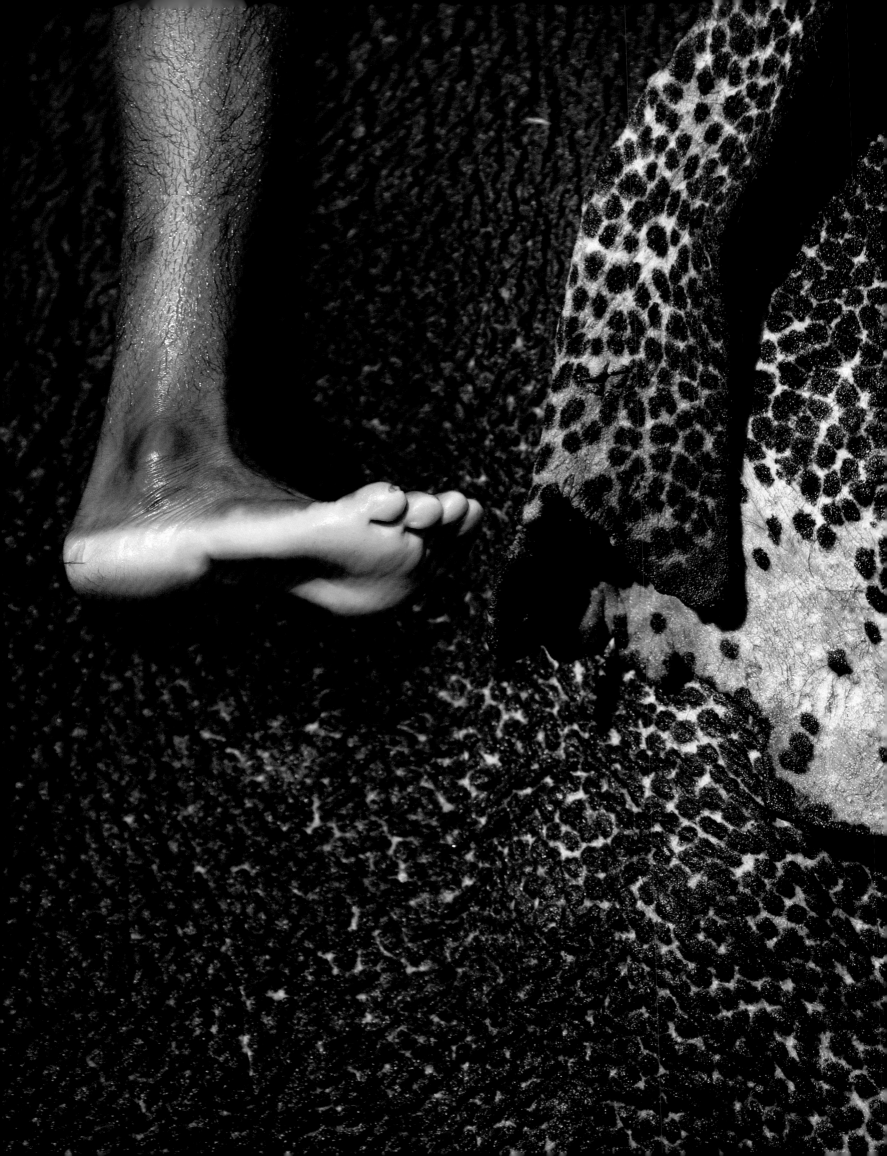

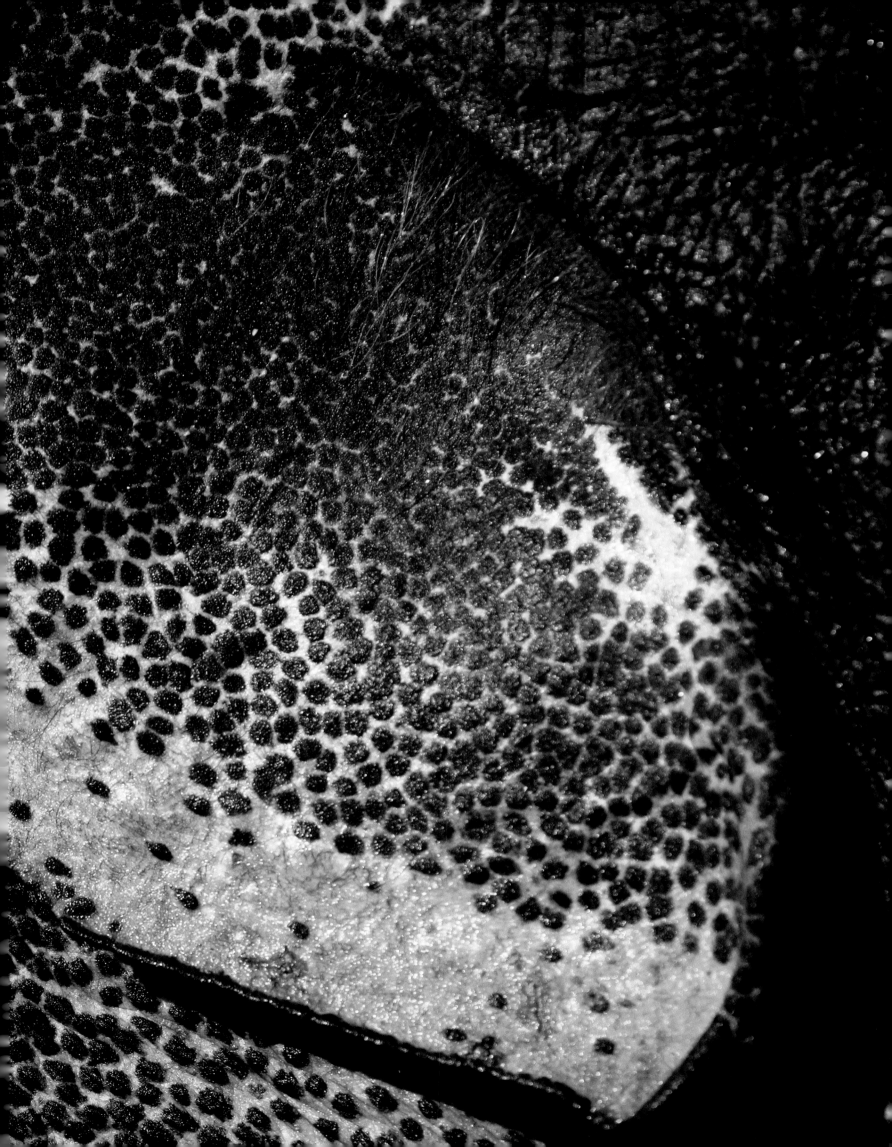

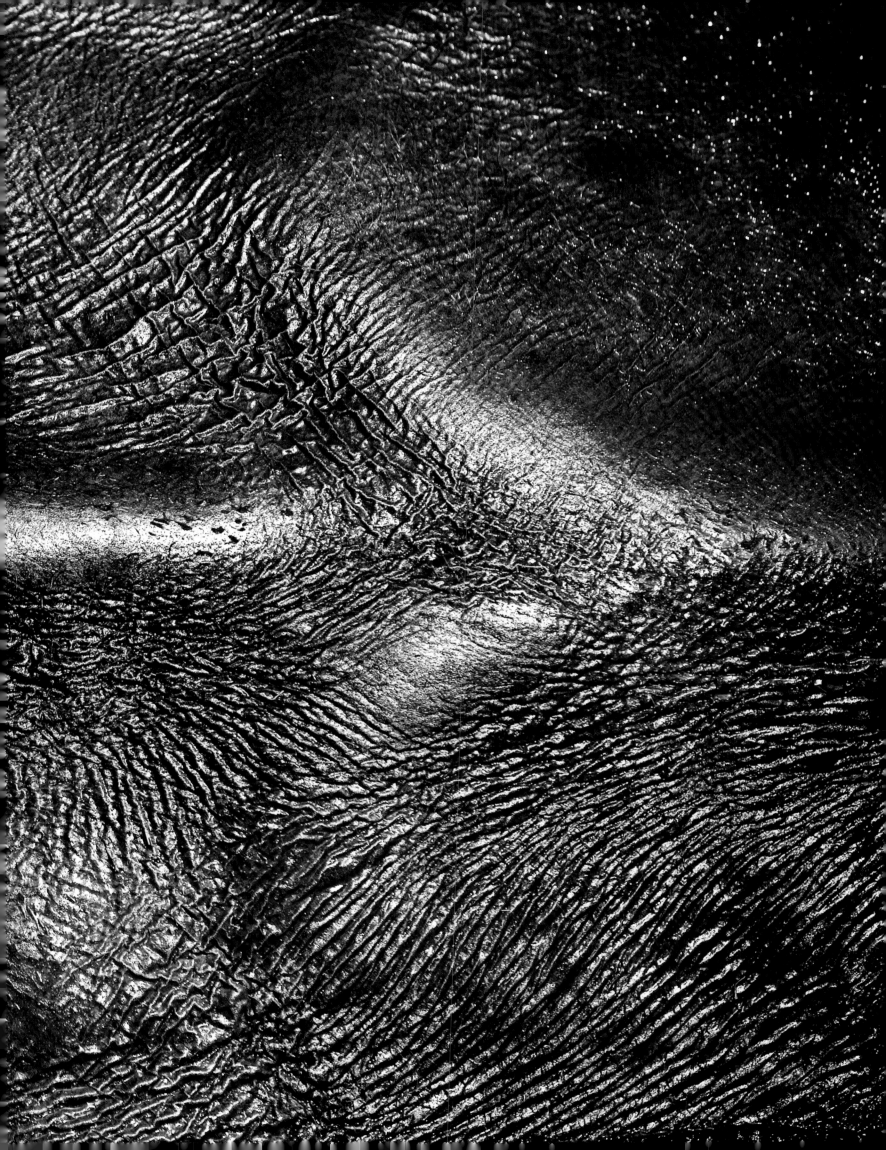

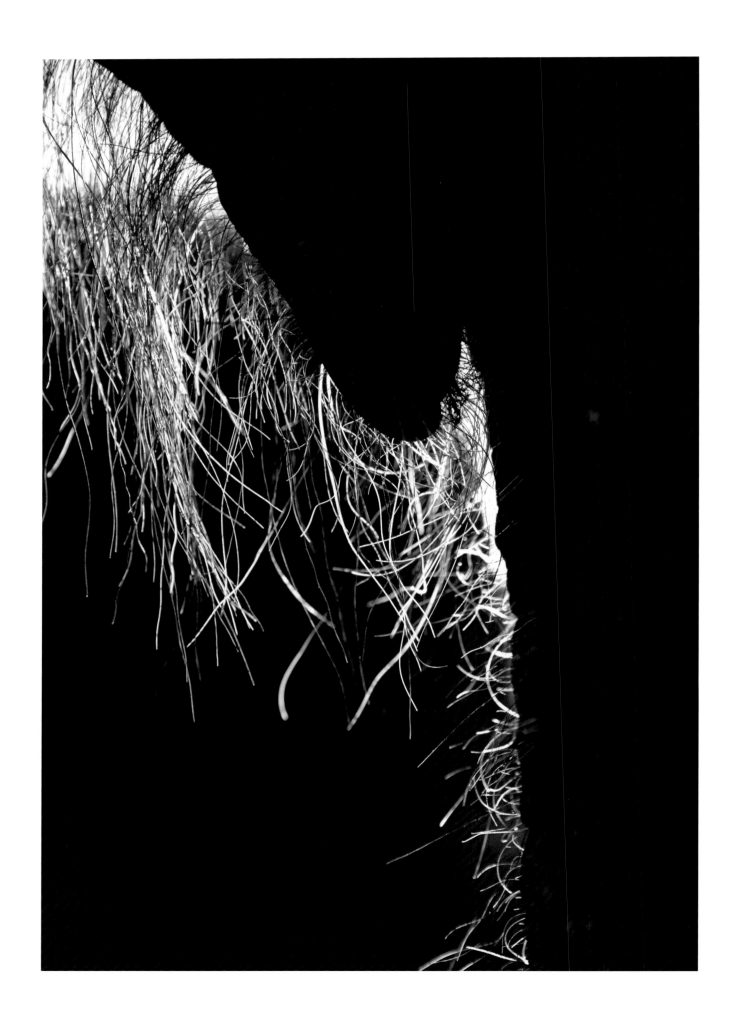

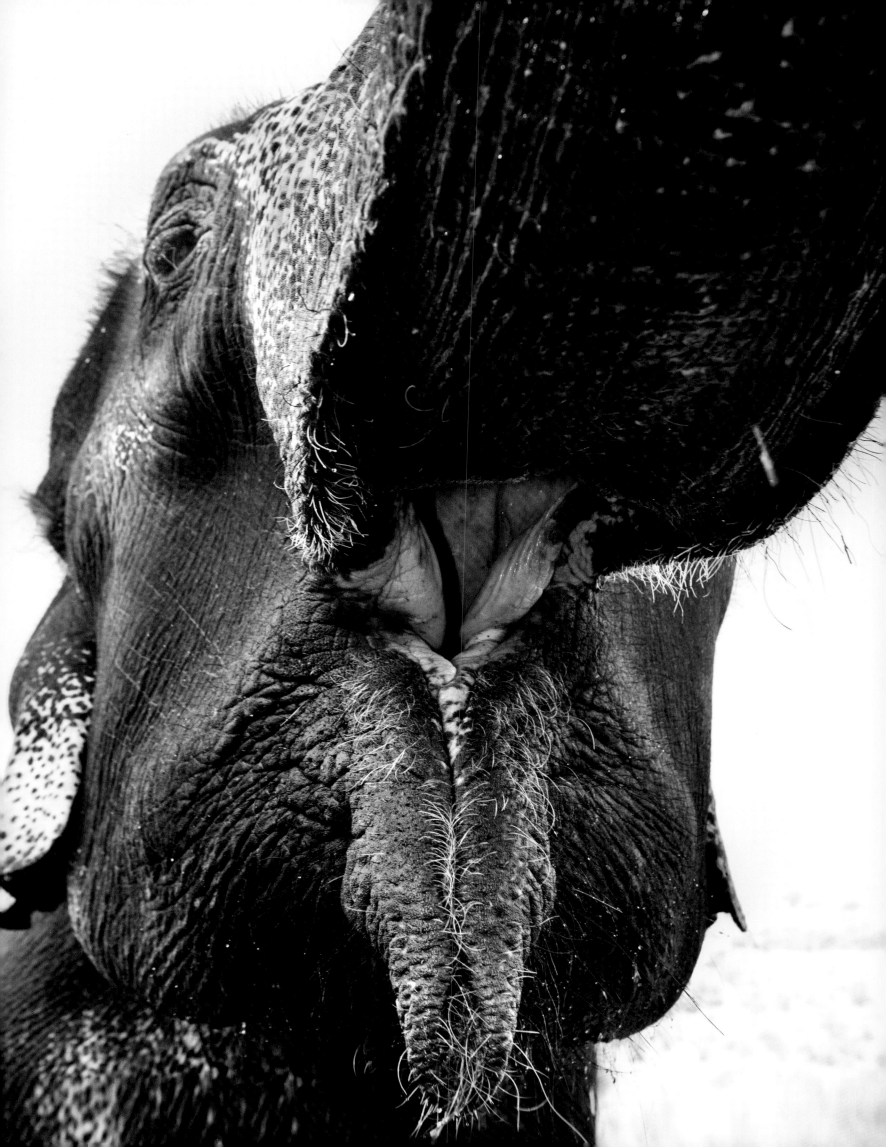

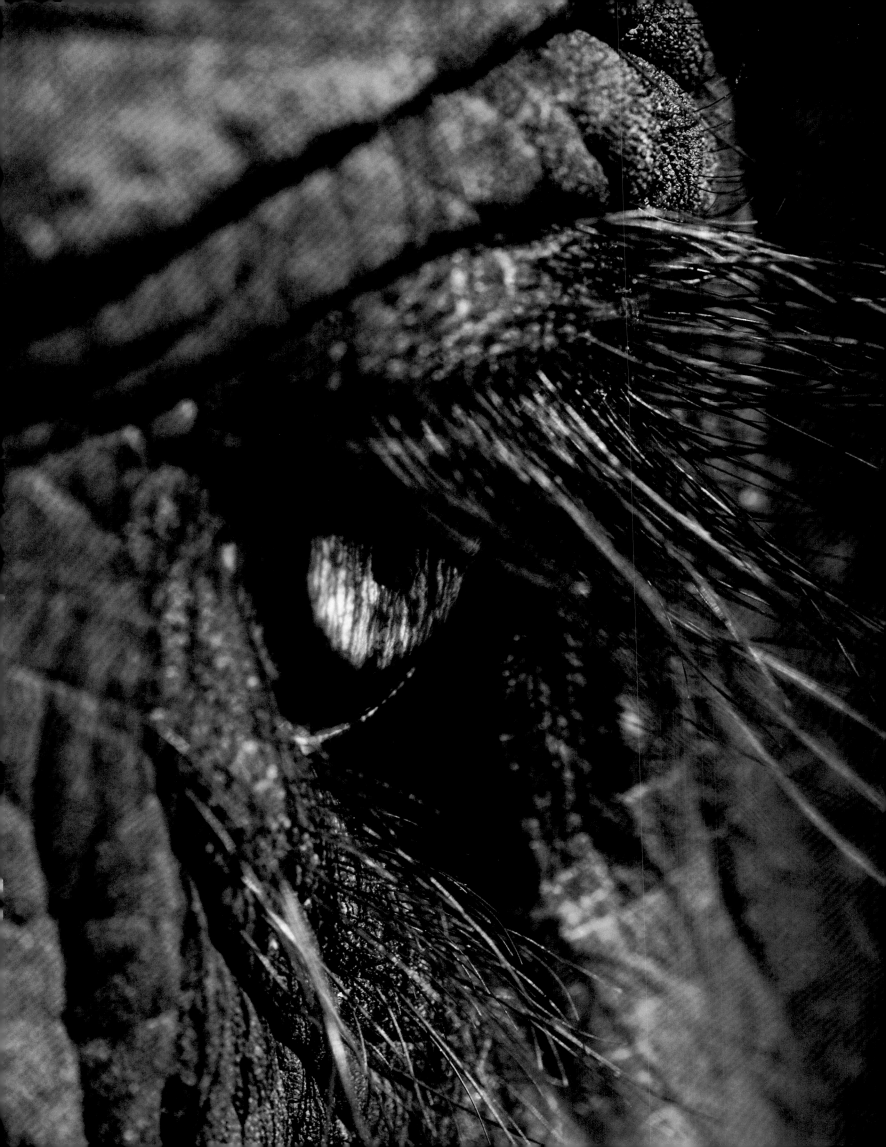

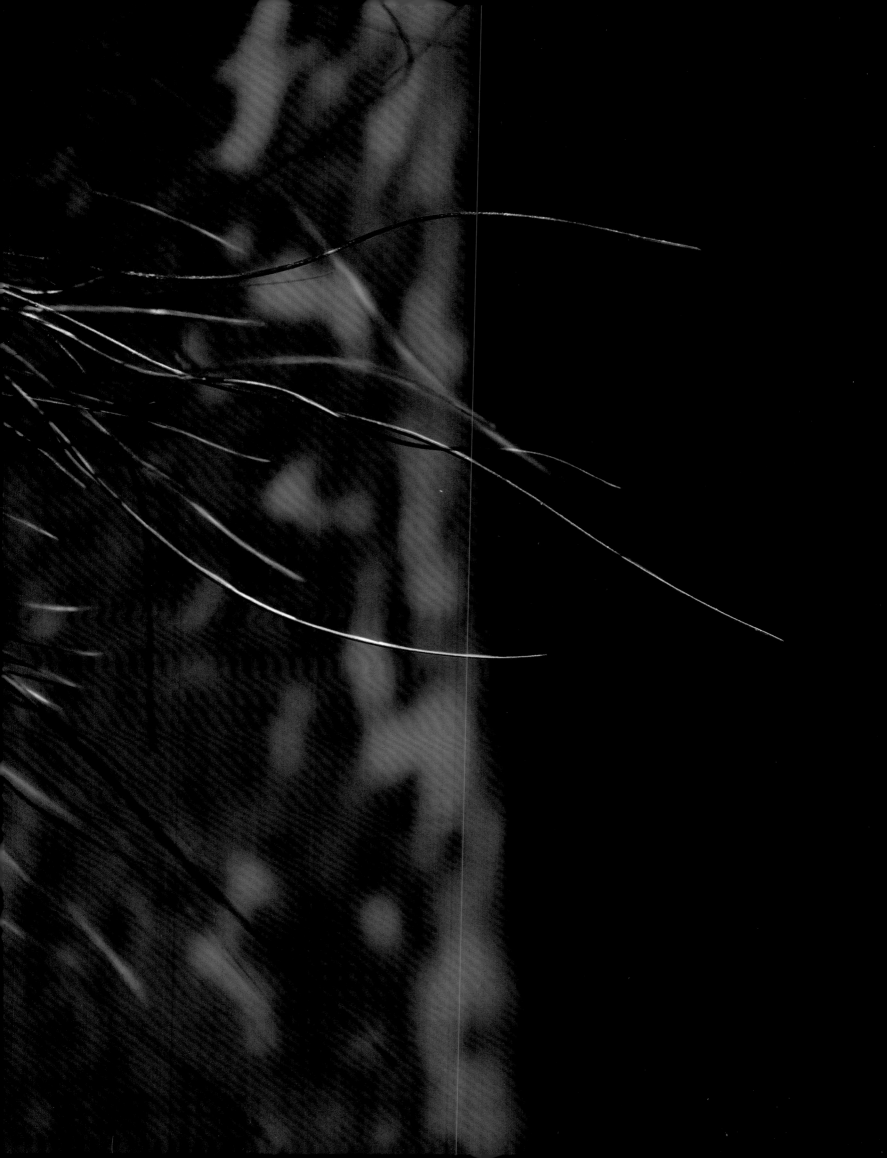

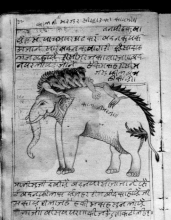
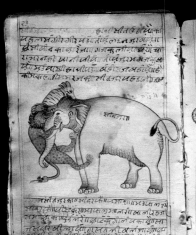
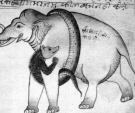
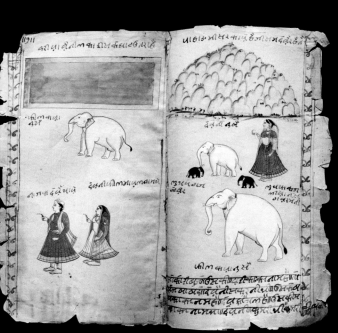
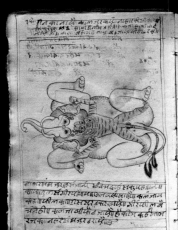
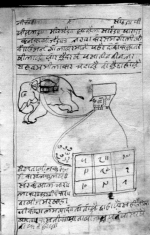

Each year in Rajastan, India, an elephant festival is held in the city of Jaipur, and I was fortunate to spend time there watching the celebrations. There was great excitement during the build-up to the event which culminated in a large, colourful procession at the local stadium. An elephant-painting competition was held at the Amber Fort, in which mahouts and elephant owners vied energetically with each other, each team striving to show off the most spectacular, colourful and richly decorated elephant the world has ever seen. I marvelled at the patience shown by the elephants, as they allowed themselves to be decorated while surrounded by a noisy, jostling crowd. About twenty elephants stood close together, barely moving in the sultry heat of the afternoon, each quietly enduring many strokes of the brush for several hours during the painting. The bright primary reds, yellows and greens contrasted with the dark grey skins, glowing with a vivid luminosity. I, and most of the crowd, were particularly drawn to one elephant, who had a magnificent tiger painted on her face. It was designed in such a way that the elephant's eye doubled as the tiger's eye, so creating an exquisite, living *trompe-l'œil*.

The elephants' tolerance was exemplary, and again made me think about the personal dynamics that take place between elephant and mahout. In the run-up to the festival one morning, I saw an elephant and his mahout in the river below the Amber Fort. The elephant ran into the water like an excited labrador, joyously splashing as he played in the sunshine. He radiated happiness, and when he eventually settled down, the mahout began to wash him in the river.

On the morning of the festival I visited the home of Mr Abdul Rasheed and his family, long before sunrise, and watched them begin the lengthy process of preparing for the big moment. I was treated to typical Indian hospitality – offered copious amounts of food and sweet tea while one of his elephants was made ready. She was initially washed and scrubbed with much attention to detail, and as the sun rose behind her, the backlit hairs on her body glowed with great intensity for a moment before the light became harsh and the oppressive heat began to dominate the day. As layers of paint were applied, children started to gather around the elephant or watched from the nearby

Beautifully handwritten and illustrated, this unique book of elephant management has been passed down through generations, and is still used today by Mr Abdul Rasheed of the Indian Elephant Development Society in Jaipur.

Jaipur Elephant Festival

189

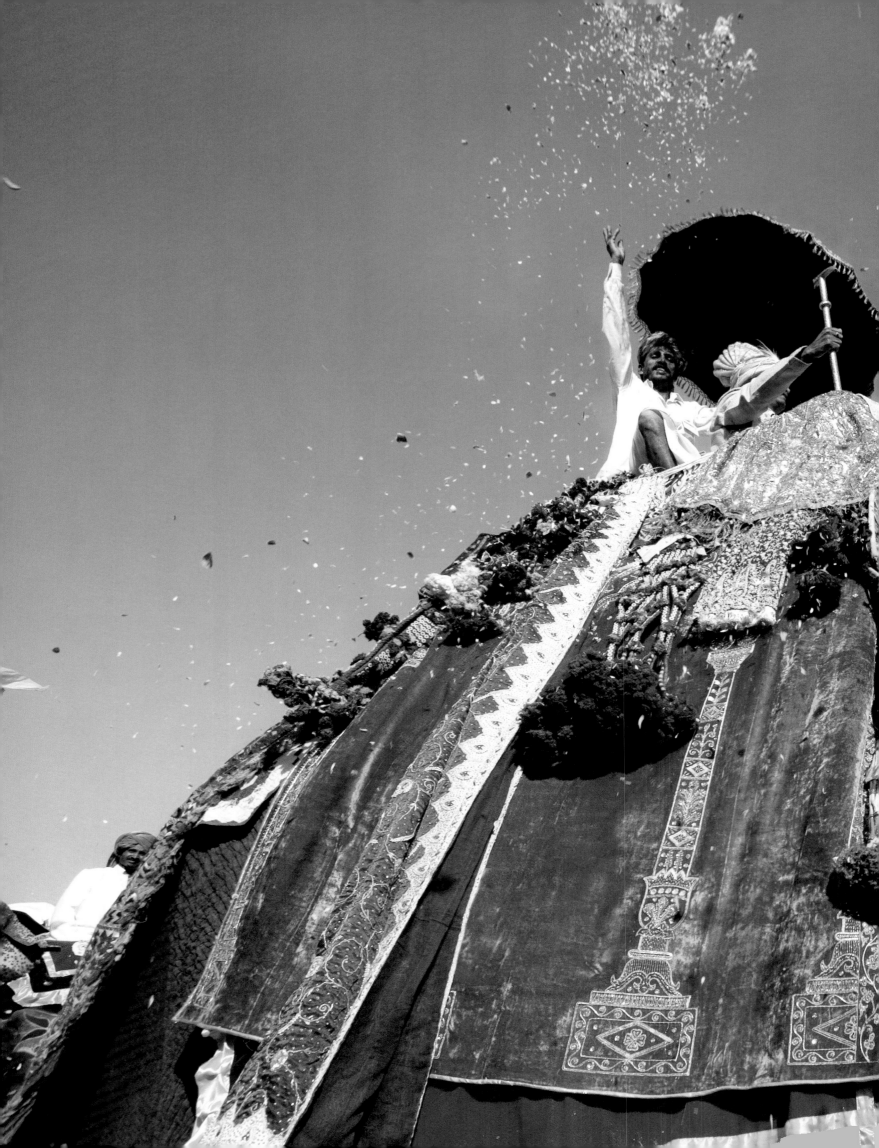

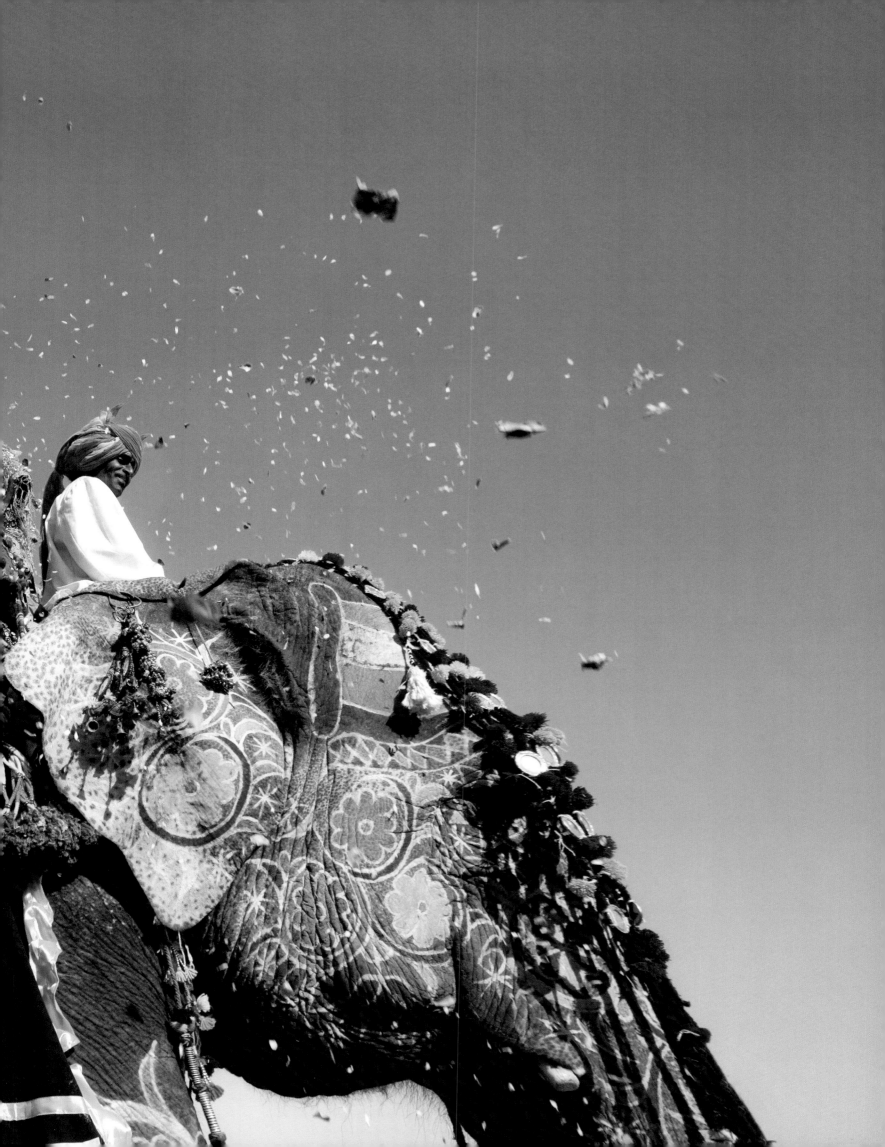

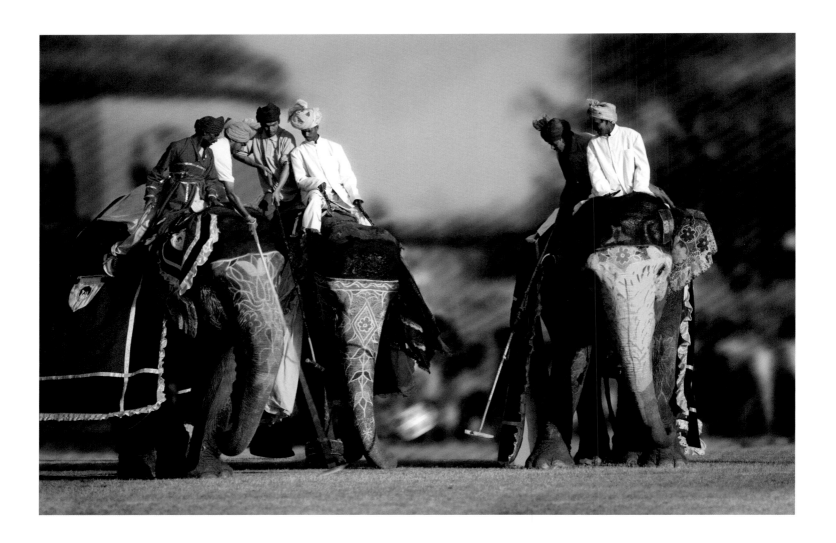

balconies. Tea continued to flow. I noticed Mr Rasheed referring occasionally to a book. It was an old, dog-eared notebook that had obviously been passed down through several generations. Beautifully illustrated and written by hand, it was a definitive and unique elephant handbook. Produced long ago, it was clearly assembled with the same care and attention I was witnessing while the elephant was being decorated in the street.

It was late afternoon before the parade took place. Beforehand, all the elephants gathered outside for the final preparations. They were preened and fussed over, covered in glittering ornaments and brightly coloured embroidered fabrics. Some were given a final coat of startling pink on the toenails. Then, amid great fanfare, they entered the stadium. There was much music and dancing as the elephants, along with camels and horses, were paraded ceremoniously, until the procession finally halted in front of a platform. Here a shield was awarded to the best decorated elephant. There were races, a tug of war and eventually a polo match. Mahouts, dressed in saffron with red turbans, wielding long-handled mallets, played from the backs of the elephants, scoring goals with a football.

In the fading light, the festival came to a close, and the crowd shuffled out of the stadium, back into the chaos of the city streets. It was all over so quickly.

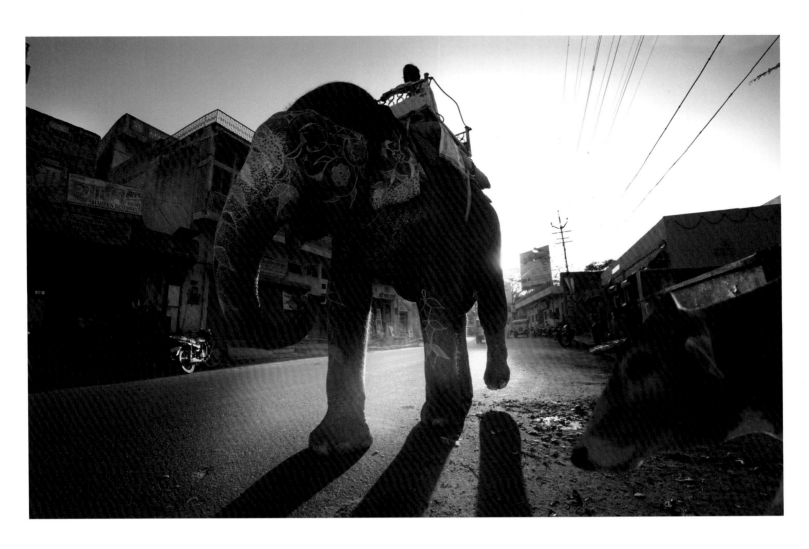

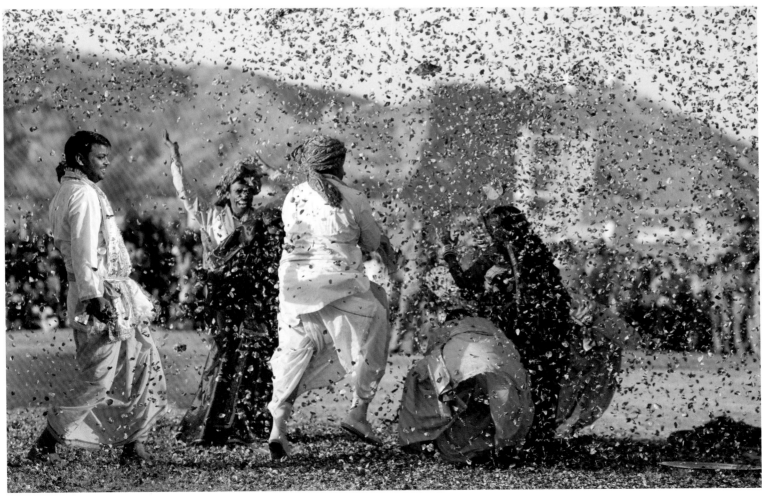

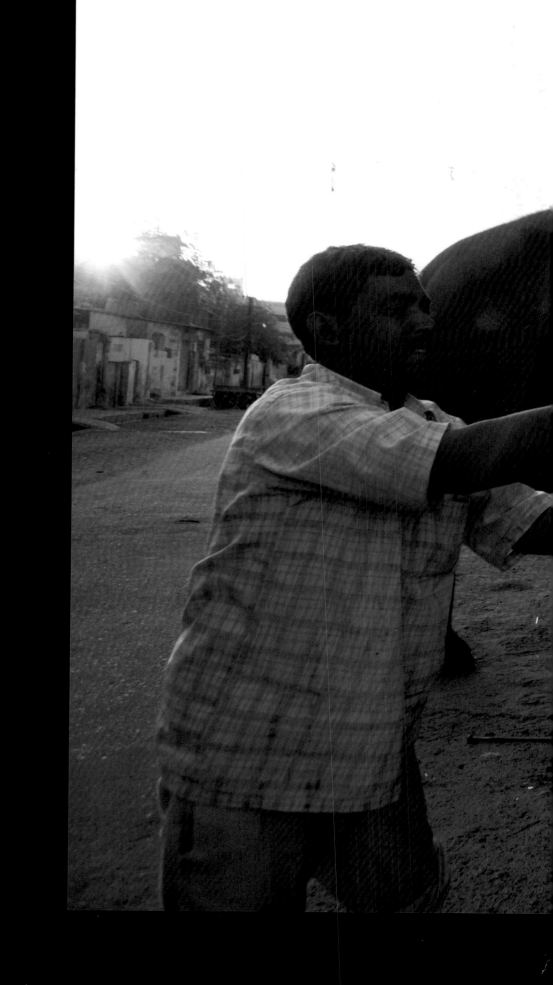

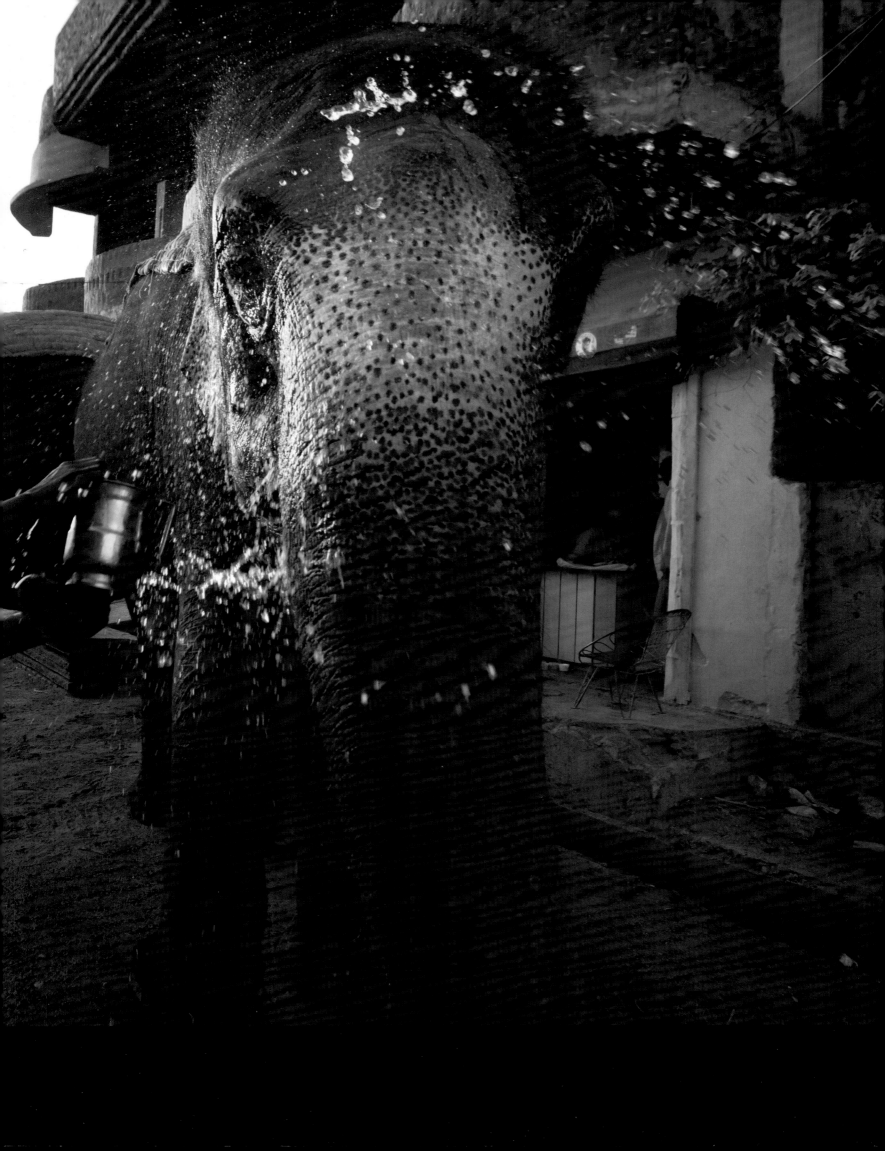

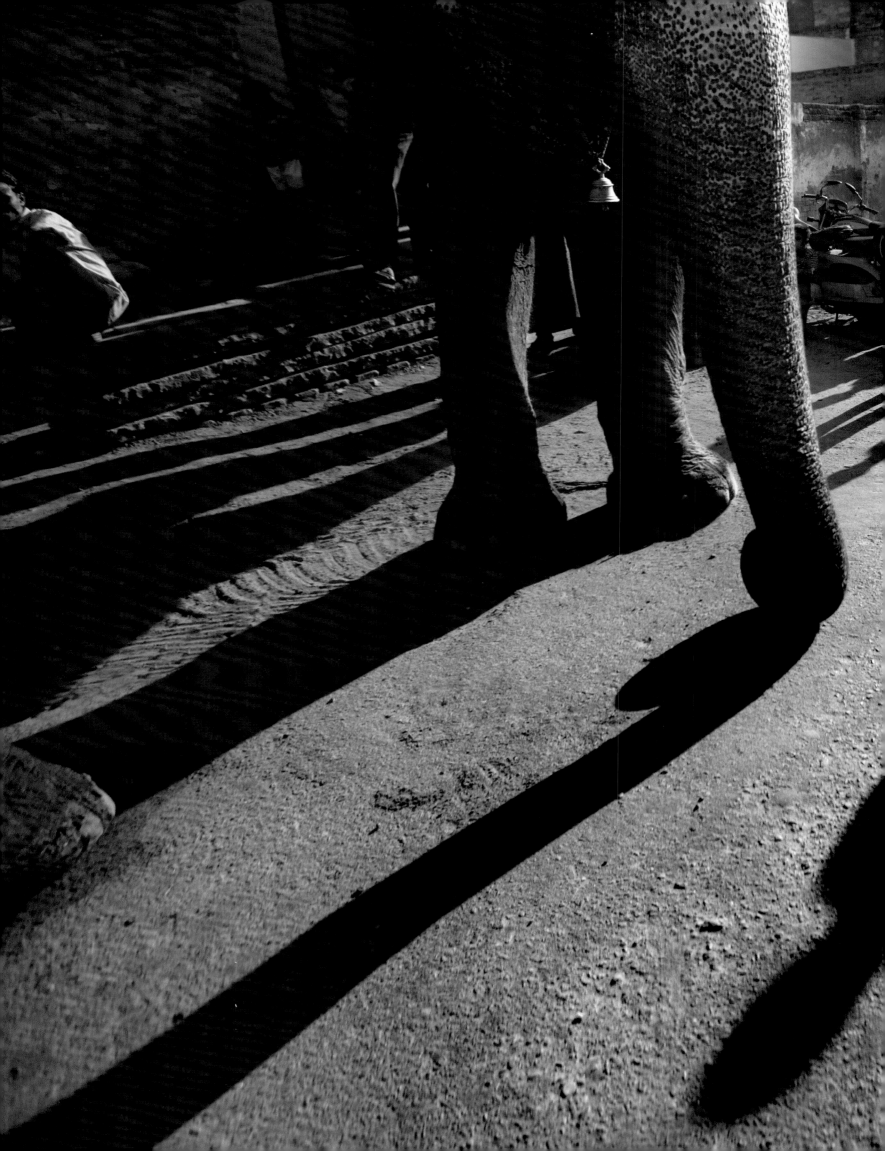

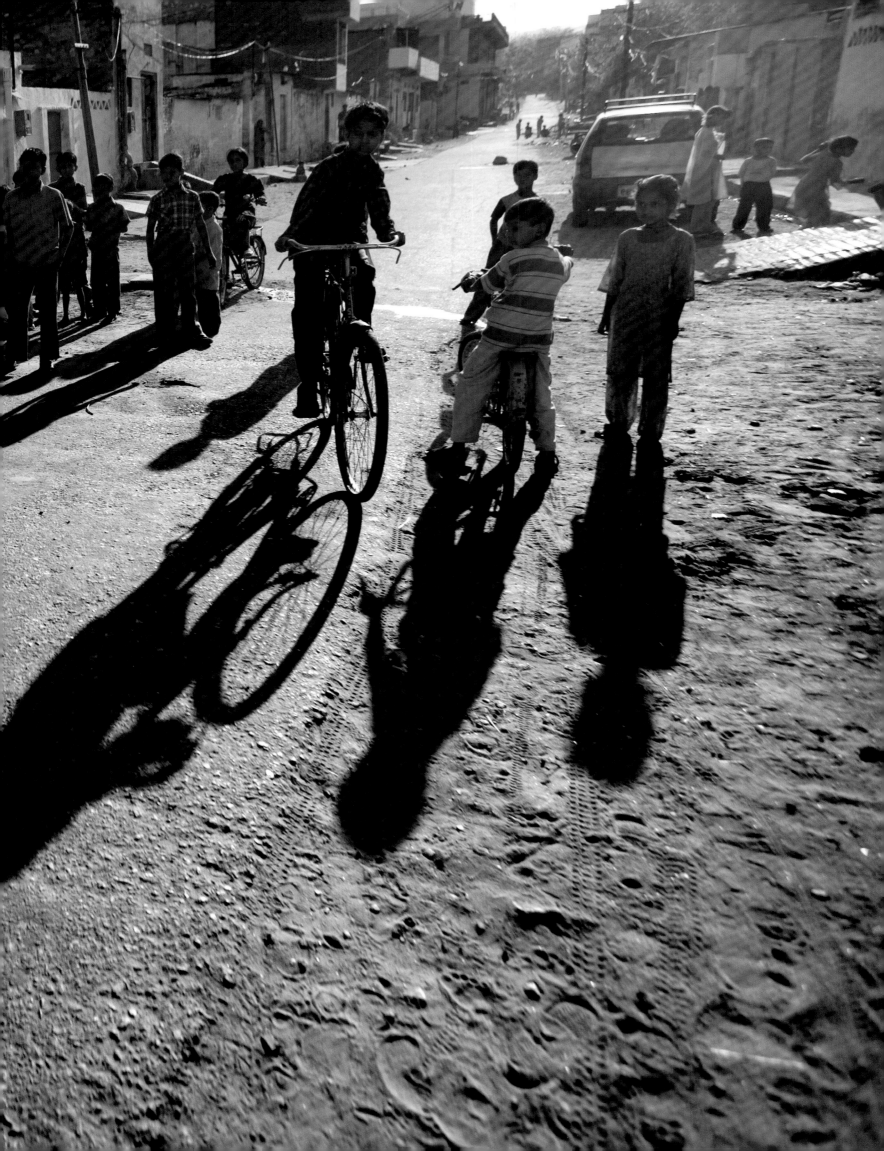

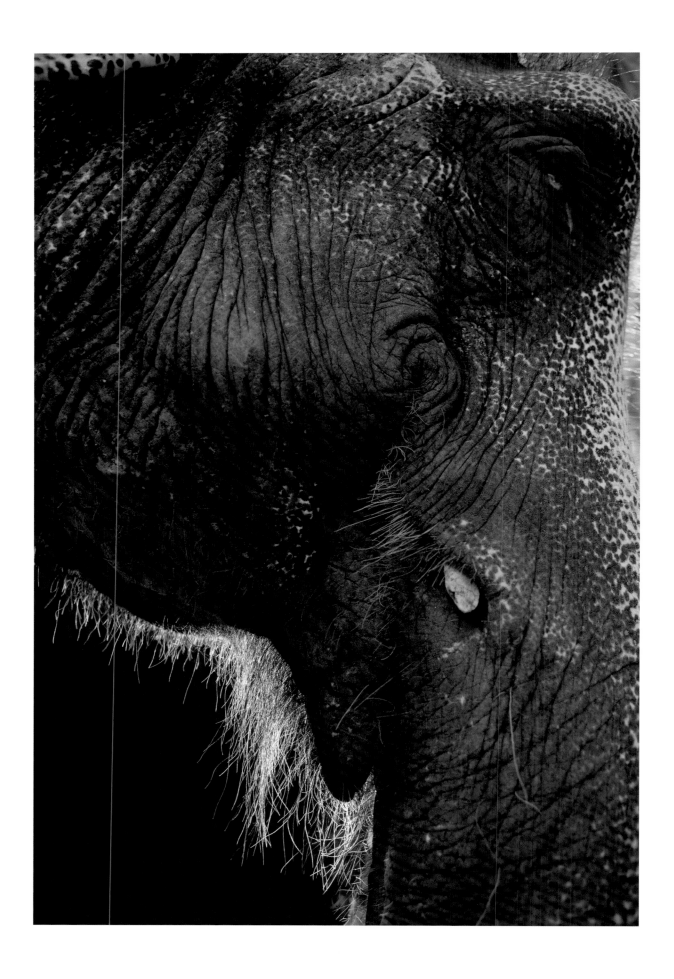

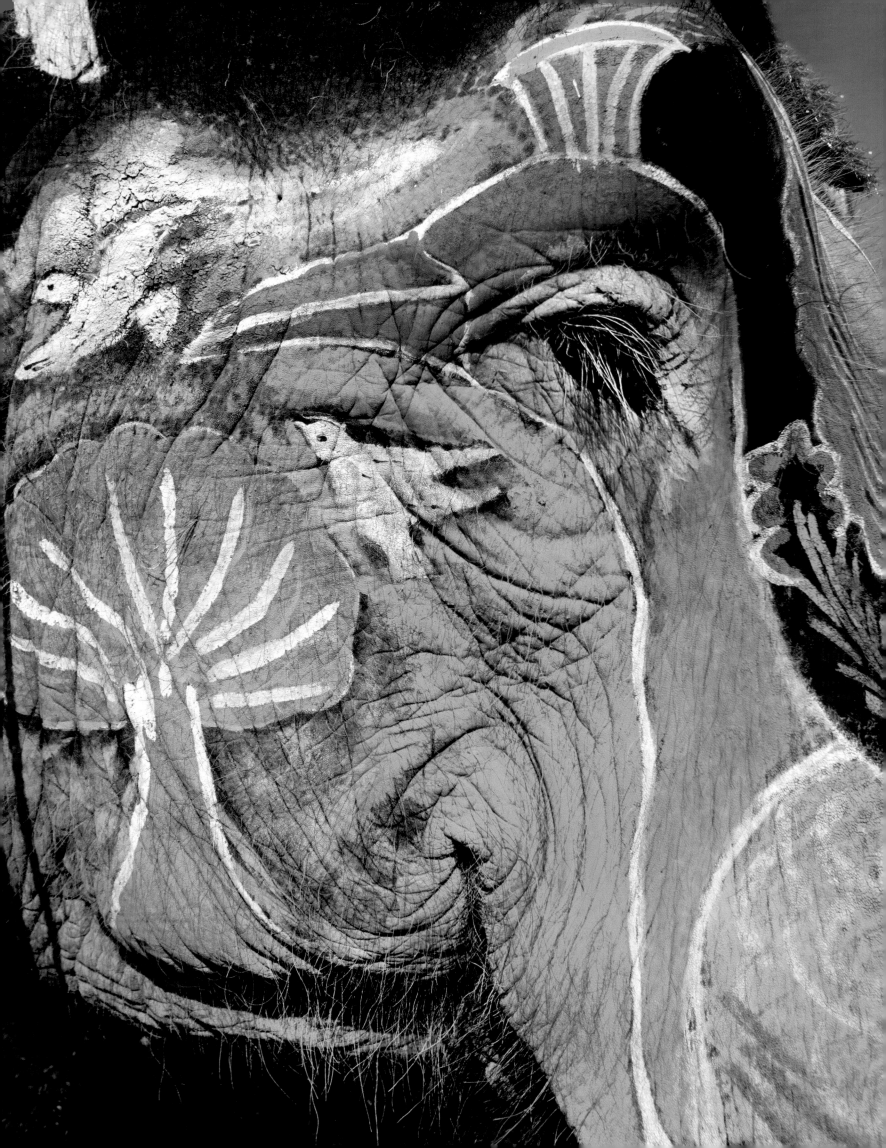

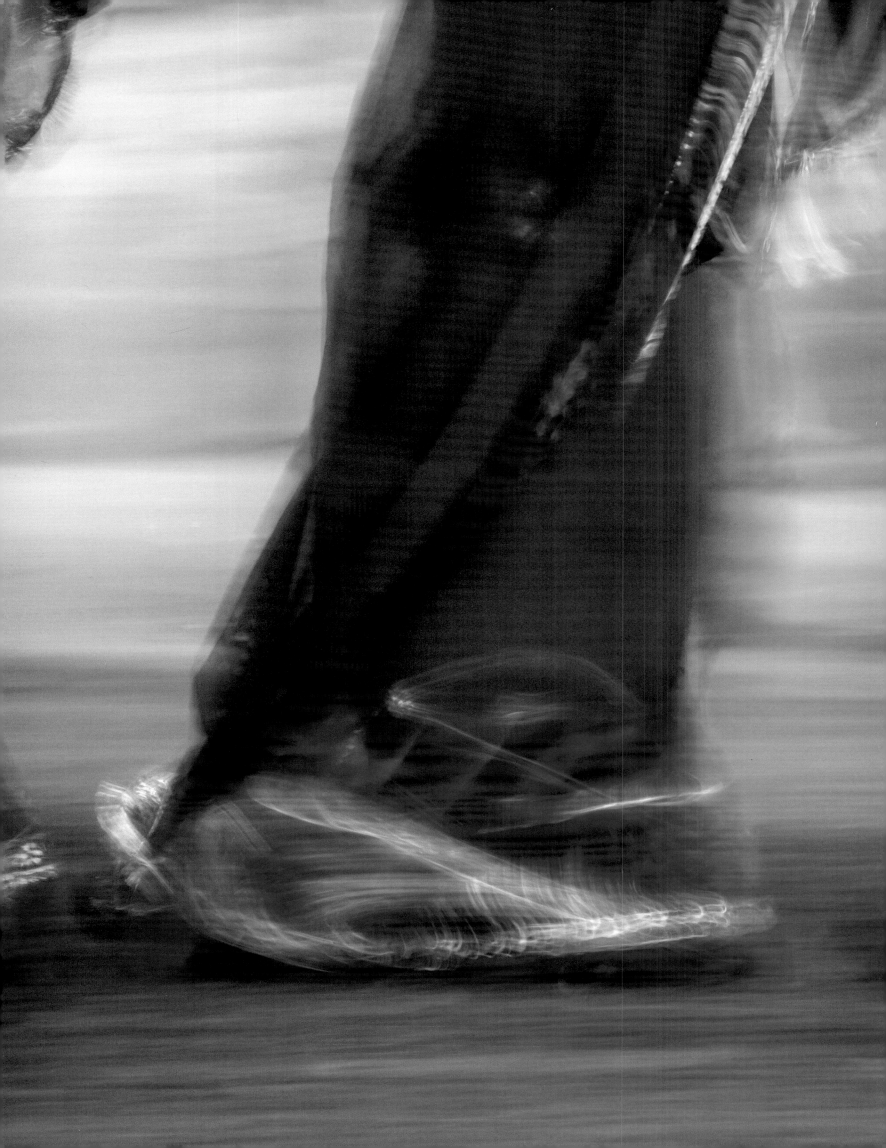

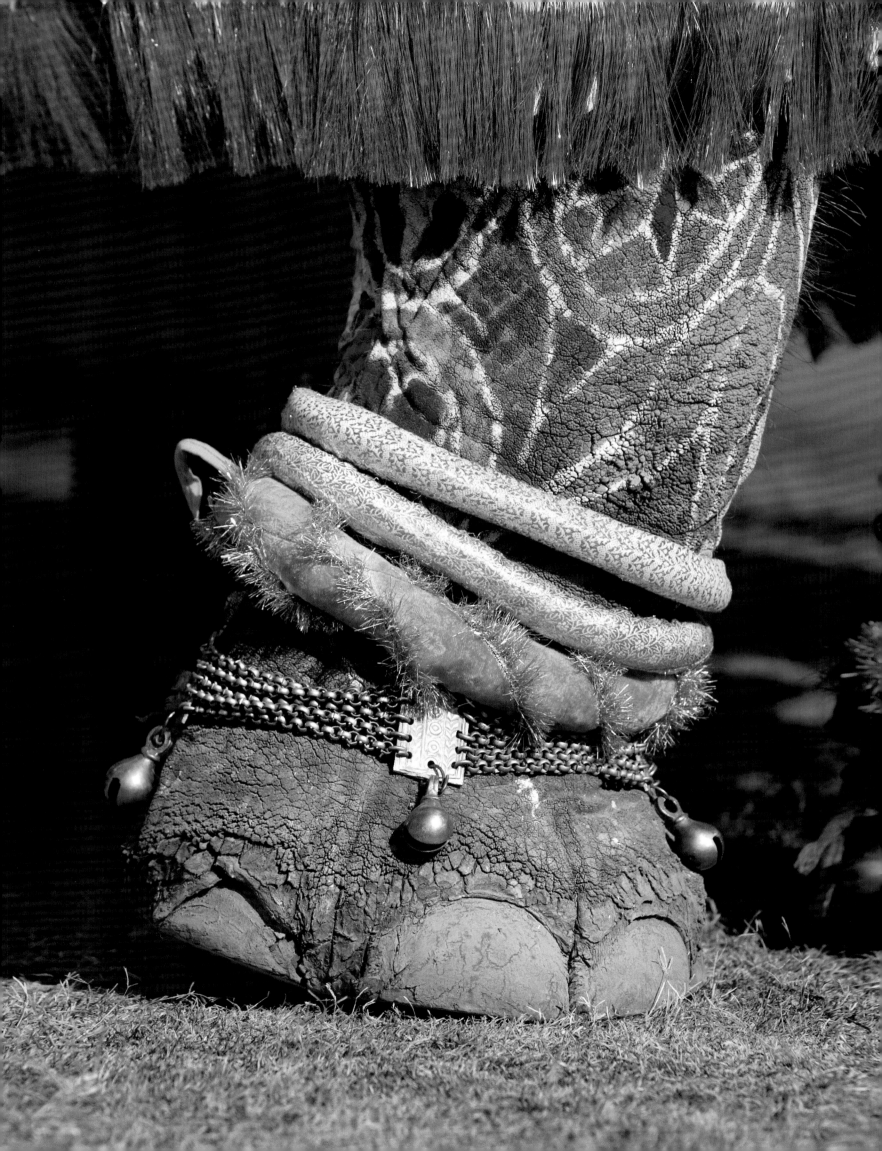

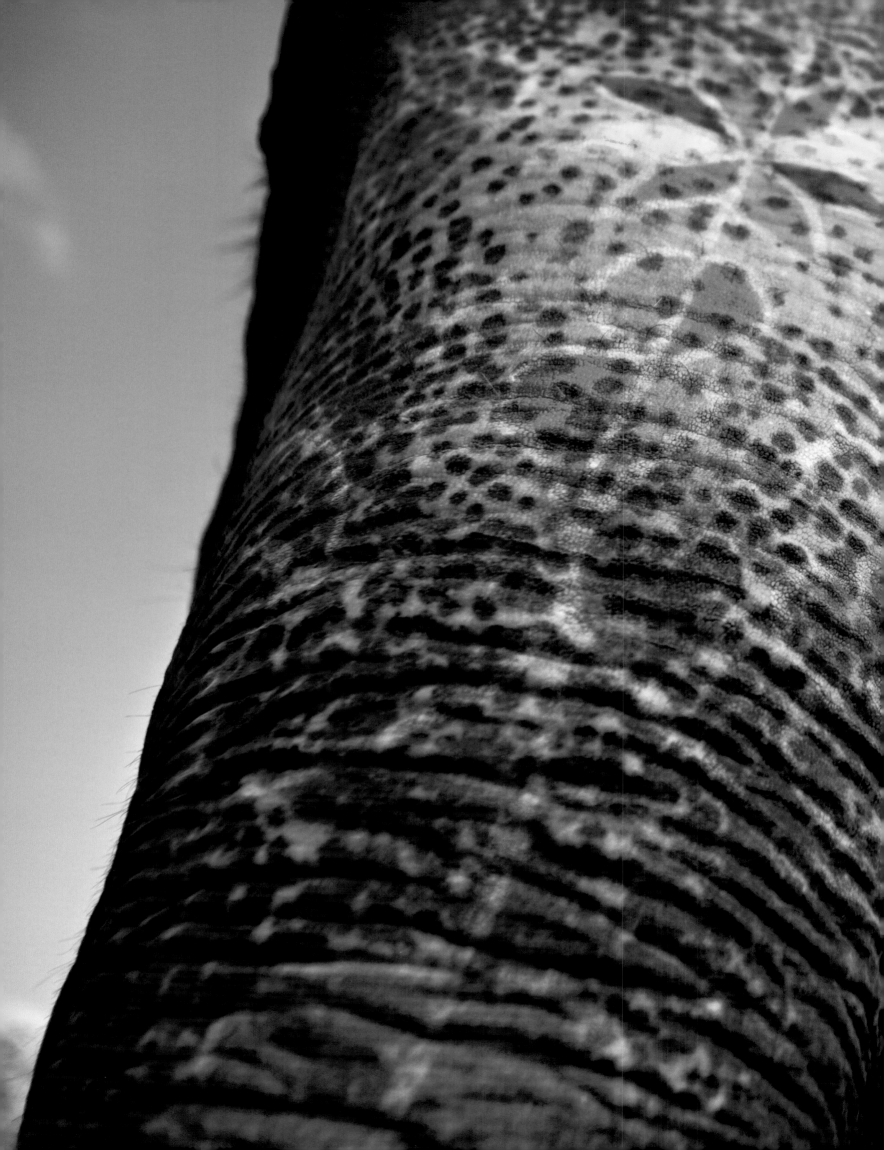

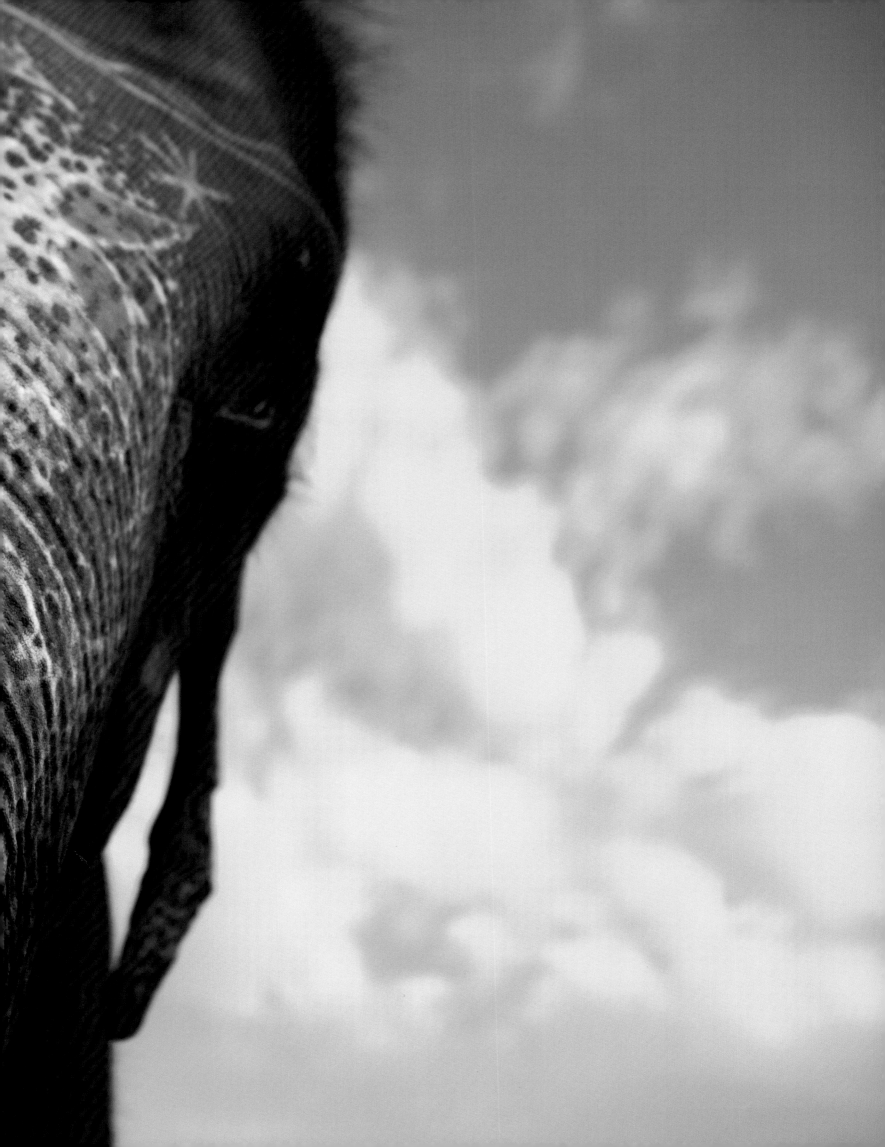

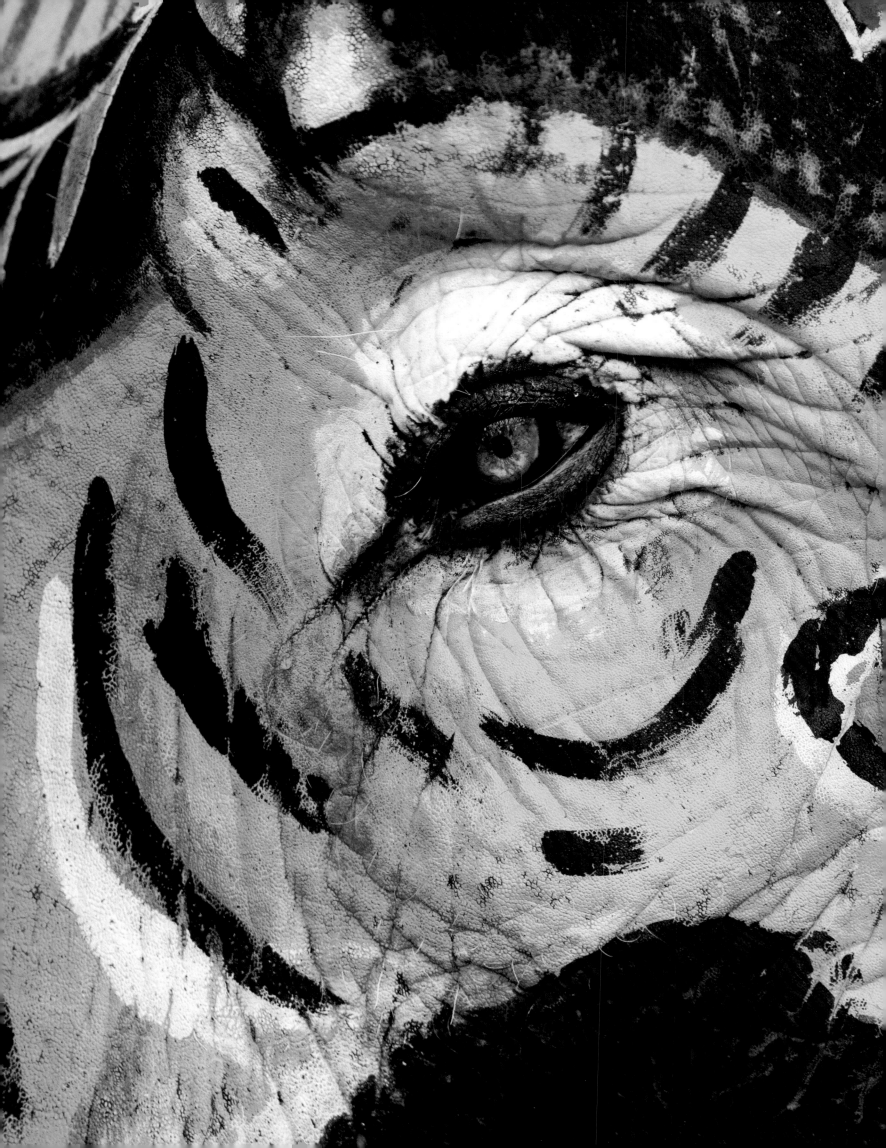

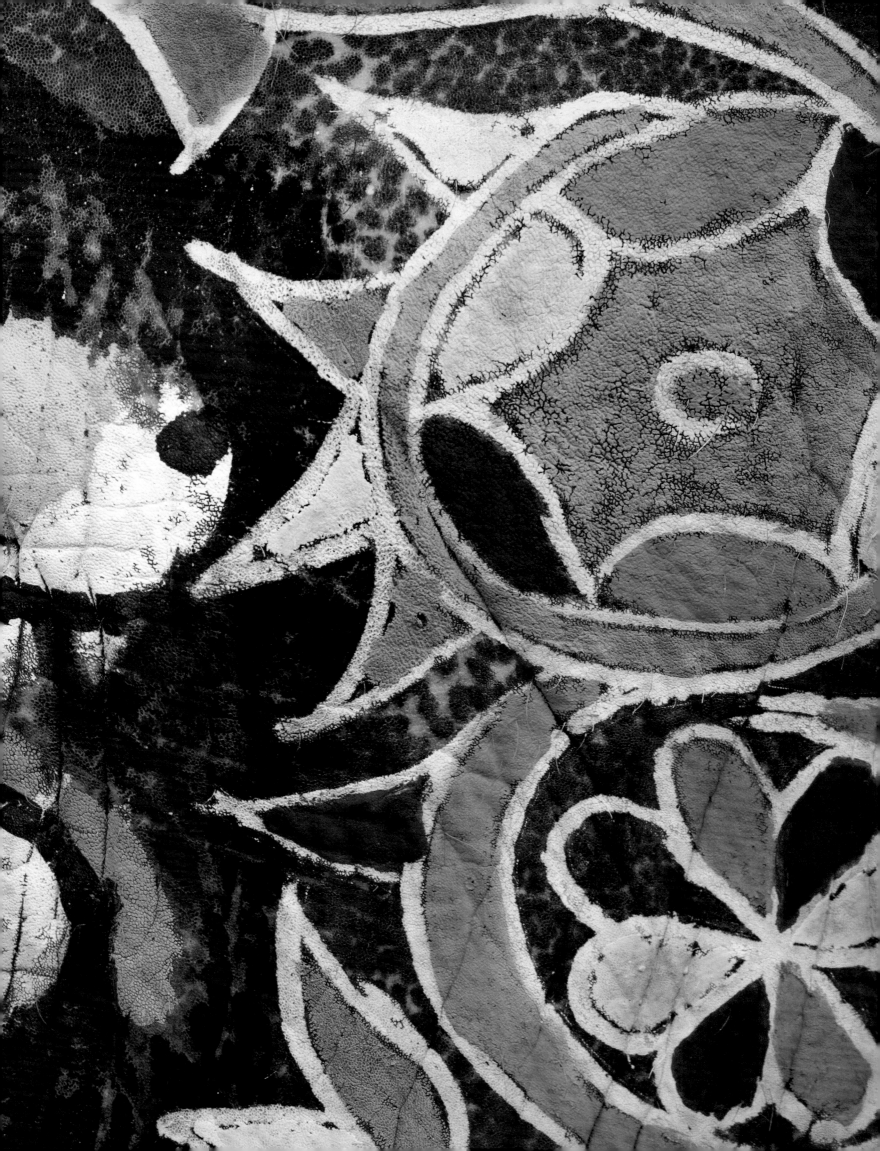

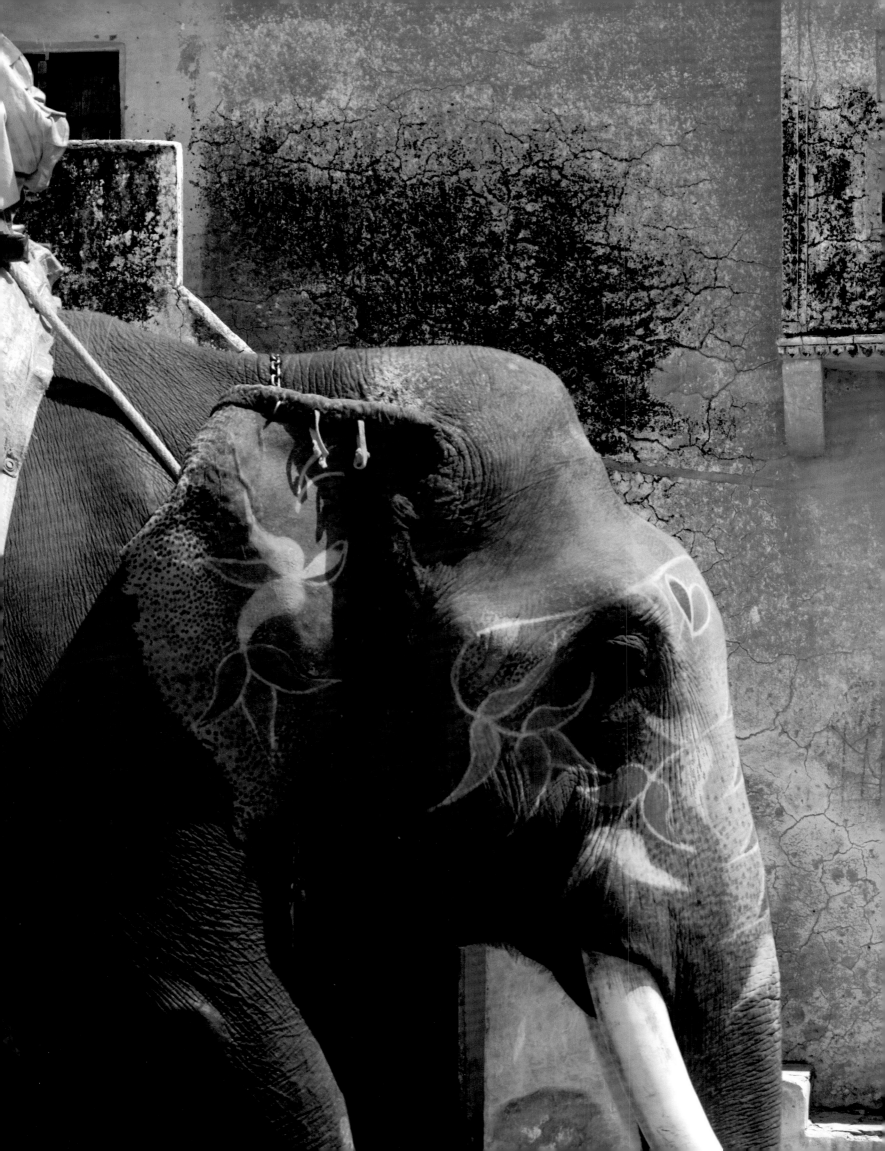

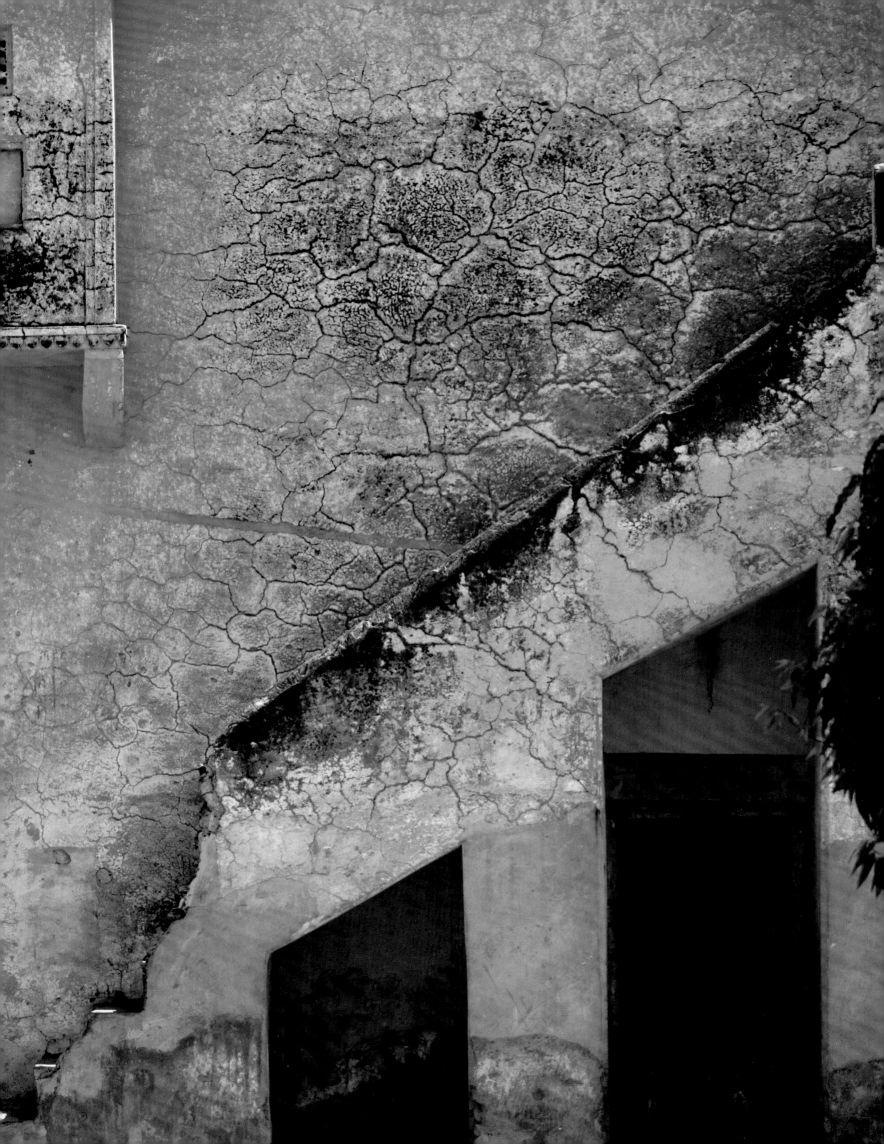

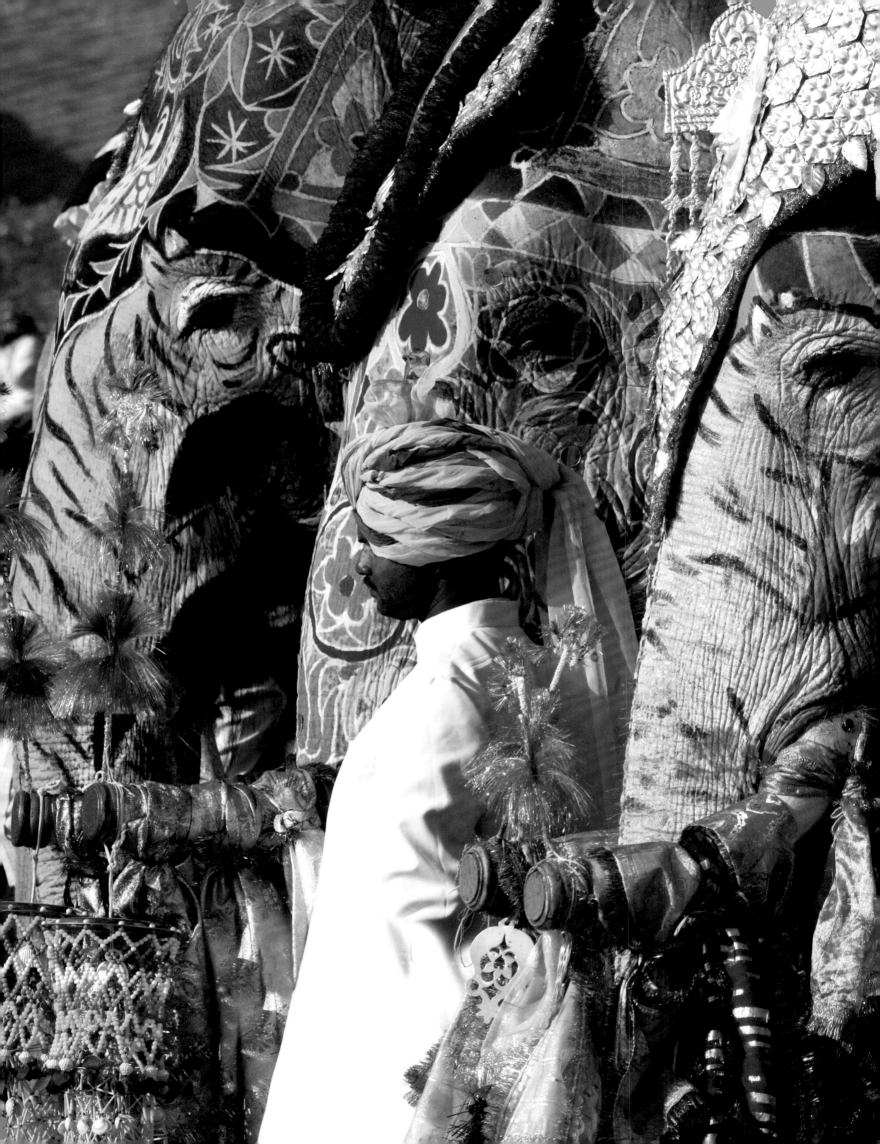

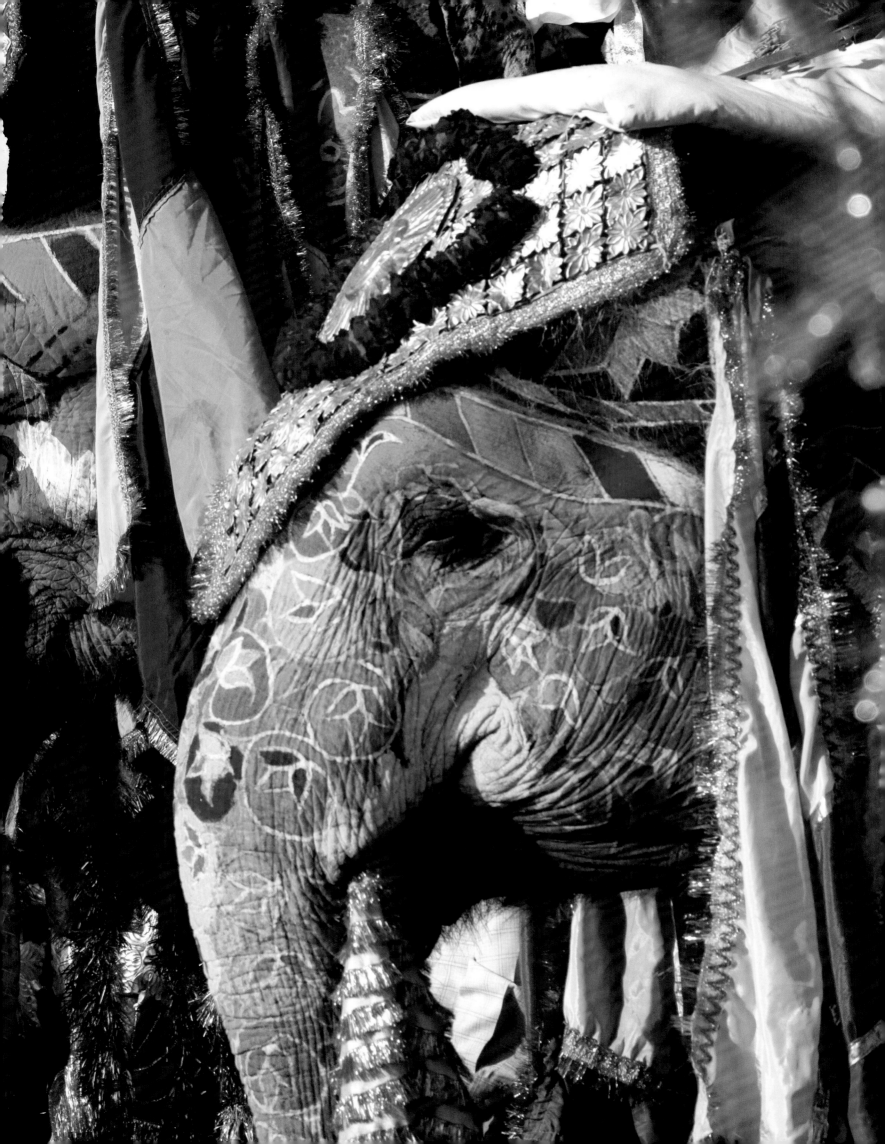

Conclusion

My journeys to the lands of the elephant have been rich and invigorating.
I have learned much, and feel humbled by the encounters I have been fortunate
to experience. This book is a personal story, told with pictures which represent
my quest to discover the very quintessence of the elephant. As I travelled, my
fascination for these creatures grew profoundly. The challenge to photograph
them in a new and refreshing way constantly tested my creative ability. Ultimately, the pictures are my primary statement about elephants: the exhilaration of
encountering another being, so physically different, yet in many ways so similar.
Perhaps that's what all my work is about – finding someone, something, that
I recognize in my heart and respond to: an acknowledgment of the fact that
our planet is shared. Watching elephants is meditative, giving us a deeper sense
of our place as an integral part of nature, and not its centre. They teach us to
marvel at the multiplicity of life, and become more compassionate and positive
in our outlook. As the most dominant of all species, we have both a collective
and individual duty of care. A world without elephants would be a world with
a shattered soul.

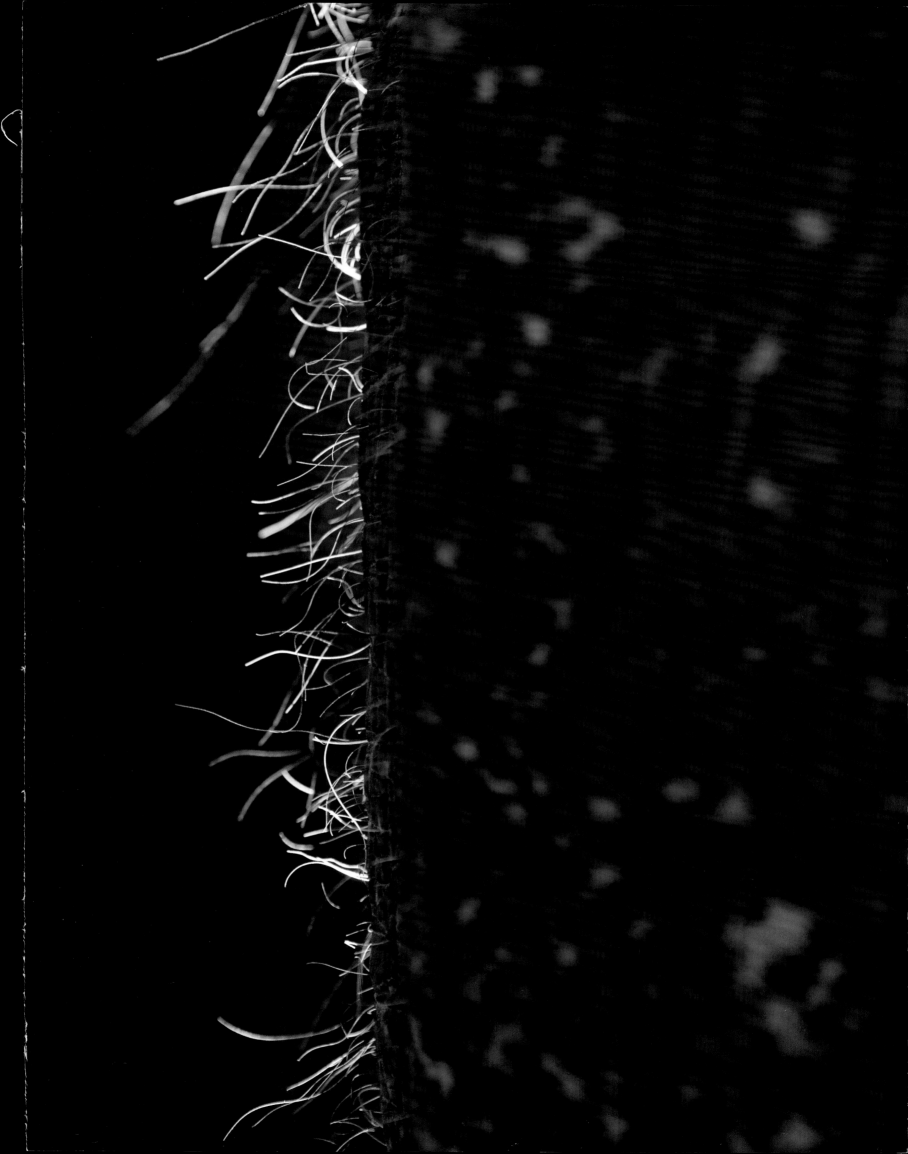

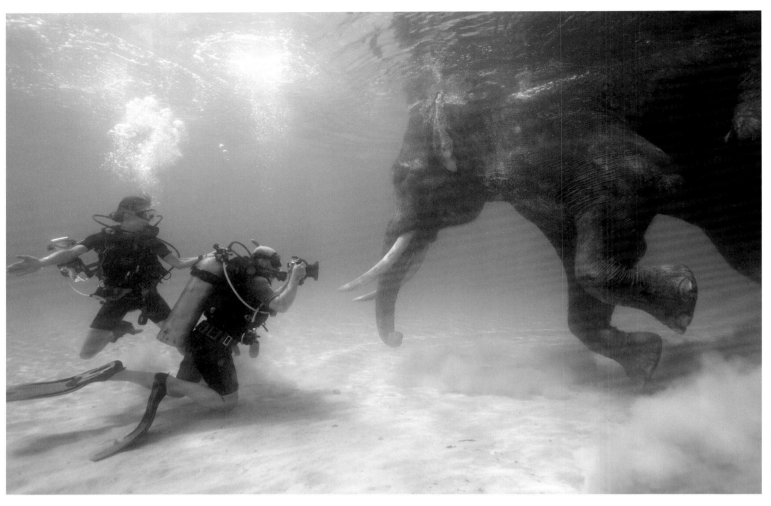

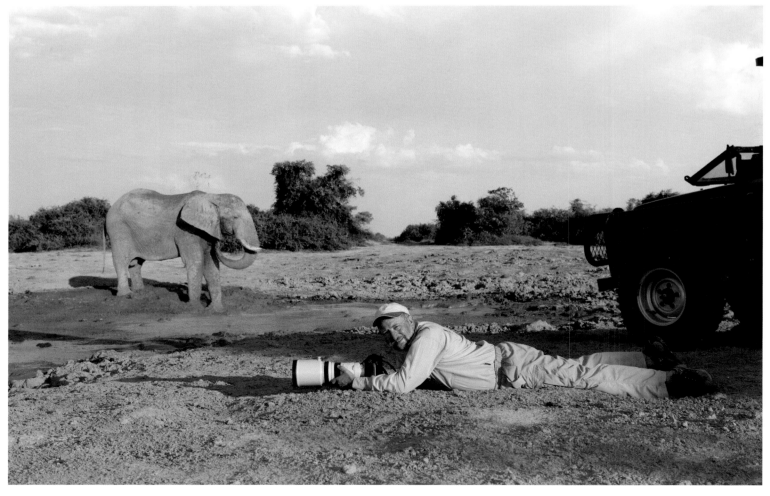

Elephants are wonderful subjects to photograph. They differ widely from place to place, and are endlessly fascinating to watch. I have photographed them in many parts of sub-Saharan Africa and the Indian subcontinent, and mostly travelled with local guides who understood elephant behaviour better than I, and advised me on all aspects of the shoot. I learned never to underestimate elephants, always respecting their right of way and was particularly wary when infant calves were present.

Each of the many trips required meticulous planning. Flying in a microlight over Kenya's Amboseli National Park involved complex negotiations with the authorities to get permission. It was undoubtedly worthwhile, as it ranks among the most exhilarating photo shoots I have ever undertaken. In Botswana's Okavango delta it took several helicopter trips to locate and photograph elephants from the air. Aerial photography requires a pilot with skill and understanding, who can safely manoeuvre an aircraft under the direction of a demanding photographer. I suffer from vertigo, and cannot go near the edge of a cliff without experiencing dizziness. Yet I will remove the door of a helicopter and lean out as far as my harness will allow, shooting straight down, while the beating rotor forces a crushing downdraught onto my body. The lure of an image is intense.

Some countries I visited many times, and often spent long hours waiting for elephants to display interesting quirks of behaviour. In Africa we persevered, day after day, determined to improve on the previous day's photo shoot. I build close friendships with my guides, in circumstances where a good sense of humour is essential for the survival of our mutual sanity. In India, where I mostly photographed domesticated elephants, I liaised closely with the mahouts, who were always accommodating and understanding.

During the production of this book, photography underwent revolutionary changes. I started with traditional film cameras, later moving to digital cameras. Digital capture and printing tools allow photographers to interpret their experiences on an artistic level which was considerably more difficult and time-consuming in the pre-digital age. While such tools are a pleasure to use, they are no substitute for a creative eye. My approach is intentionally aesthetic, as opposed to scientific, and while I enjoy exploiting the latest technology, I recognize that it merely sets new benchmarks to surpass. The American photographer, Ansel Adams, spoke of the negative being like a musical score, and the print akin to the performance. I, too, believe that images are like music, and in this book I have attempted to compose a harmony within the narrative of the pages. Print-making is a joy, and sometimes I spend hours meticulously controlling the appearance and luminosity of prints, while listening to my hi-fi.

While on location I use Canon single lens reflex cameras and lenses, and endeavour to update them as frequently as possible. A technological breakthrough may ultimately make the difference between capturing a great image, or missing it altogether, a lesson I have learned to my peril. I switched from film to digital, in what seemed like a nanosecond after the resolution of film was surpassed by pixels, and never looked back. Images are backed up onto three portable hard drives and a laptop. In the pre-digital days I slept on planes while travelling home; now I often view images on my laptop and arrive home exhausted.

Lenses vary from 15 mm fisheye to 500 mm, and I shoot with two camera bodies, with a third on standby in case of a breakdown. In general I prefer low angle images of elephants, and have a periscope attached to the viewfinder, a configuration that allows me to place the camera on the ground to get the lowest possible viewpoint. I am as fascinated by the intricate details in the folds of the skin as I am by the enormous size of elephants, so I might switch from a close-up lens to a wide angle in a matter of seconds.

I am likely to take my cameras out in sandstorms, when common sense dictates that they should be well-protected in a hard case, so I am perhaps justifiably neurotic when it comes to backups and spares. An additional camera, spare lenses and backup hardware always accompany me, with consequential excess baggage problems at airports.

My love and admiration for elephants continued to grow as this project developed. One incident sticks in my mind, and serves as a poignant reminder

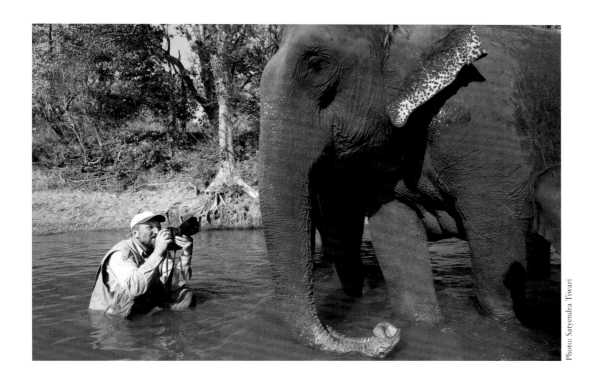

of the need to respect elephants. I spent two months working in Kenya with a guide called Tomanka Ole Selempo and together we toiled to get good photographs. One day, as we drove cautiously towards a herd of elephants, I sensed he was unusually nervous. We strategically positioned ourselves so that I could photograph the elephants walking towards us. I noticed several cows and many calves of varying ages, the youngest of whom seemed about two weeks old. We turned the engine off and waited. Elephants move quickly, and it was not long before they surrounded our vehicle in a spectacular display, and I was using all three cameras to capture as many images as possible. Without warning, Tomanka started the engine, and gently moved away. Quite uncharacteristically, he had not allowed me time to complete my photography. Later, over a cup of coffee, he revealed that he had once seen an irate matriarch trample a close friend to death. As he spoke, I was reminded that when I look through the viewfinder, peripheral vision is lost, and the adrenalin rush during a rich visual experience can easily lull me into a false sense of security. Elephants are fiercely protective towards their young, and family groups with babies should always be treated with extreme caution.

Despite the risks, I feel extraordinarily enriched by the opportunities I have had to photograph elephants at such close quarters. Though I have not travelled to every place where elephants live, with every photographic project there comes a point where the photographer has to let go, and, for a while at least, put down the camera to publish the work. With this particular project, I was reluctant to make that break, because my work with elephants will never be complete. Such is the appeal of the elephant.

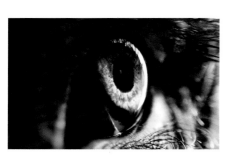

p. 1

Close-up of the knowing eye of an Asian elephant in Jaipur, India.

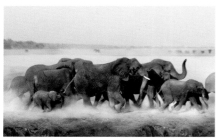

pp. 4–5

Racing to reach the thirst-quenching Chobe river in Botswana, a family herd stirs up clouds of dust.

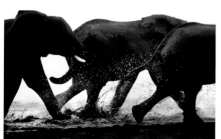

pp. 6–7

A group of elephants splash through the shallow margins of the Chobe river in Botswana.

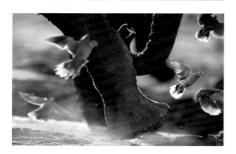

pp. 8–9

Cape turtle doves in Savute, Botswana, are disturbed as dust is thrown up by an elephant's feet.

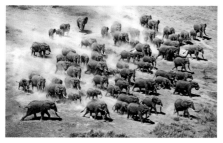

p. 13

Aerial view of an elephant herd, seen from a microlight, Amboseli National Park, Kenya.

pp. 14–15

Resplendent decorations for the Jaipur elephant festival, India.

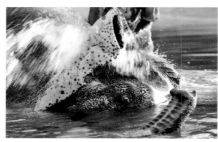

p. 17

An early morning bathing session with a mahout highlights the pink translucence of an elephant's ear in the Andaman Islands, India.

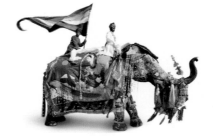

pp. 18–19

Appearing huge in such close proximity, an adult bull elephant in Savute, Botswana, heads straight for the camera.

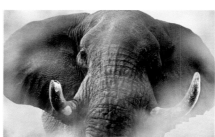

pp. 20–21

Having quenched his thirst, a large bull in Savute, Botswana, walks away from the rest of the bachelor herd, scattering a flock of doves into the air.

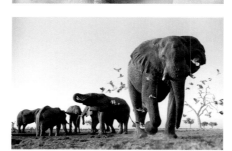

p. 22

Dusty and thirsty after a long walk to the waterhole, elephants are lit by the bright light of the camera's flash in Savute, Botswana.

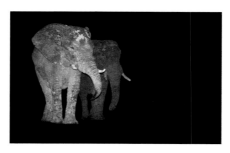

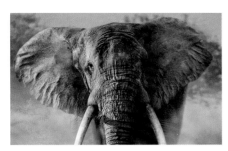

pp. 25

A cloud of dust rises under the feet of a charging elephant in Etosha National Park, Namibia.

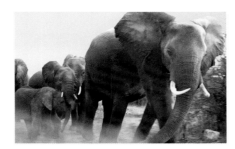

pp. 42–43

Calves of varying ages jostle for position behind the lead elephant in Chobe, Botswana.

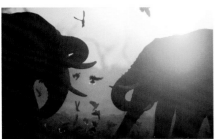

pp. 26–27

Engulfed in the warm light of the rising sun, elephants and doves cluster around a waterhole in Savute, Botswana.

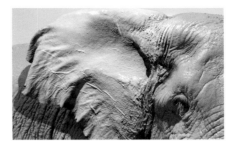

p. 45

An African elephant's ear bears an uncanny resemblance to a map of Africa. Savute, Botswana.

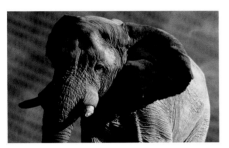

p. 33

An individual plods wearily through the dry, dusty terrain of Etosha National Park in Namibia.

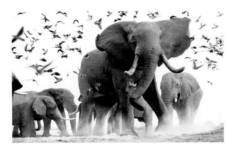

pp. 46–47

A flock of Cape turtle doves swirl around a bachelor herd at a waterhole in Savute, Botswana.

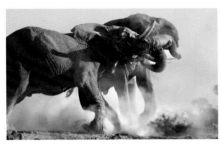

pp. 34–35

Dust swirls around the feet of a pair of fighting tuskers in Savute, Botswana.

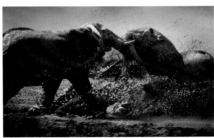

pp. 48–49

Mud flies and tusks clash as two bull elephants vie for position at the waterhole in Savute, Botswana.

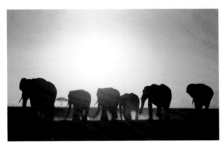

pp. 36–37

Dawn breaks in Kenya's Masai Mara, as elephants trail across a dusty landscape.

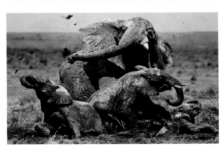

pp. 50–51

Joyously splashing and rolling in the harsh midday heat, an elephant family in Kenya's Masai Mara, crowds into a small mud hole.

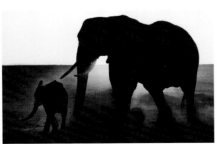

pp. 38–39

A mother in the Masai Mara keeps a watchful eye on her young calf.

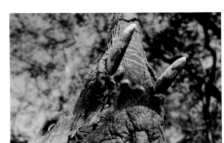

p. 52

A young elephant calf in Kapama game reserve, South Africa, stretches to reach the succulent leaves on higher branches of the tree.

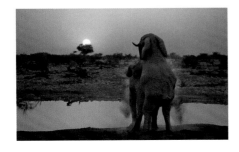

pp. 40–41

Silhouetted against a pink sky reflected in still water, a pair of elephants mate as the sun sinks below the horizon in Etosha, Namibia.

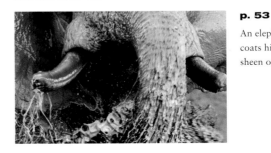

p. 53

An elephant in Savute, Botswana coats himself with a silvery sheen of glutinous mud.

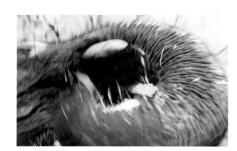

p. 54

In Kapama game reserve, South Africa, an elephant calf sweeps his trunk down into his mouth as he eats.

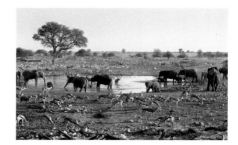

pp. 70–71

Herds of elephants, springbok and other antelope gather at a waterhole at dusk in Etosha National Park, Namibia.

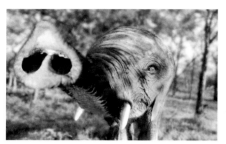

p. 55

Filled with curiosity, a young calf in Kapama, South Africa, explores the camera with the tip of his trunk.

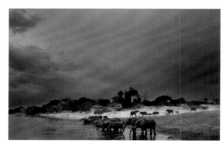

pp. 72–73

A shaft of sunlight breaks through heavy cloud, highlighting a small area on the bank of the Chobe river in Botswana.

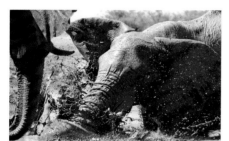

pp. 58–59

Coating their skins with mud helps to keep elephants cool and free from parasites. Savute, Botswana.

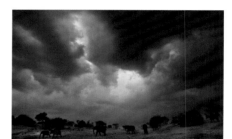

pp. 74–75

Dramatic clouds threaten an imminent early summer downpour in Chobe, Botswana.

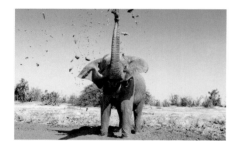

p. 63

This elephant spraying mud over his back in Savute, Botswana, may have lost one of his tusks during a fight.

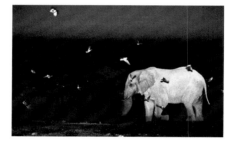

pp. 76–77

Birds and elephants share a waterhole in Etosha, Namibia. The fading light hangs in the sky, creating a dramatic red backdrop.

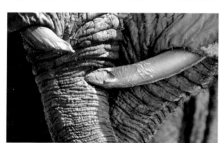

p. 64

Covered with a liberal coating of mud, a pair of elephants affectionately entwine trunks in Savute, Botswana.

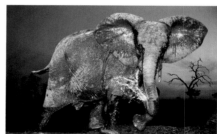

pp. 78–79

The artificial light of a flash reflected back from the elephant's eyes give him a rather manic appearance. Savute, Botswana.

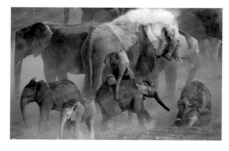

pp. 66–67

Dust engulfs the playful antics of young elephants as they frolic on dry earth around a waterhole in Etosha National Park, Namibia.

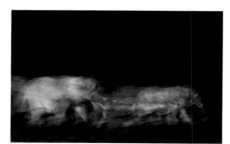

pp. 80–81

A pale blur in the dark night: illuminated by torchlight, a moving herd in Savute, Botswana, is captured by a long exposure.

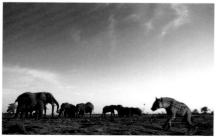

pp. 68–69

A spotted hyena prowls cautiously near a waterhole in Savute, Botswana, as he waits for the elephants to leave.

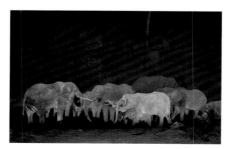

pp. 82–83

Ghostly grey figures stand in the water at night to drink in Savute, Botswana.

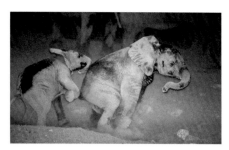

pp. 84–85

In Etosha National Park, Namibia, two boisterous calf elephants gambol at night.

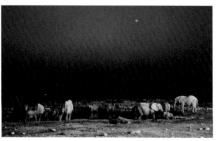

pp. 86–87

Beneath a new moon, elephants drink in Namibia's Etosha National Park, in the stillness of the African night.

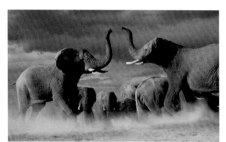

pp. 88–89

Under the watchful eyes of other members of the bachelor herd, two bull elephants confront each other in Savute, Botswana.

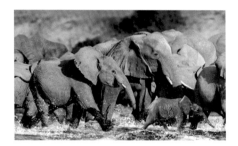

pp. 90–91

A spirited family herd, comprising adults, juveniles and infants, splashes through the Chobe river in Botswana.

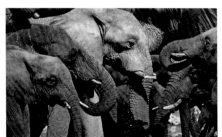

pp. 94–95

Tightly packed in the narrow space, elephants quench their thirst at a man-made trough in Etosha National Park, Namibia.

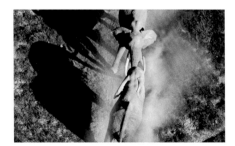

p. 99

The drama of a fight is captured in an aerial view from a microlight in Amboseli National Park, Kenya.

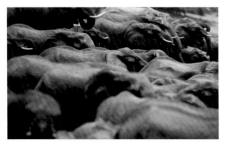

pp. 100–101

Looking across the backs of a herd in Chobe, Botswana, the varying colours of their coating of dust are clearly evident.

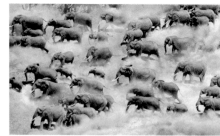

pp. 102–103

Eager to reach the life-giving water of the swamps in Amboseli, Kenya, running elephants raise clouds of dust.

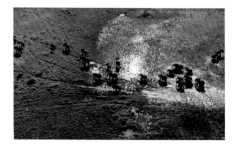

pp. 104–105

The watery landscape of the Okavango delta in Botswana is formed by run-off from the distant Angolan highlands, which flows inland for 1,000 miles.

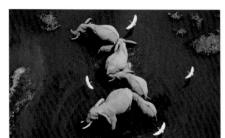

p. 107

Egrets circle over elephants as they wallow in Amboseli's abundant swampland in south-eastern Kenya, fed by melt-water from snow-capped Mount Kilimanjaro.

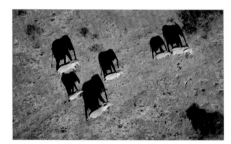

pp. 108–109

An aerial view captures long shadows cast by the early morning sunlight in Amboseli National Park, Kenya.

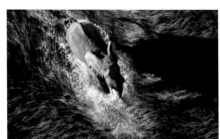

p. 111

Surging through the swampy grassland, an elephant is seen from a helicopter in the Okavango delta, Botswana.

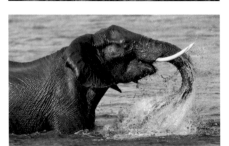

pp. 112–113

Sun sparkles on wet skin and spraying water in the Chobe river, Botswana.

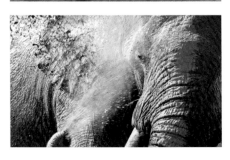

pp. 114–115

Repeated spraying builds up a thick protective coating of mud. Savute, Botswana.

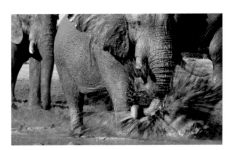

p. 116

In Savute, Botswana, a slow shutter speed blurs the motion of spraying mud.

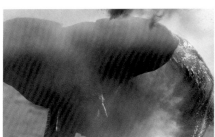

p. 117

Partially obscured by the fine, powdery cloud, an elephant dust-bathes in Chobe, Botswana.

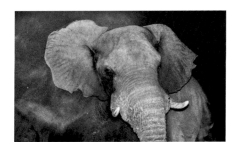

p. 118

Night-time in Savute, Botswana. The tip of his trunk appearing dark where it is wet, an elephant stirs up the dust.

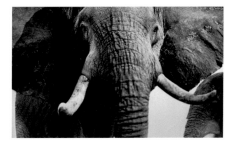

p. 119

From a low-angled viewpoint in Savute, Botswana, an elephant appears unnervingly large and powerful.

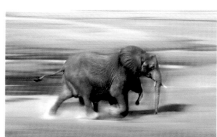

pp. 120–121

A slow shutter speed captures the motion blur of a mother and calf near the Chobe river in Botswana.

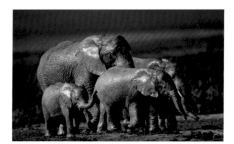

pp. 122–123

The reddish-brown earth of Addo National Park in South Africa gives muddy elephants an appearance of being chocolate-coated.

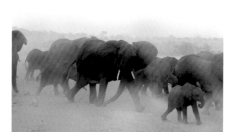

pp. 124–125

It is the dry season in Botswana's Chobe, and fine, powdery dust, stirred up by a myriad of feet, hangs in the air.

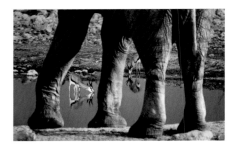

pp. 126–127

Framed by towering legs, springboks drink, reflected in the still surface of the water in Etosha, Namibia.

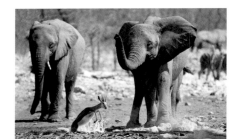

pp. 128–129

After slipping into a concrete water trough in Namibia's Etosha National Park, a springbok struggles frantically to escape.

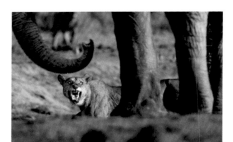

pp. 130–131

Wary of the superior size of the elephant, a lioness snarls a warning as she drinks from the waterhole in Savute, Botswana.

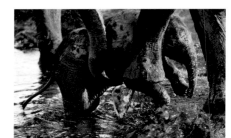

pp. 132–133

A mother's gentle foot and trunk help an infant to regain his footing on the steep bank of a waterhole in Chobe, Botswana.

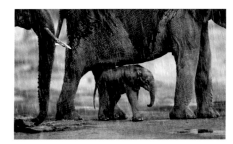

pp. 134–135

A young calf shelters beneath the reassuring bulk of his mother during a downpour in the Masai Mara, Kenya.

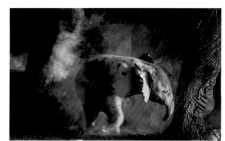

pp. 136–137

Late afternoon sun in Etosha National Park, Namibia, highlights the suspended dust surrounding a tiny elephant calf.

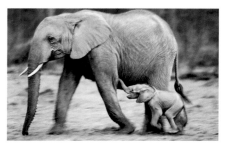

pp. 138–139

A baby struggles to keep up with the long strides of his mother in the Masai Mara, Kenya.

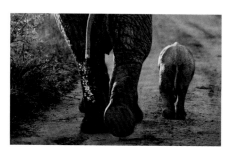

p. 141

Rear view of an elephant cow walking with her young calf in the Kapama game reserve, South Africa.

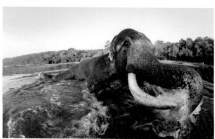

pp. 142–143

A large bull in the Andaman Islands, India, wallows contentedly in warm water.

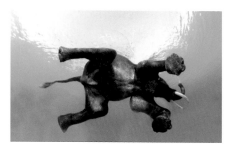

pp. 146–147

Viewed from directly below, this swimming elephant in the Andaman Islands is an unusual and somewhat incongruous sight.

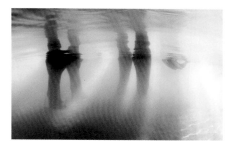

pp. 149

An elephant stands in shallow water in the Andaman Islands, India. Seen from below water level, his legs appear surreal.

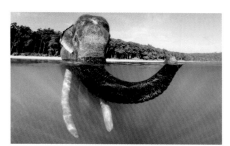

pp. 150–151

This photograph in the Andaman islands, half-in and half-out of the sea, illustrates how water distorts and magnifies.

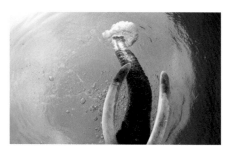

p. 153

Like people, some elephants enjoy swimming for pleasure, using their trunks as snorkels. Andaman Islands, India.

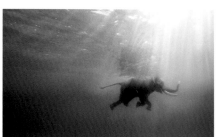

pp. 154–155

Rays of sunlight filter through blue water, highlighting a male elephant as he swims in the deep ocean off the Andaman Islands.

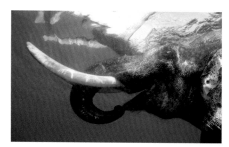

pp. 156–157

A close-up view of a large tusker captures the gleam in his eye as he swims by, Andaman Islands, India.

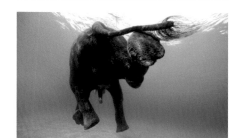

pp. 158–159

In the Andaman Islands, logging elephants were occasionally taught to swim in order to cross the sea from one island to another.

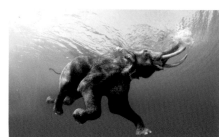

p. 161

Tail and legs flying, an elephant swims on enthusiastically in the warm blue waters of the Andaman Sea.

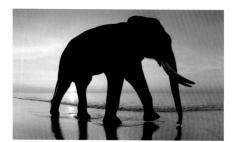

p. 162

Clearly reflected in wet sand left by a retreating wave, this large tusker takes an evening stroll along the beach in the Andaman Islands, India.

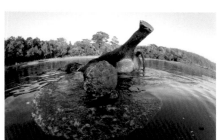

p. 165

An elephant joyously rolls over in the water during bath-time, Andaman Islands, India.

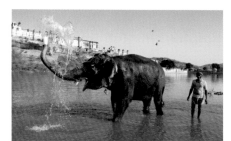

pp. 166–167

Below the Amber Fort in Jaipur, India, mahouts wash their elephants in the river.

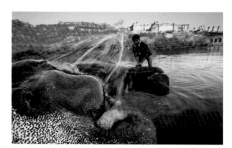

pp. 168–169

Thorough washing requires intimate interaction between mahout and elephant. Jaipur, India.

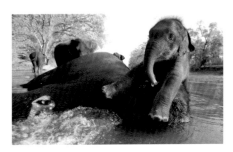

pp. 170–171

A young elephant playfully climbs over his mother as they bathe in a river in the Kanha National Park, India.

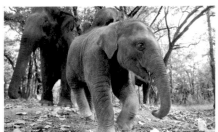

pp. 172–173

An inquisitive young elephant confidently approaches the camera in Bandhavgarh National Park, India.

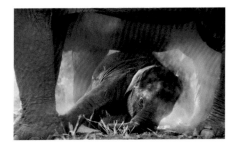

pp. 174–175

A baby elephant in Bandhavgarh, India, rolls playfully in the dust, surrounded by a protective forest of legs.

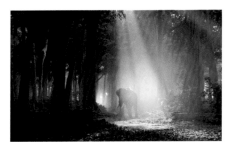

pp. 176–177

Shafts of sunlight penetrate tall trees, illuminating the early morning mist in the Andaman Islands, India.

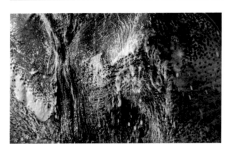

p. 178

Water drips from an elephant's head during the daily washing ritual in the Andaman Islands.

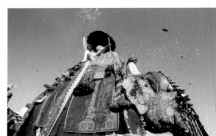

p. 179

A slow shutter speed captures the watery blur at bath-time. Andaman Islands, India.

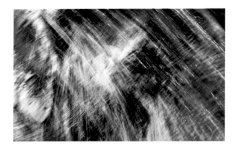

pp. 180–181

The pale underside of the mahout's foot is mirrored in the pink margins of the elephant's ear, Bandhavgarh, India.

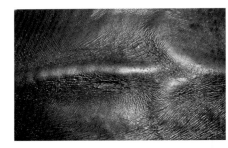

pp. 182–183

The pattern produced by the backbone of a bathing elephant in Kanha National Park, India, looks uncannily like a pointing arrow.

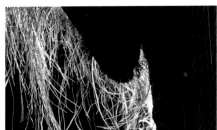

p. 184

Long hairs around an elephant's mouth are backlit by early morning sunlight in Jaipur, India.

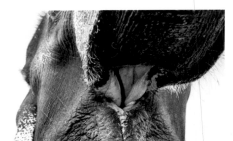

p. 185

Beneath the looming trunk, a close-up shows an unusual view of an elephant's mouth. Jaipur, India.

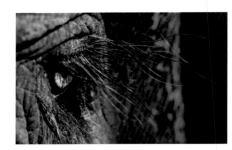

pp. 186–187

Long, wiry lashes above an amber-coloured eye are revealed in amazing detail. Jaipur, India.

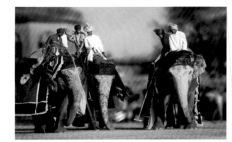

pp. 190–191

Handfuls of coloured paper are flung into the air during a parade at the elephant festival in Jaipur, India.

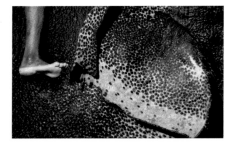

p. 192

A polo match, played on elephant back using long mallets, rounds off the festival in Jaipur, India.

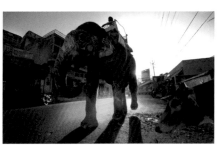

p. 193

Walking home through quiet streets after a long, tiring day at the Jaipur elephant festival, India.

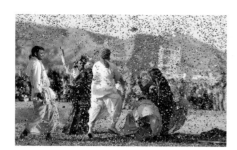

p. 193

People dressed in brightly coloured garments throw coloured paper in the air during the festival in Jaipur, India.

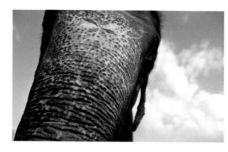

pp. 202–203

An elephant looks enquiringly down his trunk at the Jaipur elephant festival, India.

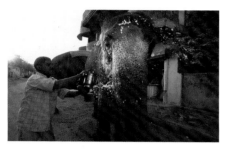

pp. 194–195

Early morning on the day of the Jaipur festival in India, and preparations begin with a thorough wash before the elephant is decorated.

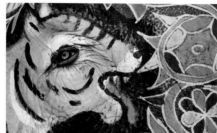

pp. 204–205

The elephant's eye becomes the eye of the tiger during the elephant painting competition at the Jaipur festival, India.

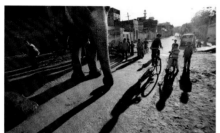

pp. 196–197

Though not such an unusual sight, elephants in the streets of Jaipur, India will often draw a crowd of inquisitive youngsters.

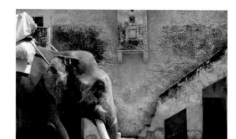

pp. 206–207

Walking in the Amber Fort in Jaipur, India, before the elephant painting competition.

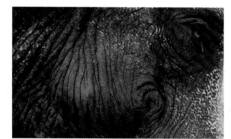

p. 198

Backlit profile of an elephant before the painting for the festival begins in Jaipur, India.

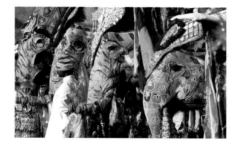

pp. 208–209

Richly decorated elephants line up in the stadium during the Jaipur elephant festival, India.

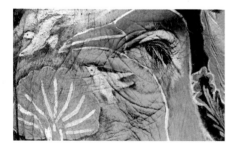

p. 199

A peacock is painted with his eye represented by the elephant's eye, Jaipur festival, India.

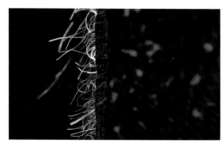

p. 211

A close-up detail of an elephant's trunk, backlit by the morning sun, reveals coarse, bristly hairs. Jaipur, India.

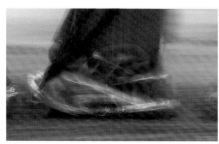

p. 200

A blur of colour, a woman dressed in a gold-trimmed sari dances in the parade at the Jaipur elephant festival, India.

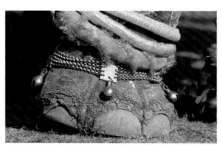

p. 201

Pink toenails and a string of silvery bells are all details that contribute to the rich adornment for the elephant festival in Jaipur, India.

Acknowledgments

This book is the result of the collective enthusiasm of a large team of people to whom I am indebted. For their practical help in the United Kingdom, I thank Kathy Bloom, Phil Jones, Janice Wickenden and Steve Warren. In Africa, I worked with Joseph Gichanga, Alexis Peltier, Peter Perlstein, Des Pretorius, Steve Turner and Tomanka Ole Selempo. In India, I am grateful to Elisa Babetto, Nick Garbutt, Abdul Jameel, Hamid Khan, Shahid Khan, Umeed Mistry, Abdul Rahuf, Abdul Rasheed, Akshay Raywat, Samit Sawhny, Satyendra Tiwari, Dharam, Nasru, Shabbir, Shuklu and Vishnu. I gained an insight into elephants from the work of eminent writers and scholars, including Jeffrey Masson, Martin Meredith, Cynthia Moss, Katy Payne, Joyce Poole, Martin Saller, Eric Scigliano, Mark Shand, Raman Sukumar and Yukio Tsuchiya.

I thank all at Thames & Hudson for sharing my passion, and in particular, Jamie Camplin and Aaron Hayden.

My memory is not as proficient as the average elephant, and I often failed to take notes during the years I spent on this project, so there are people who may have been erroneously omitted from this list. My heartfelt thanks and appreciation go to you all.